TRADITIONAL CHRISTMAS RECIPES OF SPAIN

Malcolm Coxall

*"Christmas has come
and it is fit that we should feast,
sing, and be merry!"*

Cornelio Books

Published by M.Coxall - Cornelio Books
Copyright 2013 Malcolm Coxall
First Published in United Kingdom, Spain, August 2013
ISBN: 978-84-940853-9-0

This is book is dedicated to Conny,
whose patience and knowledge made it all possible.

This book is sold subject to the condition
that it shall not, by way of trade or otherwise,
be lent, re-sold, hired-out, or otherwise circulated
without the publisher's prior consent in any form of
binding or cover other than that in which it is
published and without a similar condition
including this condition being imposed
on the subsequent purchaser.
Also available for Kindle
and as an eBook (in full colour)

Contents

Preface

1.0 An introduction to Christmas cooking in Spain
    1.1 The geography of Spain and its Regions
    1.2 A culinary History of Spain
        1.2.1 Historic Gastronomic Influences
    1.3 The culinary Geography of Spain - Region by Region
    1.4 Traditional ingredients
    1.5 Christmas in Spain
        1.5.1 The Run-up to Christmas in Spain
        1.5.2 Timetable of Christmas Festivities and Meals

2.0 The Recipes - an Introduction
    2.1 Starters, Salads, Vegetables, Gazpachos
    2.2 Soups
    2.3 Main Dishes
        2.3.1 Goat's Meat
        2.3.2 Lamb
        2.3.3 Rabbit
        2.3.4 Pork
        2.3.5 Poultry
        2.3.6 Stews and Fricassees
        2.3.7 Casseroles
        2.3.8 Fish
    2.4 Sweets and Confectionary
    2.5 Breads and Tortillas
    2.6 Christmas Drinks
    2.7 Seasonal Tapas, Canapés and Ibéricos

3.0 Dining, Serving and Restaurant etiquette in Spain

List of recipes - Spanish names
List of recipes - English names

About the author

Preface

For any traveller crossing Spain, it very quickly becomes obvious that every region has its very own specialities of which it is proud. But if we look a little more closely, we can see that this diversity is even deeper, because every province also has its own specialities. Indeed, when we really begin to look carefully, we see that every village also has its own range of localised recipes and Christmas customs, some of which are extraordinary and quite unique.

This comes as a pleasant shock to the jaded palate of the average "Western" visitor, who is much more used to the very limited and boringly homogenous range of "Christmas fare" that gets dragged out yet again when the "festive season" comes around.

Indeed, our "Western" Christmas dishes seem to have been designed deliberately to remove any sense of national, regional or local variation. The limited range of Christmas dishes that is left to us now seems to be part of a process of industrial "standardisation". We "Westerners" have lost our own food diversity and now we seem hell-bent on helping the multi-national food corporations to turn everything we eat into just a slightly different flavour of the same pulp.

If you think this is an exaggeration, just sit down and count the number of traditional Christmas dishes that you can think of from your own country. Then look at the index of this very incomplete book and I think you will see what I mean.

Gladly, this industrialisation of food has not happened in Spain to the same extent. So, for anyone interested in food, Spain is an amazing treasure trove of food diversity, centuries old evolution, dynamic and imaginative cooking, with a love of traditional food combined with an open-minded attitude to experimentation and a range of ingredients that many a chef can only dream of. On this theme, I now come to mention how this book came to be written.

In an impetuous moment I thought what a nice idea it would be to write a book that recorded the traditional Christmas recipes of Spain, so that others may rediscover these dishes, these techniques and the joy of local cookery and baking. For me, Christmas in Spain is such an atmospheric time of year, especially in a country so diverse and so deeply appreciative of a really good fiesta, properly executed with excellent food and jollity. So much about Christmas in Spain is deeply traditional and yet totally spontaneous, that the idea of a book that passed on the culinary delights of this annual feast seemed like an excellent idea.

But it didn't take very long to realise that what had seemed like a fairly straightforward exercise in researching and documenting the traditional recipes of an Iberian Christmas, was actually developing into a potentially gargantuan work involving not only the humble cookery, but also needed an appreciation of ancient and modern European history, agriculture, economics, climatology and sociology. After visits to a just a handful of villages in Andalucía, we realised that it would be almost impossible to ever truly, fully document all the traditional Christmas dishes of a country like Spain.

Why is this? The reasons are several. Firstly, Spain has an incredibly wide agricultural and gastronomic diversity. It would be a life's work to define all the traditions of even a single festival like Christmas throughout Spain.

Secondly, this is a country where traditions operate at the village level and so the task of documenting this tradition is really spread across thousands of villages and towns which are often very, very different. After all, this is a country which has both deserts and wetlands, where temperatures range from -20°C to +45°C degrees, which has snow-capped mountains only kilometres away from arid vineyards, where the weather varies from the rainy and stormy Galician coast to the blistering aridness of Andalucía, where one province grows cabbages and apples and another produces rice and mangoes.

Finally, the task is made much more complicated by the cultural history of Spain. The country has seen invasions and occupations by almost every Mediterranean civilisation over the last 3000 years and the influence of these invaders still resonates in traditional agriculture and cookery.

For all these reasons, Spain just isn't homogenous enough to write a *simple* book about "Traditional Christmas recipes". The whole story of Spanish food and cookery is a great deal more complicated than that.

However, we decided to continue with the task anyway and to start to document the better known Christmas dishes from around Spain, region by region. We figured that even though this is just the tip of the iceberg, these recipes still represent a good start and we would still have a large, diverse and delicious collection of recipes.

Since the inception our only problem is where and when to stop! Every time we think we are ready to publish this book, we find another trove of local Christmas dishes we hadn't seen before….. Someone tells us of a little known cheese dish from northern Extremadura or a different way of making a capon stuffing in Castilla-La Mancha with wild mushrooms, etc. etc.

Of course there is a limit to this and so at some moment we had to stop the research and actually just publish this book - with the firm promise of a second edition, and maybe a third… or even fourth!

Not all of the recipes we have included here are strictly confined to Christmas; many are used during other religious festivals as well. For example, there are many recipes which also appear in Semana Santa - Holy Week - Easter.

In these cases, the recipes are found during both religious celebrations because of the traditional Catholic rules on meat abstinence which prevailed until the 20th century. Despite the lifting of these rules some people still practice the abstinence from meat on the Christmas Eve "vigil" and many delicious meatless recipes have been created around these rules over the centuries and become traditional favourites.

Some of the recipes have been included because they are popular regional winter recipes, which will certainly be eaten during the days and weeks of Spain's very long Christmas festival. For example, Garlic Soup is a much loved winter soup in Castilla, and whilst it is one of the simplest, cheapest dishes imaginable, it is also very popular and tasty. Certainly it will be eaten during the Christmas festivities, even it isn't part of the more grand dinners of the Nochebuena (Christmas Eve) or Noche Vieja (New Years Eve).

We have also included a few recipes from Southern France that have gradually become assimilated into Northern Spanish cuisine and are now traditional in Spain. Some of these recipes actually originated in Spain, were brought back to France by various means (such as the returning Napoleonic armies), made popular in France and then returned to Spain - Onion soup is one such recipe. We make no apologies for this. Food knows no borders.

Another category of dishes we have included here are those which are regional favourites and which are often only made around the Christmas period because they are fiddly or time-consuming, and it is only at this time of year that enough time can be spent in the kitchen to make such elaborate dishes. This is the case with some of the traditional dishes which are much in demand when family members return home for the Christmas celebrations and hanker nostalgically after their favourite regional seasonal dishes. For example, we have an Asturian dish with chestnut and homemade cottage cheese that needs to be prepared over at least 2 days. This is a far cry from convenience food and often doesn't get to be made, except at Christmas when there is time for the kitchen and plenty of willing helpers.

One conclusion that we did reach, having researched the traditional Christmas foods of all the regions of Spain, is that many of the remaining Northern European festive dishes actually originate in Spain. In fact, we also noted that many of these "Christmas" dishes actually have their origins not in Christian culture, but in Moorish traditional cuisine. The use of almonds and spices in bakery, the combination of fruit and nuts in cooking meat are still features of many mainstream European recipes to this day, yet they are directly adopted from the Hispano-Moorish kitchen. Indeed, many of the sweets so deliciously preserved and prepared in the convents and monasteries of Spain to this day actually began their life in the kitchens of the great caliphates of Damascus and Baghdad. Turrón, for example, is thought to have been an emergency ration to feed Moorish soldiers on their long marches to conquer Spain. It is now proudly produced in a wonderful range of turrones in the ancient Monasterio de Santa Clara, to name but one.

And so, in conclusion, we have begun to research and document some of the better known regional Christmas recipes of Spain. And whilst we know the task is unfinished, we do hope that you enjoy what we have discovered and that we have an opportunity to expand this collection in the coming years.

Enjoy these delightful recipes and may we wish all our readers a sincere "Feliz Navidad!"

---oOo---

1.0 An Introduction to Christmas cooking in Spain

What is "Spanish" cookery? It doesn't take long to realise that any book about "Spanish cuisine" is actually a bit ambiguous. "Spain" may be a political reality, but from a cultural, culinary, historical or social point of view the idea of a single homogenous culinary tradition called "Spanish cookery" is actually nonsense. Spain has as many culinary traditions as it has villages. They may be related and sometimes similar, but they are actually all quite individual in some respect.

In fact, what really exists in Spain is a group of very different regions (many of which used to be countries in their own right) with all kinds of cultural, historical, hydrological, climatic, agricultural and geographical differences that now find themselves loosely strung together in a rather artificial bureaucratic alliance called Spain. Despite the best efforts of Franco, the sense of being Spanish is low in the average person's view of their "homeland". For most Spanish people the first allegiance is to family and village, then their province, then their region and after that usually comes Europe. "Spain"- the country- as a source of cultural alliance has simply never gained the enthusiasm that the Spanish right-wing wished for. Thus, every region in Spain has several good reasons why it is not that interested in being Spanish, but many good reasons to be proud of their own village, their province and their region. This situation is not that unique to Spain. You can find similar attitudes in Germany, Italy and yes, maybe even in parts of the "United" Kingdom.

Why so different? Each Spanish region is quite different to its neighbours for many reasons. They often have some traditions in common, but equally every region has many traditions which are very peculiar to them and that goes, of course, also for how they cook and what they eat.

They say that the north of Spain "stews", central Spain "roasts" and southern Spain "fries". And this is quite an accurate analogy both with regards to the weather as to the cooking habits. The south of Spain is the home of the majority of olive and olive oil production and frying is a fine art in this part of the country. Northern Spain is much colder than any other part of the country, and the most emblematic dishes in these regions are the "Potes" or the warming stews. Central Spain is full of herds of sheep and goats and roasting these is a central part of the culinary tradition.

But it isn't just the climate that makes for differences. A lot of them have to do with geographical isolation. Even today, with modern autovías and high-speed trains, many parts of Spain are very isolated even from their own provincial capitals, and even more so from their regional and national capitals. Spain has very difficult terrain in places and this isolation means that small communities have to rely on their own resources for food and other supplies. This attitude of self-reliance is very strong in Spain and is one of the reasons that over the centuries a great deal of culinary diversity has developed, even at the village level. After all, if your village is in the mountains and has a lot of goats, beans, wild thistles and wine, it is logical that dishes will be developed that exploit these food products.

Another reason for the very imaginative and diverse recipes that one finds in rural Spain is poverty. Despite the apparently wonderful climate, Spain has a lot of agricultural disadvantages in many areas. A shortage of water in some areas may be compounded by catastrophic rainfalls in that same area. Spanish weather can be quite extreme and crop failures are quite common. The history of Spain tells of a long succession of famines - many of them caused by natural disasters as well as by civil strife.

These frequent bouts of poverty have made for some very imaginative cooking, including Christmas cookery. Very little gets wasted in a Spanish kitchen, whether it is stale bread or sour wine - in Spanish cookery there is a recipe for everything edible that enters the kitchen. Take the sweet fritters made with the limp outer leaves of curly kale that are normally discarded, or the dozens of recipes that call for breadcrumbs from stale bread, or the meat or fish stocks made from all kinds of unmentionable waste parts of fish or pork. Generally speaking, the Spanish cook works with what they have and over the centuries this has given rise to some extraordinary and delicious recipes like cold almond soup and fresh grapes..... a much sought after dish that originated as a field dish made on the land by the workers harvesting almonds and grapes.... All they needed to bring was water and garlic!

Sometimes scarcity is the mother of invention and in Spain, over the centuries there has been a lot of invention!

Why so sweet? In the past, Spanish Christmas food was characterised by being quite simple and dominated by a lot of sweet dishes and cakes. This is still true today, but more complex main dishes have gradually entered the culinary tradition. Nonetheless, the amount and range of traditional sweets which are available over the festive period is phenomenal. Many of these are very traditional, many are based on almond, dried fruits and honey and all of them are unapologetically sweet. Why is this so? Well there are several possible explanations for this, ranging from quite innocent to slightly sinister. Here are the two main explanations:

- Many Christmas recipes originated in peasant kitchens when feeding the workers. They needed to deliver nutrition and calories to support the extremely hard work on the land. Sometimes, this meant serving warming high-calorie foods and sometimes it meant making sweet foods to give instant energy to the workers. This was especially true in the winter, and so many Christmas foods are sweet and fatty.

- The Church was (and is) keen to associate Christian festivals with pleasant sensations in the mind of its parishioners, like good food. This was especially imperative when the Christian monarchs invaded the Moorish lands of central and southern Spain and found it very hard to persuade the Muslim inhabitants to convert to Christianity. For the same reason the mosque of Córdoba had a Christian cathedral inserted into the centre of it - simply because the Christian monarchs had failed to stop attendance at the mosque, so they decided to put a church in the middle of it, with the hope of persuading the Muslims to convert. In the same way, sugar was used as a lever to entice the notoriously sweet-toothed Muslim population over to Christianity. For this very same reason many of the Christian monastic settlements and convents took up the making of confectionary - and to this day there are scores of convents and monasteries still making some of Spain's most exquisite, delicious and ancient sweets

Whichever of these explanations you care to believe, we are all the beneficiaries of history and Spain has the most extraordinary range of Christmas sweets in Europe. The recipes we present here are just a tiny sample of a huge range of Spanish Christmas confectionaries. Some of these are so unique that they command their own EU enforced D.O. status to protect their quality and reputation. I have to say: it all somewhat eclipses mince pies and Christmas pudding!

Why so much Fish? Fish is a big Christmas favourite throughout Spain. Again we have the influence of the church to thank for this. As a result of centuries-old abstinence from meat on Christmas Eve (which was considered to be a night of vigil keeping), fish and non-meat dishes came to dominate the menu on the evening of Nochebuena. Whilst these religious rules have long since been abolished, the custom lives on - mostly because so many delicious recipes developed over the centuries to accommodate the absence of meat.

Why so many almonds? Almonds are so synonymous with Christmas throughout Europe, that it is hard to imagine Christmas without them; whether it's Weihnachtsstollen in Germany or marzipan on Christmas cakes in England. It is most obvious in Spain, where almost every conceivable Christmas dish is a potential candidate for the addition of almonds. Obviously, Spain is a large producer of extremely good quality hard-shelled Mediterranean almonds and these almonds are harvested just a couple of months before Christmas. But why are almonds so popular at Christmas? Well, the primary reason is that they are fresh and they arrive in vast quantities - therefore, they must be eaten. But a second reason is that almonds have a very high protein content and when the end of the summer finally comes, there is a temporary gap in the production of other sources of protein. This is easily filled by using almonds. It is a saying in Spain that a handful of almonds is worth a small beef steak. That might be a slight exaggeration, but the concept is correct - almonds are an excellent food and a good stop-gap in lean times like mid-winter. They travel and store well and they are delicious and versatile.

---o0o---

1.1 The Geography of Spain and its Regions

Origins of the Autonomous Regions: Whilst Spain is considered by outsiders to be a single nation, most Spanish people see themselves primarily as being citizens of their region; not only politically, but also culturally, socially and historically. For much of its recent history, Spain has been a country of conflicting identities; on the one hand a national identity hinging on the concept of Spain as a single country; on the other hand a network of regional identities, with many parts of Spain displaying distinct regional characteristics, and even using their own distinct languages.

A united Spain: In the time of Franco, the vision of Spain as a single united country prevailed, and was even enforced. In the modern post-Franco era, Spain has taken the path of devolution, creating, "autonomous communities" with their own parliaments, institutions, taxes, cultural identities and even languages. In the last decades, since the return of democracy to Spain, much of central government power has been devolved to the autonomous regions. But despite these recent political changes, there are much more fundamental reasons why the regions have retained their very individual characters.

Cultural Diversity: Spain's modern regions are based on ancient historical and geographical borders. In some cases, the regions were actually independent nations in their own right in the past, like Galicia, Cataluña, Aragón, País Vasco, etc. There are also several active languages in daily use in the Spanish regions such as Catalán and Euskera (Basque), not to mention Galician and Aragonese. What we refer to as "Spanish" is usually referred to as "Castellano" inside Spain to distinguish this language from other regional languages in daily use.

Geographic divisions: Apart from the political, cultural and historical divisions within Spain, the geography of the country also maintains enormous economic and agricultural diversity, and this directly impacts on the culinary traditions of the regions. Obviously, the Canary and Balearic islands are geographically separate from the Iberian Peninsula, but even within the mainland the differences between regions are quite profound.

One of the main reasons for the diversity of the country is geographic accessibility. Spain is a big country by European standards and it is also the second most mountainous country in Europe (after Switzerland). It is therefore quite an inaccessible land. Indeed in the 19th century it was said that it was faster and easier to get from Barcelona to Havana in Cuba than it was to get to Madrid from Barcelona.

Many geographic and climatic obstacles have resulted in the existence of many relatively isolated and self-sufficient communities throughout the peninsula. During the Franco period, the country was largely isolated from the rest of Europe. The inherent logistical difficulties meant that the country was obliged to be even more self-sufficient. This isolation gave rise to the development of localised food production, which in turn created many local food industries, many of which survive to this day and promote a vast diversity of food products; a lot of which are made in a unique, traditional way and are of exceptional quality.

Social Diversity: As you travel across Spain you very quickly realise that every town and village in Spain has its own speciality products and local recipes: whether it be a wine, a honey, a type of cake, some meat product, liquor, dried fruit or one of a thousand other food products or recipes. This extraordinary diversity has been largely lost in most of Northern Europe, where the push towards uniformity in food is now almost complete.

In this book we have chosen to look at recipes in terms of regional differences, but there are many examples where a traditional dish in one village is made quite differently in a village just 10 kms away and "always has been". So we should probably have researched recipes by village rather than by region or province. However, the latter would be a project taking a lifetime and an awful lot of food sampling!

The Autonomous Regions of Spain: To get a feeling for the differences between regions and how they affect the culinary traditions of the region, we will describe each one a little later in the book. But for now take a look at the basic geography of Spain and its regions.

Here are the Spanish autonomous regions:

    Andalucía
    Aragón
    Asturias
    Canarias
    Cantabria
    Castilla y León
    Castilla-La Mancha
    Cataluña
    Extremadura
    Galicia
    Islas Baleares
    Comunidad de Madrid
    Región de Murcia
    Navarra
    La Rioja
    Comunidad Valenciana
    País Vasco
    Ceuta y Melilla

1.1.1 A Map of the Regions of Spain

1.1.2 A Map of the Provinces of Spain

Most regions are divided into several provinces.

1.2 A culinary History of Spain

Here is a brief timeline of the history of Spain:

- 32000 BC: First human beings arrived in the Iberian Peninsula from Africa
- 900 BC: Phoenicians settle the Iberian Peninsula and founded Cádiz.
- 800 BC: Bastuli (Celtiberian) settlements.
- 770 BC: Founding of Malaka (Málaga) by the Phoenicians.
- 600 BC: Greek settlements along the coast.
- 500 BC: Carthaginian (Punic) settlements in Spain.
- 218 BC: Region invaded by Rome.
- 19 AD: Roman invasion completed. Peninsula becomes known as Hispania.

- 1st-5th Century: Hispania supplies Rome with food, olive oil, wine and metal.
- 476. Foundation of the Visigoth kingdom by invading Germanic tribes.
- 500: Rome in decline, invasion by Byzantine, Germanic and Visigoth pirates.
- 624: Byzantine expulsions.
- 711-718: Muslim Arab conquest of southern Spain.
- 10th Century: Moorish control of the entire Iberian Peninsula except Asturias
- 1085: Alfonso VI from Castilla conquered Toledo from the Moors.
- 1094: The Castilian knight El Cid conquered Valencia from the Moors.
- 1138: The Kingdom of Portugal was established
- 1228: Moorish influence was reduced to the Kingdom of Granada.
- 1487: Final siege of Mālaqa (Málaga) by the Catholic monarchs.
- 1484-1501: Mudéjar period, in which Muslim converts were given protection.
- 1481: The founding of the Spanish inquisition - the suppression of Jewish and Muslim practices in Spain.
- 1492: Capitulation of King Boabdil of the Kingdom of Granada.
- 1492: Wider colonisation of the conquered Kingdom of Granada by Christians from other parts of Spain begins.
- 1492: Columbus' discovery of the Americas.
- 1609: Phillip II of Spain decreed the Expulsion of the Moriscos - the Christian "ethnic and religious cleansing" of Spain.
- 16th-18th century: Large parts of conquered regions are depopulated and in economic decline.
- 18th century: Period of economic recovery for Spain.
- 1808-14: Napoleonic Wars.
- 1898: Loss of the final Spanish colonies.
- 1931-1936: Spain's First Democracy: The Second Republic
- 1936: Spanish civil war. Many brutal atrocities from the Francoist military dictatorship against the largely Republican population caused severe reductions in agricultural development and production.
- 1978: Democracy returns to Spain.

---oOo---

1.2.1 Historical Gastronomic influences

Phoenician influences: The Phoenicians were a sea-faring people and most of their settlements were on the sea or close by. Malaka (Málaga) was an important part in many of their trade routes, as was Cádiz.

- Muscatel: The Phoenicians are believed to have introduced the Muscat grape into the province of Málaga. The grape (*vitis vinifera*) is believed to be the oldest cultivated variety of grape in the world.

Roman influences:

- Olives: The Romans originally introduced the cultivation of olives into southern Spain.

- Food preservation: Rome was very interested in having food produced in Hispania. Therefore, during the occupation by Rome, they introduced various methods of food preservation to prepare the food for the long sea voyage back to Rome or to other parts of the empire. Drying, salting, pickling and marination were used to preserve fruit, meat and fish for transport and storage. Some of the original techniques are still in use today.

Arabic influences: There are many culinary and agricultural influences which were introduced into al-Ándalus during the Moorish era:

- Irrigation: The Moors were experts in the design and construction of irrigation and water storage systems for agriculture. Many of their constructions are still in use to this day.

- Olives and Olive oil: The Arabs extended the planting of olive trees in al-Ándalus, and olive oil was an important part of the economy during the Moorish era.

- Sugar: Arab traders introduced sugar cane cultivation to Andalucía (from India).

- Oranges and Lemons: Arab farmers brought oranges and lemons for cultivation in Andalucía.

- Almonds: An Arab caliph of Córdoba is believed to have brought almonds to Andalucía from Syria to beautify the city of Córdoba as a present for his bride. The almonds of southern Spain are still considered to be of the world's best quality.

- Herbs: The use of herbs in dressings and sauces was introduced by Arab cooks.

- Spices: The trade routes to the east which ran from Andalucía, through Africa and central Asia to China were controlled by the Moors, and this allowed for the importation of many spices into Spain which are still in daily use today. These included cinnamon, saffron, cloves, bay leaf and nutmeg. The use of these spices revolutionised cookery in Spain.

- Cotton: The Moors introduced the cultivation of cotton into Andalucía.

- Dried fruit in savoury dishes: The frequent use of dried and/or fresh fruit in savoury recipes is a tradition brought to Spain by Arab cooks of the Levant. Dried figs and raisins became common in savoury dishes.

- Figs: The modern cultivated fig was introduced by Arab agriculturalists into southern Spain.

- Fruit drying: The Romans introduced and the Moors developed fruit drying. Primarily this was done to prolong the life of excess fruit production, both for transportation and for over wintering. However, the drying process also altered the food's taste and this gave rise to many new and interesting recipes, especially those which use fruit in sweet and savoury combinations, so much loved by Moorish cooks.

- Rice: The improvements in irrigation made by the Moors allowed for the introduction and cultivation of rice. Together with the use of saffron, the making of paella was actually pioneered by the Moors.

- Wines: Whilst wine production was discouraged with taxes, it was not consistently outlawed during Moorish times (sometimes on the contrary, in fact).

- Asparagus: Ziryab (the blackbird), was a Baghdadi Arab musician to the court of Córdoba. He was also keenly interested in food and invented many new Andalusí dishes, which survive to this day. He was responsible for elevating the humble spring weed called asparagus to the status of a delicacy. (This man actually deserves a whole book dedicated to him alone - he was really an extremely clever, inventive and colourful person of enormous talent).

Christian influences: The gradual Christian invasion of al-Ándalus brought many changes to the territories they occupied:

- Pork: The lifting of the Muslim prohibition on pig meat brought about a new culinary repertoire of fresh and preserved meats, like cured hams, chorizos and other cured meat products.

- Wine: The taxing of wine production was relaxed and the wine industry in the Christian occupied territories was encouraged in order to generate revenue for the Christian monarchs.

The influence of the Americas: The discovery of the Americas brought many changes to the diets of everyone in Europe, but especially to the agriculture of the sub-tropical areas of Andalucía and the Mediterranean coast:

- Tomatoes, peppers, cucumbers, aubergines, potatoes, chillies, and many tropical fruits come originally from the Caribbean and the Americas. It's hard to believe how we managed before these ingredients arrived. They revolutionised the diet in southern Spain and gradually in all of Europe.

---oOo---

1.3 The culinary geography of Spain - Region by Region

Because of the great variations in climate and geography, every region of Spain has its own speciality ingredients and dishes. Here we describe the geography, a little history, and something about the regional agriculture and iconic products, ingredients and dishes for each region with a special focus on Christmas dishes:

1.3.1 Andalucía

Geography: Capital: Sevilla. Andalucía is the southernmost region of continental Europe. The second largest of Spain's seventeen autonomous communities, Andalucía stretches all the way across the south: from the Atlantic Ocean at the province of Cádiz, past the Straits of Gibraltar to the Mediterranean at Almería province. Andalucía has the largest population of any region, but most of it is concentrated along the coast and in the Guadalquivir valley. Despite coastal developments, Andalucía remains a magnificent and wild region of great diversity, with mountains, hills and plains. Andalucía's climate is similar to North Africa's with balmy winters and often searingly hot, dry summers.

History and Culture: The region has some of the richest cultural heritage in Spain. This is the old Arab territory of al-Ándalus, heartland of the brilliant Moorish civilization that dominated Spain for nearly 700 years and left its mark on Andalucía's landscape, on its people, and, naturally enough, on its food. It was the last European fiefdom of the Moors, and al-Ándalus boasts some of the finest historic remains of Moorish culture. The Moors continued in Andalucía until 1492, when the invading Christian armies finally overcame them in Granada. It was in the same year that Christopher Columbus first set foot in the Americas. The great Moorish heritage of Andalucía survives to this day in the many Alcazares, Alcazabas and other constructions, but most famously in the Mezquita in Córdoba and in the Alhambra in Granada - both of which are very impressive world heritage sites.

Food Economics: Andalucía is one of the poorest regions of Spain, particularly away from the coastal tourist areas of the Mediterranean coast between Málaga and Marbella. Behind the coast, much of the region is very hilly and mountainous, culminating in the snowy peaks of the Sierra Nevada, some of the highest mountains on the Spanish mainland. Between the Sierra Nevada and the coast lie the Alpujarras, where the last Moors of Spain hid when expelled from the city of Granada. To this day, the area with its white villages clinging to hillsides, is very similar to parts of Morocco.

Northern and eastern Andalucía are sparsely populated; many parts being characterised today by endless olive groves. Other parts of eastern Andalucía are dry and virtually a desert. Just inland from the port of Almería lies the Desierto de Tabernas, the only area in Europe that is officially designated as a desert. The most fertile part of Andalucía is the central valley of the river Guadalquivir which flows east to west from Jaén province through Córdoba and Sevilla, reaching the Atlantic coast in the province of Cádiz. Though the flow of the river is very seasonal, the Guadalquivir and its tributaries sustain huge agricultural activity throughout the area, including the production of Sherry, which comes from the area around Jerez de la Frontera in Cádiz province.

Though the olive groves of Andalucía originate with the Romans, it was nonetheless the Arabs who put a permanent stamp on Andalucían olives and oil. We know that from the language: the words *aceite, aceitunas, almazara*, meaning oil, olives, and the olive mill - all come directly from Arabic. Jaén, one of Andalucía's eight provinces, is today the leading olive oil producer in the world.

Typical Food Products: Every one of Andalucía's provinces has its own specialities, depending on the local conditions. We will now take a closer look at these ingredients and dishes:

> **Caracoles en salsa:** These seasonal delicacies are popular in many parts of the region: Snails, often cooked in a minty, spicy tomato sauce.
>
> **Langostinos de Sanlúcar:** These are large prawns from the mouth of the Guadalquivir, often served grilled or baked.
>
> **Escabeche de sardinas from Almería:** vinegar-infused roasted sardines.
>
> **Sardinas and salmonetes:** These are fresh sardines and small red mullet, best served hot from a grill set over the embers of an open wood fire.
>
> **Caldo de perro:** This is a fish stew from Cádiz, typically flavoured with the juice of bitter (Seville) oranges.
>
> **Olive Oil:** Olive oil is oil obtained from the olive (Olea europaea), a traditional tree crop of the Mediterranean Basin. Spain is the world's number one producer of olive oil. Pressed from about 260 different cultivars, the oil is prized around the world. Andalucía accounts for about 80% of Spain's olive oil production.
>
> **Alcachofas y Patatas a la Cordobesa:** This is an artichoke and potato stew with saffron and garlic, from Córdoba.
>
> **Alboronia from Jaén:** This is a mixture of vegetables: courgettes, garlic, aubergines, onions, peppers, and tomatoes.
>
> **Jamón de bellota, jamón de pata negra:** Jamón de pata negra refers to the variety of pig from which these prized hams are made. The most famous hams are produced in Huelva province from the meat of the semi-wild Iberian pigs. This is considered to be the finest ham in the world. "Bellota" refers to the acorns (bellotas) on which the pigs feed for the last months of their lives and that contribute to giving the ham its distinctive characteristics.
>
> **Cazuela de Arroz and Cazuela de Fideos:** These casseroles are from Málaga, and consist of rice or pasta, pan-roasted with saffron, fish and shellfish.

Puchero: This is an Andalucían stew made with lots of vegetables, including pumpkin, courgettes, and green beans.

Caldereta de Chivo: This dish is from Málaga and made with lamb or kid goat baked with cinnamon, cloves and peppercorns.

Pato a la Sevillana: This is a braised duck with oranges, olives, and spices, from Sevilla.

Gazpacho: A deliciously refreshing combination of stale bread, olive oil, ripe tomatoes, garlic, peppers, and vinegar, served cold in the hot summer months.

Ajo blanco: Another cold soup, made with crushed almonds and garlic.

Pipirrana from Jaén: This is a finely chopped salad made with tomatoes, cucumber, onions, peppers, and sometimes flavoured with cumin and vinegar.

Almendras: Almonds were introduced into Andalucía by the Moors and the quality of these Mediterranean almonds is unsurpassed. They are full of flavour and used in many Andaluz dishes. Marcona almonds are a small, round type and prized for their flavour and texture.

Sherry ("Jerez"): There are many different types of sherry and the whole subject is worth a book by itself. *Fino* is a dry, pale-coloured wine that may be served as an aperitif. A similar sherry is *Manzanilla*, which is lighter and drier than Fino and has a lower alcohol content.

Sherry Vinegar: Sherry vinegar (*Vinagre de Jerez*) is produced in the Jerez region of Cádiz known as the "sherry triangle". The same Palomino Fino grapes used to produce sherry are used in the making of sherry vinegar. To be called "vinagre de Jerez" according to the D.O., the sherry vinegar must undergo ageing for a minimum of six months, and must have a minimum acidity of 7 degrees.

Christmas in Andalucía: This is the land of some extraordinary and world-famous hams and chorizos. These include the legendary Ibérico hams from the Sierra de Aracena in Huelva, and the Serrano hams of the Alpujarras. Today these exquisite products of great quality are often brought to the table for the Christmas and New Year celebrations.

In Andalucía it's common to have turkey and seafood for the main Christmas Eve dinner. Especially along the Andalucían coast, the famous and excellent prawns of Sanlúcar de Barrameda, Huelva and Cádiz are a popular festive main course for the dinner on Nochebuena.

There are many traditional sweet Christmas dishes in Andalucía, usually made with a combination of almonds, sugar, figs and honey and many spices such as cinnamon, cloves and anise. These include various sweet fritters like the "alfajores andaluces" of Medina Sidonia and "pestiños". There are lots of types of Andalucían shortbreads and biscuits - like the "polvorones" and "mantecados" of Estepa, and there is a huge variety of sweet doughnuts of every conceivable flavour, like the delicious "Roscos de vino".

---oOo---

1.3.2 Aragón

Geography: Capital: Zaragoza (Saragossa). Landlocked Aragón is a sparsely-populated region which is mainly rural, with agriculture wherever possible. However, in its dry hilly areas, there is little more economic activity possible beyond grazing and in places where the land is accessible, forestry.

Aragón begins high in the snow-capped Pyrenees along Spain's mountainous border with France. From steep heights Aragón descends through foothills into broad plains along the banks of the Ebro river, including near desert regions like Los Monegros, then rises again to the much lower Sistema Ibérico in the south. There are just three provinces in the region, Huesca in the north, Teruel, in the south and Zaragoza in the middle, sited on an ancient crossing of the Ebro River.

Aragón is a landscape of stunning vistas that include medieval hilltop villages and ancient -ruined- fortifications, old drover roads where shepherds move their flocks between winter and summer grazing. There is very little tourism.

History and Culture: This part of Spain is, like most regions, rich in history and culture, particularly visible in the Moorish and Mozarabic heritage of Zaragoza, the Mudéjar heritage of Teruel, and the ancient castles such as the Romanesque fortress at Loarre.

Food Economics: The northern parts of Aragón are made up of the Pyrenees which, on this southern side, are fairly dry and arid. Narrow valleys with rocky gorges are characteristic of this region. South of the Pyrenees, the wide Ebro valley around Zaragoza (or Saragossa) is a fertile agricultural region. In the south-east, between the fertile agricultural plains and the coast, lies a dry hilly area of Mediterranean pine forests and olive groves.

Aragón is a strongly agricultural region. It is famous for having a very straight-forward cuisine. Its traditional recipes are very much reliant on meat, especially lamb and pork, and include fresh meats as well as the long-cured hams and chorizos.

Aragonese agriculture is very diverse. The green mountain pastures of Aragón produce lamb and many sheep's milk cheeses. The plains of the river Ebro are full of wheat and barley. The southern area of Aragón produces excellent olive oils, made mostly with the "empeltre" and "arbequina" varieties of olive. The region also boasts full-bodied red wines with three D.O. wines in Zaragoza: "Campo de Borja", "Calatayud", and "Cariñena". As mentioned, Aragón is home to a number of fine cheeses, including the most notable, Tronchón, mentioned in Don Quijote for its quality.

Typical Food Products: Let us look at the dishes and ingredients in more detail:

> **Recao**: a country dish made with white beans, rice, and potatoes, liberally flavoured with garlic, hot pimentón (paprika), and chorizo.
>
> **Pollo or cordero al chilindrón**: chicken or lamb braised in a rich sauce of sweet red peppers, tomatoes, and fine jamón serrano from Teruel.
>
> **Perdiz al chocolate**: Partridge with a sauce thickened with bitter chocolate, most likely directly related to the chocolate brought back from the New World.
>
> **Menestra a la pastora**: This is a thick, country-style lamb stew, rich with vegetables such as artichokes, peas, fava beans, potatoes, onions.
>
> **Black truffles and wild mushrooms**: from the Maestrazgo region of Teruel.
>
> **Truchas**: Trout from the swift high mountain streams of Aragón.

Cecina: This is a cured salty beef or salty goat meat.

Magras con tomate: This is a farmhouse dish of lean slices of Teruel ham, lightly fried and covered with tomato sauce.

Melocotones de Calanda (Calanda Peaches): Aragón is famous for the quality of its peaches, and these Calanda peaches have their own controlled denomination and are the best in Spain.

Migas: These are fried breadcrumbs, like similar dishes from Castilla and Andalucía. In Aragón migas are served with diced ham, chorizo, bacon, or morcilla (black pudding), often with chocolate to thicken the sauce.

Christmas in Aragón: The most typical Christmas dishes of Aragón are cardo (thistle) with béchamel, or "cordero al chilindrón" - chilindrón lamb, "bacalao al ajoarriero" - a salted cod dish, and various versions of stuffed capon.

Popular sweets include the traditional "guirlache de Aragón" - nougat of Aragón, or the "crespillos" of Barbastro.

---oOo---

1.3.3 Asturias

Geography: Capital: Oviedo. For most of its length, the coastline of northern Spain is hilly or even mountainous. Behind a narrow and fertile coastal plain, the terrain rises steeply into the mountains of Cantabria and Asturias, known collectively as the cordillera Cantábrica, culminating in the Picos de Europa, dramatic, very rocky mountains with deep valleys and soaring peaks. The area has been nicknamed "Switzerland on the sea", on account of the proximity of high mountain peaks, green valleys, and the Atlantic Ocean.

Tourism was slow to develop here, and the northern coast of Spain has not seen too much of the mass tourist development of the "Costas". There are long stretches of relatively unblemished coastline, with fields and meadows coming right down to the edge of the sea or, in most cases, the cliff tops. Like Galicia, Cantabria and Asturias are parts of what is known as "Green Spain" (España Verde) on account of their oceanic climate. They are small regions, just including the coastal areas and the northern slopes of the Cantabrian Mountains.

History: Asturias has a very difficult geography. This is the primary reason why even modern Spaniards say that Spain begins with Asturias, simply because it was the one region never conquered by the Moors, and it was the region from which the long drawn-out saga of the Christian invasions of Moorish Spain began.

Food Economics: Asturias' geography gives it both a rich agricultural hinterland and also a valuable source of seafood, including bígaros (periwinkles), mussels, shrimps, spider crabs, and sea-urchins. It has a rainy Atlantic climate, with mild winters. High green pastures make for excellent dairy production. Asturias is well-known for its array of cheeses, many of them aged in limestone mountain caves.

Apart from the excellent seafood, the region also has beautiful fresh-water trout and salmon. However, the more important and emblematic products from Asturias include cider, cheeses and beans.

Cider: Like neighbouring Cantabria, Asturias is not a wine-producing region. However, the most popular drink of the area is cider, made from one or more of 22 different varieties of apple permitted in the Denomination of Origen (D.O.). In fact, there's a whole culture around sidra, which is ideally served in a sidrería, a cider bar, poured from a green bottle held at a great height in order to aerate the drink. Traditionally, the most popular varieties are unfiltered, unpasteurized, cloudy, amber-coloured, and only lightly alcoholic.

Cabrales - Cheeses: There are more than 25 different varieties of cheese produced in Asturias, including the deeply veined, blue-green "cabrales", made from a mixture of cow's, sheep's, and goat's milk.

A lesser known cheese called "gamoneu" (gamonedo) is a bit dryer, also made with a mixture of milk. Then there is "afuega'l pitu", which is made from un-pasteurized cow's milk. These cheeses are manufactured under the standards of their own D.O. system. They are some of the world's best cheeses.

Fabada asturiana: This is a bean stew often said to be the national dish of Asturias. This is a large and hearty one-pot bean stew made with beans that are grown for the purpose around Villaviciosa, Pravia and Cangas. These are large, plump white beans. In a proper fabada, the beans are cooked for hours with spicy chorizo, lacón (cured pork shank), perhaps salted unsmoked bacon, morcilla (blood sausage), and flavoured with saffron and sweet unsmoked paprika (pimentón).

Typical Food Products: Here we take a closer look at the main ingredients and recipes of Asturias:

> **Casadielles**: These sweet pastry fritters are filled with chopped walnuts and flavoured with anis liquor.
>
> **Pote asturiano**: White beans, potatoes, and curly kale, stewed in an earthenware pot with morcilla (black pudding) and chorizo.
>
> **Arroz con leche**: This is a sweet rice and milk pudding, often with a grilled crust.
>
> **Frixuelos de manzana**: These are delicate crepes rolled around a filling of chopped apple.
>
> **Escanda**: This is an ancient type of wheat, almost extinct, similar to spelt or to a type of durum wheat called "emmer", popular in Asturias.
>
> **Caldereta asturiana**: This is a fish stew made from whatever fish is available plus onions, parsley, and white wine.
>
> **Merluza a la sidra**: These are fillets of hake poached in Asturian cider, served with potatoes and clams.

Christmas in Asturias: The area is well known for its production of chestnuts, cider, goat's meat, apples, honey, mushrooms and cheeses. Typical Christmas dishes include kid goat in cider - "cabritu a la sidra", cream of crab soup - "Crema de andaricas", free-range chicken with chestnuts - "pitu", and the Asturian "potes" - rich winter stews served with chorizo and black pudding.

There is no shortage of sweet dishes, including "casadielles" - anis flavoured pasties made with ground walnuts and honey, "Borrachinos" - sweet cinnamon dumplings, as well as chestnut purées and various spiced apple dishes.

---oOo---

1.3.4 Islas Baleares

Geography: Capital: Palma de Mallorca. The Islas Baleares are actually 15 islands lying between the Spanish east coast and Sardinia, some 80 to 140 miles off the coast of Spain. Only four of the islands are very important: Menorca, Mallorca, Ibiza and Formentera. The

Balearic climate is pure Mediterranean, very mild: an annual average of between 16 °C and 17.5 °C, with more than 300 days of sun per year and seasonal rains. The summer period is hot and dry and the annual rainfall varies across the islands, from 350mm in the south to 1,500mm in the high areas on the Sierra de Tramuntana mountain range. However, most of the islands receive between 450mm and 650mm of precipitation over the year. The rains, stable temperatures and sunshine make for good agricultural conditions, and for the rapid tourist development which the islands have experienced in recent decades.

History and Culture: Each island has its own character, but all together they share many characteristics of Cataluña, especially in culinary, cultural, and linguistic matters.

Over the centuries, the islands were a stopping place on almost every route through the western Mediterranean, but especially on the route from Barcelona, Marseille, and Genoa to North Africa. This has given rise to many cross-cultural influences. The islands experienced a similar history to the Spanish mainland, including the arrival of Phoenicians, Romans, Visigoths and Moors and finally the latest Christian crusaders of the middle ages.

Food Economics: Despite the modern tourism, it is still possible to tease out the roots of a delightful traditional cuisine with many time-honoured products of the sea and the land. Some examples of the islands' notable production:

Olive oil is an important agricultural product in the islands. These oils are often of excellent quality and are mostly made from the local "empeltre" and "arbequina" varieties of olive.

Despite this, pork fat is also very important in island cookery and is the basis of one of the most highly regarded pastries, the ensaimada. This a sugared breakfast bun made from a light, sweet, yeasty dough.

Wine from the Balearic Islands: There are two denomination of origin (D.O.) wines in the Baleares, both from the island of Mallorca: "Binissalem Mallorca" and "Plà i Llevant". Both are excellent.

Menorca, the outermost of the Baleares, is still more agricultural than the other islands. The very popular cheese called Mahón (named after the capital of the island) originates here. It is said to derive its quality from the process of aging in underground caves for six months to two years. This gives the cheese an exceptional buttery flavour.

Typical Food Products: Let us take a look at some of the specific ingredients and recipes which are most typical of Las Islas Baleares:

> **Cocas**: This is somewhat similar to pizza, and is an open tart, topped usually with roasted sweet red peppers and trampó (a mix of peppers, onions and tomatoes). It is similar to the cocas of Cataluña, but in the islands they are always rectangular.
>
> **Sobrasada:** This is a soft, deep red, spiced, garlic sausage made from the meat of the islands' black pigs. These are related to, but not the same as, the semi-wild Ibérico pigs of mainland Spain.
>
> **Ensaimadas**: Spiral-shaped yeast buns, traditionally served at breakfast, with powdered sugar on top.
>
> **Trempó (or trampó)**: This is a salad of sliced tomatoes, onions and green peppers.
>
> **Tàperes (capers)**: Capers are the flower buds of the caper plant, which, after being pickled in vinegar, are used in sauces and garnishes.
>
> **Mayonnaise (mahónesa)**: It is believed that this sauce was actually invented in Mahón, capital of Menorca; hence the name mahónesa.
>
> **Caldereta de langosta**: This is a seafood stew, based on local lobsters, cooked with peppers, onions, tomatoes, and garlic.
>
> **Tumbet**: This is a dish of fried courgettes, aubergines and red peppers, baked with potatoes in a tomato sauce. It is similar to ratatouille.

Christmas in the Baleares: The most typical Christmas dishes in the Baleares are turkey, chicken or pork, but there are other popular and more traditional dishes like pasta shell soups and stuffed suckling pig which are typically Mallorcan. One ancient sweet called "Cuscussó" is also a Christmas favourite in Menorca, originating in the Arab era and made with butter, honey, sugar, bread crumbs, chopped almonds, cinnamon and lemon zest. In addition, there are the so-called "Pastissets" which are a pastry shaped like a flower with five petals, made with sugar, butter, egg yolks and flour, about 6 cm. in diameter. They are white on the outside and yellow on the inside and traditionally served for Christmas and important family gatherings.

---o0o---

1.3.5 Basque Country / País Vasco / Euskadi

Geography: Capital: Vitoria (Gasteiz): Despite the reputation of the region for its violent separatist movement ETA, the Basque country is actually the most prosperous region in Spain (by GDP per capita) thanks to its industry, tourism and agriculture. There are two official languages in the Basque Country, Basque (Euskera) and Spanish (Castellano). The Basque language is completely different from Spanish, which explains why many places in the Basque area have two quite different sounding names. The region has two big industrial and commercial cities, the ports of Bilbao and San Sebastian (Donostia). Between them, the rocky Atlantic coastline offers a number of small resorts that have seen little development in recent decades.

The northern half of the Basque country is hilly - the Basque hills being the westward extension of the Pyrenees. But unlike the Spanish Pyrenees, the Basque hill country benefits from more rainfall, making it a very green and wooded area. The hills and valleys are dotted with small villages and isolated farmsteads. The southern part of the Basque Country, the province of Álava, south of the coastal mountains, enjoys a much more continental climate. Most of the population of Álava is concentrated in the Vitoria conglomeration. Beyond the capital city, the area is largely agricultural, particularly on the flat expanses of the upper Ebro valley.

Food Economics: Apart from its agricultural and marine wealth, the Basque country lays claim to the greatest density of Michelin star chefs in the world: Just between the towns of San Sebastian and Bilbao, there are 17 Michelin stars awarded to restaurants that are world famous.

Typical Food Products: Coming down from the lofty culinary heights of Michelin stars, the region has a great wealth of traditional cuisine of more plain cooking, of hearty country and fish dishes, with meats (mostly lamb and beef) and fish grilled over wood fires, and many local bean stews.

A well-respected local drink is the cider of the Basque country which is served foaming in the glass in sidrerias. But in addition, the Basque Country, which isn't usually noted for its wines, does include the province of Álava, which is actually the home of the Rioja Alavesa, one of La Rioja's premier wine districts.

Apart from this distinguished red wine, the Basque Country is noted for "txakoli", a white wine made along the coast west of San Sebastian and a lively accompaniment to the robust cuisine of the region, especially when sampling tapas ("pintxos") in the old towns of San Sebastian or Bilbao.

Typical ingredients and dishes:

> **Kokotxas de merluza**: Hake fillets ("kokotxas") are sautéed with olive oil and garlic with the cook's gentle but constant swirling motion of the pan creating an emulsified sauce for the fish.
>
> **Perritxikos**: These are prized mushrooms of the Tricholoma family. They are only available during the spring season and are usually sautéed with garlic and parsley, or served mixed into freshly scrambled eggs.
>
> **Pimientos de Gernika**: These are small, sweet green chillies (similar to Galicia's pimientos de Padrón) from the Basque town of Guernica, usually grilled "a la plancha" and sprinkled with salt.
>
> **Alubias de Tolosa**: This is a bean stew made with the black beans of Tolosa, cooked together with spicy green peppers (*guindillas*), garlic, and pork ribs.
>
> **Piperrada**: This is a mixture of garlic, onion, red peppers, tomatoes, and fresh herbs, all cooked together and served with a slice of jamón serrano or scrambled eggs.
>
> **Bacalao a la vizcaina**: A favourite cod dish from Vizcaya province, this is salted cod cooked with dried sweet red peppers, garlic, diced ham, and parsley.
>
> **Txistorra**: These are finger lengths of chorizo served as a tapa with sparkling Txakoli.
>
> **Bacalao al pilpil**: Fried cod: As the cook swirls the pan, the salt cod releases gelatine combining with the garlic-flavoured oil to make a creamy fish sauce.
>
> **Txangurro:** This is spider crab served stuffed with its own meat baked in a savoury, peppery, tomato sauce, with hot paprika and brandy.

Christmas in the Basque country: Christmas dishes in the Basque region are quite distinctive and tend to be dominated by fish dishes. But there are other traditional, non-fish, dishes. These include a cabbage stew seasoned with oil and garlic, and fattened capons.

The region also has some interesting sweets which include "kapoizopa" (Guipúzcoa) which is a dessert soup made with milk sweetened with honey. Also typical of the festive season are jams or fruits cooked in wine. Vizcaya is famous for its dried fruit compotes, rehydrated in wine with cinnamon.

---oOo---

1.3.6 Islas Canarias

Geography: Capitals: Las Palmas de Gran Canaria and Santa Cruz de Tenerife. Las Islas Canarias are an archipelago located just off the north-western coast of Africa, some 100 kilometres west of the border between Morocco and the Western Sahara. The Canarias are one of Spain's 17 autonomous communities and are one of the outermost regions of the European Union. The islands include: Tenerife, Fuerteventura, Gran Canaria, Lanzarote, La Palma, La Gomera, El Hierro, and some smaller islands.

The volcanic islands of the Islas Canarias curve in a 300-mile-long isolated archipelago. They are an integral part of Spain and have been so since the 15th century when this remote group of islands became an important stopover point on the routes to the New World. Lying at the northern edge of the northeast trade winds, the Canaries were a natural port of call for ships setting off into the Altlantic.

History and Culture: The aboriginal population, called Guanches, has almost completely disappeared, and is thoroughly assimilated with Spanish and others who settled the islands from the 15th century onwards.

Food Economics: The climate is quite mild as a result of the Atlantic influences, and the islands produce a large amount of tropical foods like bananas, pineapples, avocados and mangos, as well as the more traditional agricultural products like almonds, tomatoes, chilli peppers, potatoes etc.

The islands are generally very mountainous and agriculture tends to be confined to the coastal strips. However, many micro-climates exist on the islands with localised rainfall varying quite extremely in places. These micro-climates provide a lot of agricultural opportunities for a large variation of crops. The islands are volcanic and the soil is very fertile if irrigated.

Goats are ubiquitous on the islands; their milk going into a number of cheeses, their meat an important source of locally grown protein. Thus there are many quite ancient goat meat dishes still very typical of the islands. One recipe for goat stew (olla de cabrito) was a Sabbath dish for the so-called crypto-Jews of the islands; conversos, forcibly converted to Christianity by the Inquisition, but who continued to practice Judaism in secret. It's an ancient recipe, with ground almonds mixed with fenugreek, and nutmeg added at the end.

One of Spain's great cheeses which has its own D.O. is called "majorero", and is produced on the island of Fuerteventura. Here a native breed of goats, called majorero produces an excellent milk yield. "Majorero" is a raw milk cheese with a creamy texture and flavour. It is mild when young, but the cheese grows spicier and more fragrant as it matures. It can be aged up to 60 days or more, when it is usually protected with olive oil and paprika. Similar cheeses are produced throughout the islands, sometimes with the addition of sheep's or cow's milk, but only the true "majorero" have a D.O.

Typical ingredients and dishes:

> **Conejo en salmorejo (rabbit in a salmorejo sauce)**: This is rabbit marinated in a combination of wine, oil, vinegar, garlic, cumin and paprika, and then roasted in a clay pot.
>
> **Miel de Palma (Palm honey)**: This is not really honey at all, but is a sweet palm-sap syrup, thickened by boiling, used in many island sweets.
>
> **Papas**: More than 20 varieties of potato are grown in the Canarias, most of them papas antiguas (old varieties) like "negra yema" and "bonita" that came directly from Peru, i.e., not through Spain. The volcanic mountainous soil produces small, thin-skinned varieties with pink, yellow, or white flesh, all of which are valued for their sweet flavours.
>
> **Almogrote**: This paste is made from aged, hard cheese ground in a mortar with olive oil, garlic, chillies, and often tomatoes. It is served on bread or with potatoes.
>
> **Bienmesabe**: This is a thick sauce for ice cream and other sweets made by caramelising sugar with ground blanched almonds, cinnamon, and lemon or lime zest.
>
> **Gofio**: Guanche influence lingers in "gofio", which is the foundation of traditional island cooking. It is a savoury ground

meal made from toasted wheat, barley, corn, or a combination of all of these, often mixed with salt or sugar. It is added to the islands' stews. Gofio is tasty and nutritious. Mixed with water it makes a fortifying drink. It is often served as a breakfast cereal, with a mojo.

Sancocho: This is an island fish stew, made with salted fish boiled with potatoes and sweet potatoes, and then thickened with cornmeal gofio and served with a green or hot mojo.

Mojos: Mojos are a basic component of the islands' cuisine - spicy sauces made with a variety of ingredients. Mojo picón, for instance, is a hot sauce with chillies, vinegar, garlic, and cumin, while mojo rojo, red sauce, is brightened with paprika, and mojo verde, green sauce, has loads of minced cilantro and parsley. Mojos are used on almost everything, from grilled or roasted meat or fish, to beans and greens, to potatoes. One popular Canarias dish is papas arrugadas, or wrinkled potatoes, made by boiling potatoes in their skins in sea water until they are coated with salt, then serving them with a spicy or green mojo.

Lanzarote lentils: These small green lentils from the island of Lanzarote are prized for their "meaty" flavour.

Christmas in the Islas Canarias: The connections between the Canary Islands and the "New World" have greatly impacted on the culinary traditions of the Canaries. For example, one very popular Christmas sweet is the "Truchas de Navidad", which is a type of baked or fried sweet potato and almond filled fritter. The Canaries also produce several other unique Christmas sweets like "Turrón de Gofio", which is made with sugar, roasted maize meal, almonds, water, honey, anise and lemon.

Another popular traditional Canarian dish with a new world heritage is "Papas Arrugadas con mojo picón". Potatoes have been cultivated in the Canaries since the 17th century when they were brought back from the Americas. The "mojo" or sauce which accompanies the potatoes is made with chilli peppers and is slightly hot and very tasty. The two are often served as a side dish or as a tapa. Naturally, at Christmas time, the islanders also take full advantage of their maritime produce with prawns being a very popular dish on Christmas Eve.

---oOo---

1.3.7 Cantabria

Geography: Capital: Santander. Cantabria is nestled between the Bay of Biscay to the north and the barrier mountains of the Cordillera Cantabrica to the south. Wedged between the País Vasco to the east and Asturias to the west, Cantabria is an integral part of "green" Spain, España Verde, the rainy north coast.

The area is characterised by the rocky shores and sandy beaches washed by the Atlantic and rolling green hills climbing to the high snow-capped peaks of the Picos de Europa. Sea and mountains are contiguous throughout this zone. From Santander, the capital, with its broad sandy beaches, it is only a short drive to climb towards the highest peaks of the Picos de Europa-the "European peaks", so called because they were a landmark for sailors returning from long times at sea.

History and Culture: Cantabria was mentioned occasionally in Roman texts of the time, but came into its own when it gained its independence from the Visigoths in 574. However, in 714 an Arab/Berber army captured the region. However, within 200 years, the region was aiding the other Northern provinces in the first attempts at an invasion of the Moorish southern areas of Spain, which were gradually occupied by Christian forces over the next 400 years. Cantabria took an active part in the colonisation of Andalucía. After a great many other tempestuous times, Cantabria finally became an autonomous region of Spain in 1981.

Food Economics: As befits the climate and the green meadows, this is a region with a lot of dairy farming. Cantabria is said to have more cattle than any other region in Spain; most of them dairy cows, grazing alongside sheep and goats on green, high-mountain pasture. They produce a rich milk that makes delicious butter and creamy cheeses. These cheeses include the spicy "Picón Bejes", the "Ahumado de Áliva" and Quesuco, smoked and unsmoked versions of the same mixed-milk cheese that are part of the over-all designation "Quesucos de Liébana".

The mountainous zones have a variety of cheeses, from creamy fresh cheeses to long-cured hard cheeses. Many of these cheeses rarely make it to markets outside the region.

The area also has many tasty hams and sausages, cured in the dry mountain air. (Chorizo de Potes, for example)

The region is well known for its stews (cocidos) to combat the cold - combinations of meat, beans, and greens braised together slowly in earthenware pots; for example "cocido montañés" and "cocido lebaniego".

The Cantabrian coastline and the fishing fleet also provide high-quality fish and shellfish from the cold waters of the Atlantic: anchovies, crabs, mussels, lobster, squid, sardines, tuna, sea bass, and hake. Most of the tuna landed here is albacore or yellowfin, caught by hook and longline, which is a more sustainable method than trawling. Santoña, a small city east of Santander, is famous for its production of very high-quality canned fish, especially oil- or brine-packed tuna and anchovies.

The local drink, as it is throughout these regions of "Green Spain", is sidra (cider). But the crowning glory, the finishing touch, is almost always a quick shot of orujo or asorujo, a powerful distilled spirit that is considered the only proper way to end a meal.

Typical Food Products: Here we take a look at the most traditional recipes and ingredients of Cantabria:

> **Picón Bejes-Treviso**: This is a special blue-veined cheese with a D.O. that regulates that it must be made from the milk of specific breeds-Tudanca, Brown Swiss, and Holstein cows, Pyrenean goats, and Lacha sheep, all grazing in the high meadows; it is aged up to five months, often in abandoned mines.
>
> **Quesucos de Liébana**: These mostly small (0.5 kg or less) cheeses, are made from mixed milk (cow, goat, sheep) from the area of Liébana in the Picos de Europa in south-western Cantabria; this over-all controlled denomination includes Picón, Quesuco, and Ahumado de Áliva.
>
> **Cocido lebaniego**: A stew made with beef as well as pork sausages, and with chickpeas from Liébana; fried breadcrumb dumplings are often added.
>
> **Frisuelos**: These are sugar-coated thin crepes from the Liébana region.
>
> **Quesada pasiega**: A rich and creamy custard made with fresh cow's milk cheese from the Pasiego valleys; traditionally quesada is sweetened with honey and flavoured with cinnamon.
>
> **Tudanca beef**: This is an ancient breed of Cantabrian cattle, well adapted to the steep mountain meadows where the cows

spend their summers. Once used as draft animals, Tudancas are now bred primarily for their meat and milk.

Sorropotún: A tasty fish stew that can be made with any firm-textured fish, but is traditionally made with onions, potatoes and fresh tuna.

Cocido montañés: This is a mountain stew made with white beans, pork, sausages, and cabbage.

Cachón en su tinta: This is squid cooked in its own ink and a tomato sauce.

Christmas in Cantabria: Christmas Dinner may be preceded by some of the region's most delicious cheeses or by a starter using prawns or shellfish.

The main course of the dinner on Christmas Eve in Cantabria is likely to consist of a stuffed turkey, roasted lamb and/or a fish dish like lobster.

There are several very popular Christmas sweets in the region, one of the most popular of them being Tostadas de Navidad, which is like a sweet French toast, also called Torrijas elsewhere in Spain.

---o0o---

1.3.8 Castilla La Mancha

Geography: Capital: Toledo. Castilla-La Mancha is another sparsely populated region, but one where agriculture is more extensive. Castilla-La Mancha, sometimes called Castilla la Nueva, is the heartland of Spain, a vast, high plateau that to the first-time visitor can appear bleak, harsh and even hostile. It is a land of big skies, rolling plains and low hills. Temperatures can be extreme, ranging from well below freezing in winter to well over 40 degrees Celsius in the summer.

Five provinces - Cuenca, Ciudad Real, Albacete, Guadalajara, and Toledo (the capital) - make up this large region, best known as home of Don Quijote de la Mancha.

History and Culture: The cultural heritage of Castilla-La Mancha has remained remarkably intact, notably with the dramatic city of Toledo, the former home of the great Spanish painter El Greco. The area around Toledo is famous for its olives.

The agricultural history of Castilla-La Mancha is a history of sheep-herding. Archaeological remains confirm that Bronze Age Spaniards lived on this Meseta nearly 4,000 years ago, raised sheep, spun wool, and used sheep's milk to make cheese. By the time of Don Quijote, in the late 16th century, sheep breeding and grazing were entirely controlled by the state-run Honrado Concejo de la Mesta, which also managed the drover roads, called cañadas, that crisscrossed Spain from north to south as vast flocks passed from winter to summer pastures and back again.

The region shared many historical events with the rest of Spain: the arrival of the Romans, the Visigoths and then the Moorish settlements, followed the arrival of the Northern Christians, centuries of conflict ending in 1214 with the consolidation of the region into the kingdom of Castilla.

Food Economics: Between the cities of Albacete and Ciudad Real vast wheat fields stretch as far as the eye can see. There are also important vineyards and other crops. Where there are hills, they are dry and barren, and windy, too; this is the country where the legendary Don Quijote roamed.

It is a perfect terrain for cereal crops and sheep. Sheep are still important in Castilla-La Mancha, although the Mesta was disbanded in 1836. But "transhumance"- the seasonal movement of people and livestock is still practiced, on a very limited scale.

Manchego cheese (D.O.) is a product of international fame, despite some years of neglect. But cheese-making has become an industry and some of the largest cheese factories in Spain are now located in the region. Small scale Manchego production however, is still carried out in regional farmhouses.

Castilla-La Mancha is also home to many important vineyards. The D.O. La Mancha is actually the largest wine region in Spain. Generally, it is seen only as a high-volume producer of wines, but over the years Castilla-La Mancha has adopted new techniques to produce better wines. All told, there are nine controlled D.O's, the best known being Valdepeñas.

The golden Manchego saffron is also a less well-known, but very important product of the region.

Typical Food Products: Let us take a closer look at the food products and typical dishes of Castilla-La Mancha:

> **Gachas and migas**: These are two popular peasant recipes: gachas are like porridge but made from wheat flour, ground lentils, and flavoured with ham, garlic, and paprika; migas are made from stale bread, coarsely ground or chopped, dampened and then fried, with the addition of ham, garlic, and sometimes a little fresh chilli.
>
> **Pisto manchego**: This vegetable stew is like ratatouille, but green peppers predominate, along with onions and sometimes tomatoes; often served accompanied with hard-boiled eggs or fried potatoes.
>
> **Queso manchego (manchego cheese)**: There are several grades of this excellent cheese, ranging from young (tierno) to very old. Queso manchego is a very tangy cheese, with the taste developing as it ages.
>
> It is made exclusively from the milk of manchega ewes, and is left to age for at least 60 days (often much longer). Cured Manchego is sometimes marinated in olive oil to make it into an even more irresistible delicacy.
>
> **Olive oil, primarily from the cornicabra olive**: Castilla-La Mancha produces about 15% of Spain's olive oil; much of it is of excellent quality. The province of Toledo is well known for its olive oil.
>
> **Tojunto**: This is a speciality of Ciudad Real; the name means "todo junto" ("all together") and refers to the way game, especially wild rabbit, is cooked all together with garlic, onion, green peppers, spices, and a dash of vinegar.
>
> **Mazapán (marzipan from Toledo)**: Arab farmers gave both almonds and sugar cultivation to Spain and it is quite likely that Arab cooks combined ground almonds with sugar to make marzipan for their soldiers to carry on long marches. These days it is made in Toledo's convents and is still delicious.
>
> **Sopa de ajo (garlic soup)**: Garlic soup is a traditional peasant soup and a favourite in country restaurants. It is made simply of garlic, bread, and water, and often coloured with saffron and enriched with an egg poached in the broth.

Azafrán (saffron): Mauve saffron flowers blossom in La Mancha late in October and the harvest of their bright red-golden stigmas begins immediately thereafter. This is the D.O. azafrán de la Mancha, said to be the finest in the world.

Gazpachos de Pastor: This is a stew of chicken and rabbit and sometimes game, cooked with garlic, tomatoes, onions, mushrooms, and green vegetables flavoured with thyme, rosemary, sweet pimentón and peppercorns, served hot with thin unleavened flatbread to thicken.

Cordero or cabrito asado (roast young lamb or goat): Following on a long Arab tradition, eating of a lamb of kid goat is considered a great treat and often a dish only eaten during important festivities.

Christmas in Castilla-La Mancha: It is very cold in the winter in Castilla-La Mancha. This fact certainly characterises the seasonal recipes of the area. Many traditional winter dishes are very high in calories, both in sugar and fats simply to manage the hard physical labour during the cold winter months. Thus, many villages in the region have locally based pork products such as chorizos, black puddings, and various cured hams and marinades.

Traditionally Christmas was the time for the first tasting of the pigs killed in the autumn "sacrificio" and many winter recipes take advantage of the plentiful supply of pork "by-products".

The main course eaten at Christmas in the region would include kid goat, lamb or roast pork dishes. Other winter dishes designed to warm include the "gachas" of La Mancha. These savoury porridges are eaten because they are very nice and high in calories; during the olive harvesting season, which straddles Christmas and the New Year, the workers need these calories to manage the strenuous work. And aside from the more practical reasons for these calorie-bombs, many of these recipes are also delicious. People love to make these dishes around Christmas time.

Sweets from Castilla-La Mancha are also plentiful and based on a rich tradition embracing Muslim, Jewish and Christian cultures. They include the famous marzipan of Toledo and many shortbread recipes (mantecados) and doughnut recipes of the region.

The cold also makes it "advisable" to take the occasional brandy or other warming spicy liquors like "resolí", which is a digestive drink of

Arab origin, now based on brandy, typical of the town of Cuenca and manufactured for centuries in Alfarnate in Málaga province.

---oOo---

1.3.9 Castilla y León

Geography: Capital: Valladolid. The old kingdom of Castilla was the area around the capital Madrid, and the historic heart of Spain. Old Castilla is now split into three regions, with Castilla y León the largest of the three in terms of surface area, though not in terms of population. Madrid itself is historically the capital of Castilla, but is now an independent autonomous metropolitan region.

Castilla y León is the largest of Spain's regions. It is the northern counterpart to Castilla-La Mancha in the south. But Castilla y León is a little different from its cousin to the south. Although it starts as a flat plain, predominantly rural and agricultural, more than a third of the territory is mountain, while the Duero, one of the peninsula's longest rivers, flows through the region from east to west on its way to the Atlantic, providing excellent vineyard soil for some of Spain's greatest red wines, including the Ribera del Duero and the popular white Rueda wines.

Food Economics: The great open expanses of Castilla are largely given over to agriculture, particularly cereals; but most of this region lies at an altitude of 800m or more, and the climate is dry and cold in winter, dry and hot in summer. Though the mountains around the Castilian mesa support pine forests, there are large expanses in the middle of the region where trees only grow naturally alongside water courses, and where irrigated farming can be practised.

Castilla y León is a community rich in food traditions and Christmas is a time when many of these traditions get a chance to be seen and tasted.

History and Culture: In the past, Castilla was a wild, desolate area, where people lived together in fortified cities or castles; many of these survive to this day, including some of the jewels in the Spanish crown. There are nine provinces in Castilla y León, most of them historic walled cities such as Ávila, Salamanca or Segovia, all classed as UNESCO world heritage sites - not forgetting the great cultural heritage of other cities such as León, Valladolid or Burgos, or the impressive Romanesque cloisters of the monastery at Santo Domingo de Silos. Since the camino de Santiago, the pilgrim trail from France to Galicia, ran through León, the region has had a long relationship with "Europe beyond the Pyrenees". For example, French Cistercian monks reputedly played an influential role in the development of wine-making along the Duero.

Typical Food Products: Pork is the staple of the local diet. Traditionally, the sacrificio (slaughter) of the family pigs, also called the matanza, took place in the winter, after which hams, sausages and other cured meats hung for months in attics and cellars, to cure and preserve. Today, most pork goes into industrial production, but the results are nonetheless excellent, especially the hams and sausages from the Ibérico varieties of semi-wild pig - the prized black pig grazed around Salamanca and Guijuelo.

Another treasured pork product, a fundamental ingredient in olla podrida or regional cocidos (bean-and-meat stews), is morcilla, a type of black pudding or blood sausage, in Burgos made with rice as a thickener and in León with lots and lots of onions. Cattle are also raised in the region and used to make cecina, a spiced dried beef that, when well made, is as popular as jamón ibérico.

In Segovia the local grills - "asadores" - specialise in "cochinillo asado", roasted suckling pig. The other speciality is lamb, also often roasted in a wood-fired oven. Sheep are an important source of milk for cheese as well. Many sheep's milk cheeses are impressive, especially soft, fresh "Queso de Burgos" and matured "Zamorano", made from the milk of "Churra" ewes that graze around the city of Zamora.

Typical ingredients and dishes: Here are some well-known ingredients and dishes from Castilla y León:

> **Sopa de ajo (garlic soup)**: This is a popular and hearty winter soup, thickened with stale bread, full of garlic and spiced with pimentón, hot or sweet depending on the cook's taste. Often an egg is poached in each portion.
>
> **Cocido maragato**: This is another one of the filling winter country pot stews. This one is made with chickpeas and many different cuts of fresh and cured pork.
>
> **Cured pork products**: These include chorizo, morcilla, lomo (cured pork loin), and longaniza, especially delicious when made with Ibérico pigs. Hams can be called jamón ibérico, jamón de bellota (meaning, free-range pigs "finished" on

acorns), or jamón de pata negra, in which the hoof has been left on the ham to show that it truly comes from this breed of black pigs.

Sopa de ajo zamorano: This is a thick garlic soup made in and around Zamora, pungent with pimentón and made more substantial with pieces of chorizo and other cured pork products. The bread absorbs the broth so that the "soup" is actually eaten with a fork.

Farinato: This is a very local, soft-textured, sweet, anise-flavoured sausage from Salamanca. It is often served with scrambled eggs.

Wines: Apart from Ribera del Duero and Rueda, there are several other important Denominations of Origin (D.O.) wines in Castilla y León. For example Cigales, north of Valladolid, is known for clarets or rosés. Toro makes hearty reds from "tinta de toro" grapes, similar to the tempranillo grape. Bierzo, in western Castilla y León, produces some whites and some hearty red wines, the latter coming from the "mencía" grape.

Cheeses: Cheese makers of Castilla y León produce some very high quality goat's milk cheeses. Amongst the best known are the ones from the Tiétar river valley south of the Gredos Mountains. Another good cheese from the region is Valdeón, a blue-veined mixture of cow's and goat's milk. It is wrapped in oak or sycamore leaves, and aged for three months in limestone caves until it has reached a creamy texture.

Christmas in Castilla y León: Iberian pork plays a big part at Christmas in Spain and the region of Castilla y León produces some "Iberíco" products of excellent quality. Apart from these Ibéricos, there are other traditional meats such as roast lamb and goat, especially in Palencia and Soria. Roast suckling pig is very popular at Christmas time. The region is a big producer of pulses such as chickpeas, beans and lentils and therefore there are many winter stews to be found in Castilla-León around the days of Christmas. The region has some famous sweet dishes including the "Mantecados" - shortbreads of Soria, and the egg dishes of Ávila - "Yemas de Ávila".

---oOo---

1.3.10 Cataluña (Catalunya)

Geography: Capital: Barcelona. Cataluña is one of the richest and, with almost seven million inhabitants, the second most populated region of Spain.

Cataluña, the north-easternmost region of Spain, is the very epitome of the Mediterranean. The area around Barcelona, Spain's second city, a thriving business city and one of the major ports on the Mediterranean, is fairly densely built-up. The heavily populated areas extend along the coast, and into the valleys northwest of Barcelona, where there is still a fair amount of heavy industry. Barcelona is linked to Madrid by the AVE, Spain's high-speed rail network, and will soon be linked to the French border, allowing direct high-speed train services between Barcelona and Paris.

Cataluña, bordering France, is the most easily accessible of Spain's regions, and the Costa Brava was the first part of Spain to exploit mass-tourism development. To the north and the south of Barcelona, the coast is a string of suburban and holiday developments, crowding in on the small seaside towns. But in the region's hinterland there are still wide open spaces and natural areas, many largely untouched by developments in the city and on the coast. There are some magnificent mountain landscapes in The Catalan Pyrenees: dramatic gorges, peaks and fantastic vistas. Much of the region is agricultural and many areas are quite remote, maintaining many localised culinary traditions.

There are four provinces in Cataluña: Girona to the north, Tarragona to the south, Barcelona the capital, and Lérida (Lleida) in the interior. The Ebro River cuts through Lérida and Tarragona on its long course to the sea.

History and Culture: The one thing that surprises many visitors when they first visit Cataluña is that people in this region don't speak "Spanish". Freed from the constraints of the Franco dictatorship, when Castilian "Spanish" was imposed throughout Spain, the Catalan autonomous governments reinstated Catalan as the official regional language, to the point where it is now generally the only language used.

The history of Calatuña goes back to the pre-Roman Iberian period, and includes the arrival of the Romans, the Visigoth invasion, followed by the Moorish colonisation in 718, which was followed by the Frankish invasion in 801 right through to the invasion of Northern Spain by the Christian Carolingian Empire, the beginnings of the Christian crusades in Spain and the middle ages. Cataluña played a big part in all the major episodes in Spanish history and this is reflected in its rich collection of historic sites, such as the UNESCO World Heritage listed mediaeval churches in the area of Tahull.

Food Economics: Cataluña boasts an excellent seafood cuisine, but also has all the meat-based and dairy ingredients of a mountainous landscape. It also has many wild mushrooms, meats from pastured lowland animals, and all the vegetables that symbolize the Mediterranean: aubergines, courgettes, peppers, tomatoes, onions, garlic, and fresh herbs in abundance.

The Delta of the Ebro, where the longest river in Spain empties into the Mediterranean, is Cataluña's most important agricultural zone and one of the large wetlands in Spain; a region of broad lagoons, salt marshes and sand dunes where rice is by far the most important crop. Rice in various forms, cooked with chicken, fish, shrimps, vegetables, sausage, or pork ribs, takes pride of place at every Catalan table.

There are also two D.O. controlled zones of olive cultivation in Cataluña: Les Garrigues, in Lérida, and Siurana in Girona. However, high quality olive oil is produced throughout Cataluña, made primarily from the arbequina olive, which has a well-known nutty flavour.

As for the wines of Cataluña, probably the best known is cava, a sparkling white wine made in the Penedès, southwest of Barcelona, according to the champagne method, but using local varieties, "xarel-lo", "macabeo", and "parellada". There are also still wines made in the Penedès, both whites and reds. The more famous red wine districts are found in Priorat, in Tarragona province, and around Priorat (D.O. Montsant).

Typical Food Products: Here is a more comprehensive list of the most important food ingredients and dishes that originate in Cataluña:

Typical ingredients and dishes:

> **Rice dishes**: Rice growing is a very important agricultural activity in the Ebro delta and so Cataluña has many rice dishes. Included in these are arrosejat (rice, potatoes, and fish, cooked together with lots of garlic and mild chillies), arròs negre (rice blackened with squid ink, often served with alioli), arròs abanda (rice cooked in fish stock, the fish served separately with quintessential alioli), and of course paella.

Fideua: This is a relatively modern dish using an ancient ingredient, fideos. These are an early form of pasta. In fideua, the spaghetti-like pasta is cooked as if it were rice in a paella together with a mixture of seafoods.

Canalons (cannelloni): similar to the Italian pasta, but with fillings that include pork, chicken breast, lamb brains and chicken livers.

Embutidos (cured pork products): These include "Jamón de Cerdaña" (Cerdanya hams), famous in Roman times, from a district in the Pyrenees; "fuet", a long skinny sausage, dry cured like salami, from the district of Vic; "butifarra" is a cooked pork sausage, white or black, in which the meat is mixed with spices like cumin or coriander.

Anxoves de l'Escala (anchovies from L'Escala): The town of l'Escala, on the Gulf of Roses north of Barcelona, is famous for its excellent anchovies. They are prepared fresh, pickled, fried or grilled in l'Escala but they may also be found salted outside the district.

Espardenyes (sea cucumbers): These rather ugly sea creatures are considered a delicacy along the coast of Cataluña. They are conventionally known as sea slugs, unappetizing in appearance, but much appreciated by their enthusiasts.

Calçots and calçotadas: Calçots are blanched onions from the town of Valls that are usually consumed in the winter months, roasted whole over a wood fire and served with a sauce, similar to romesco sauce, called salvitxada. The meal at which these are eaten is called a calçotada.

Pa amb tomàquet: This is "the" Catalan breakfast - consumed by most people and consisting of a crusty bread roll, halved lengthways, each half rubbed with a fresh tomato and sometimes a cut clove of garlic, sprinkled with olive oil and salt. It's not so dissimilar from the typical breakfast dish taken elsewhere in Spain - the tostada.

Alioli: This is a very typical sauce of Cataluña, served with rice dishes, with fish, sometimes with steamed or roasted vegetables. It is made in a mortar with fresh garlic, olive oil and salt. You may add an egg to bind the sauce, but this is neither traditional nor necessary. The mortar and pestle is the emblematic tool in the Catalan kitchen and many cooks believe that it is often superior to a blender.

Escalivada: This is another very typical regional dish similar to ratatouille, made with tomatoes, aubergines, peppers, grilled (ideally over a wood fire) and then peeled, cut in strips as a salad.

Samfaina: This dish is the same as "Escalivada", except that the aubergines, peppers and tomatoes are fried in olive oil rather than being grilled.

Esquiexada: Salting cod is a popular way of preserving cod throughout Spain, and despite the arrival of the deep freeze, salty cod remains an important traditional ingredient. It is usually prepared by soaking the cod in water overnight and then shredding it, mixing it with tomatoes and onions and serving that as a salad.

Picada: Often called a sauce, which it really isn't, a picada is added to dishes as a thickener and to boost flavour. It is composed of fried garlic, fried bread, olive oil, and nuts, pounded together in a mortar, although the ingredients may vary a lot. In other parts of Spain this is often called a majado and is the basis of many traditional dishes.

Cocas (coques): Catalan pasties with a filling, both savoury and sweet, open or closed. The open savoury version resembles a pizza in many respects and it is thought to be the original source of the modern Italian pizza. Naples (and other parts of Italy) was part of the Spanish empire for 200 years until 1714, and many Spanish ingredients and dishes were exported to Italy from Spain including pizza and many pasta types.

Suquet de peix (Catalan fish stew): This is a Mediterranean fish stew with potatoes, garlic and tomato, thickened and finished with a picada.

Romesco: In the province of Tarragona, seafood of any kind is usually served with "romesco". This is a delicious sauce made from ground mild red chillies, tomatoes, garlic, fried bread, and either almonds or hazelnuts (or sometimes both).

Mar i muntanya (sea and mountain): A favourite combination in the Ampurdán, an area in north-eastern Cataluña, is fish and meat cooked together in a kind of ragout thickened with a picada "sauce". Combinations include shrimp and snails, rabbit with monkfish, rabbit with lobster, chicken with shrimps etc.

Xocolata (chocolate): Barcelona is known for the production of excellent chocolate. The city has several world-famous chocolatiers. Also, Barcelona is one of the few places in the world where it is possible to find very old-fashioned stone-ground chocolate sweetened with cane sugar. This is the kind of grainy chocolate that the Spanish explorers brought back from the "New World".

Christmas in Cataluña: Christmas Eve and New Year's Eve dinner tends to centre on traditional dishes like roast turkey with various garnishes, "duck a l'orange", or stuffed capon. In addition, there will be an abundance of seafood dishes and dishes based on Ibérico hams, as well as on the excellent Catalan chorizos.

The most typical and traditional dishes of the Christmas season in Cataluña can be found on Christmas Day with dishes like "Escudella Catalana de Navidad " - Catalan stew, and the various traditional pasta soups and stews of the region.

December 26 (St. Stephen's day) is a holiday in Cataluña and this is the day that the Catalans typically use up the leftover Christmas food together with local pastas, such as the "Canelones San Esteban". The dishes eaten on 26th December have become quite typical of the Catalan Christmas cuisine in their own right.

Catalan sweets include a number of turrones and wafers, "barquillos"- rolled biscuits, and various rice dishes like sweet "Tortell de Reis".

---o0o---

1.3.11 Extremadura

Geography: Capital: Mérida. Extremadura borders Portugal to its west, Andalucía in the south, Castilla-La Mancha in the east and Castilla y Leon in the north. It is a large, landlocked region. The mountain areas of Extremadura are very wild and the land is generally rather poor throughout the region. Indeed, it has many harsh, arid areas of high plains, intersected by steep mountain ranges. Despite this, it also has areas of oak forest and some areas produce olives and even wheat. But the granite bedrock is never far below the surface, and indeed often breaks through in rocky tors.

Extremadura has two provinces, Badajoz in the south and Cáceres in the north.

Food Economics: Extremadura has long been the poorest region in Spain. In the past, its poverty caused much of its population to flee in search of better fortune, often to South America. Today the region remains sparsely populated; large areas are too poor to cultivate, and are given over to subsistence farming, but elsewhere the landscape consists of olive groves or stone oak forest and in the more fertile parts there are rolling fields of wheat. Despite the bleakness of some of its terrain, Extremadura has produced three of Spain's most emblematic food products: Jamón ibérico, which many claim is the finest ham in the world; Torta del Casar and La Serena, rich, creamy cheeses that have captivated cheese-lovers around the world; and "pimentón de la Vera", a smoked paprika, which is much loved by chefs and cooks both inside and outside Spain.

Jamón Ibérico: Iberian pigs were already a significant feature of the Extremadura landscape even going back to Roman times. These black pigs are an ancient breed that lives in the "dehesa". The dehesas are extensive "open" forests of different species of mainly oak trees, shrubs and pastureland, and are the natural habitat for the semi wild pigs. Their hams are variously called "jamón ibérico", "jamón pata negra" (black-foot ham for the dark hoof that is left attached to the ham to guarantee its origin), or "jamón de bellotas" (bellotas being the acorns on which the pigs feed freely during the last months of their lives).

The hams are traditionally cured in salt, hung in an airy place for several months, and then transferred to cellars for further aging before they are sold. The result is a dark, velvety meat with a very characteristic taste.

Cheeses: The Torta del Casar from Cáceres and the La Serena cheese from Badajoz are two of Spain's rarest, most unusual and most sought-after cheeses. They are made from raw sheep's milk, specifically the milk of merinos that produce only small amounts of rich milk. The cheeses are curdled with vegetable rennet from wild thistles, which gives them a subtle but pleasant bitterness. Aged for 60 days, they have a creamy texture which allows them almost to be eaten with a spoon.

Paprika: The "pimentón de la Vera", is a brick-red smoky paprika produced in the Vera valley of northern Extremadura, where the rainy climate does not allow for open-air sun-drying of peppers. In this area the peppers, ranging from very mild to hot, are harvested when ripe and dried slowly over smoky oak fires. They are then ground to a powder. The resulting pimentón has all the flavour of capsicum peppers but also has a delicious smoky flavour.

History and Culture: Extremadura is probably the least known region of Spain, even to most Spaniards. The origins of the name are obscure and many reasons have been suggested. The region has a number of beautiful old towns, including Roman Mérida, with its 15,000-seat amphitheatre and extremely long arched Roman bridge across the Guadiana River.

Extremadura is also the region from which the original "conquistadores" came, the men who first explored the Americas. Two of the most famous (or infamous) conquistadores, Pizarro and Cortés, were from this region, and they, and others like them, brought great wealth back from South America, which they spent on large country estates and prestigious palaces in towns such as Cáceres and Trujillo.

Typical Food Products: here we will take a look in a bit more detail at the traditional ingredients and dishes of Extremadura:

> **Frite extremeño or caldereta**: This is the meat of a young goat, along with its liver, chopped and braised with red peppers, tomatoes, onions, and spicy La Vera smoked pimentón.
>
> **Migas**: This is an old country dish found everywhere in Spain, but especially in the south and west. In Andalucía and Extremadura, stale bread is dampened in water, then crumbled and fried with garlic and shreds of jamón ibérico, pimentón, (hot or mild according to taste). It's a very simple dish that was designed to use up stale bread and old ham, but despite that, it is quite delicious.
>
> **Faisán or perdíz a la Alcántara**: Pheasant or partridge cooked with port or oloroso sherry, local truffles, and jamón. Not an everyday peasant dish!
>
> **Zarangollo**: This dish is made with potatoes fried in olive oil and a sauce of roasted red peppers and tomatoes.
>
> **Ibores**: This cheese is made of raw goat's milk from local breeds: Serrana, Verata and Retinta. It is a semi-hard cheese. It is often rubbed with olive oil and pimentón, and then aged for

60 days or more to produce a slightly piquant, aromatic, buttery cheese.

Sausage: Besides jamón ibérico, all kinds of sausages are made from the meat of the Ibérico pigs, including chorizo and salchichón (salami-like sausages), lomo (loin, cured like a sausage), morcón (like chorizo but with less fat), and morcillas (black puddings).

Pan de Cáceres: This is an excellent tapa and goes well with the local cheeses of the region. Pan de Cáceres is really a sweet paste of dried figs with ground and crushed almonds. A similar product to "Pan de Higo", it is found in other southern regions of Spain.

Licores and aguardientes: In the high mountain valleys of northern Extremadura, there is a tradition of producing distilled spirits from various fruits, such as figs, green apples, and especially cherries from the Valle del Jerte. The products are delicious and really preserve the true flavours of the fruits.

Christmas in Extremadura: Historically, Extremadura was a pioneer in farming turkey brought back from the Americas. In addition, Extremadura has vast areas of dehesa - semi forest grazed by the famous black foot Iberian pig - which gives rise to some of the world's best hams and all the other famous Ibérico products such as the chorizos and blood puddings, delicacies that are very often eaten at Christmas time.

Apart from these, we also have some other notable Christmas treats coming from the region. One example is "Pavo trufado", which uses the traditional Extremadura truffles. These fungi are close relatives of the famous and expensive black truffles of the genus Terfezia that are so prized in Northern Europe.

Additionally, there are a number of quite distinct festive dishes: like "Conejo de Navidad relleno" - stuffed Christmas rabbit, "lechón al horno" - roasted suckling pig, some thistle stews, "pollo en pepitoria" - chicken fricassee.

The region also produces some delicious Christmas sweets and deserts like "Rollo de Navidad" - Christmas roll, "pestiños de Extremadura" - sweet fritters, and "roscos de vino" - wine doughnuts. Another unusual traditional recipe for the season is the "Sopa Dulce del Valle del Jerte" - the Sweet soup of the Jerte Valley, which is made with fried bread, almonds or walnuts, apples, honey or mead, all cooked together in a clay pot.

---oOo---

1.3.12 Galicia

Geography: Capital: Santiago de Compostela. Galicia lies at the northwestern tip of Spain. An Atlantic coastal region, it benefits from a temperate climate and plentiful rainfall, making it the greenest region in Spain. The population of Galicia is concentrated along the coast, mostly in the cities of Vigo and A Coruña (Coruna), the major port cities. Vigo is the largest fishing port in Europe, and an industrial hub, with shipbuilding and manufacturing industries.

Away from the urban areas, Galicia has a dramatic rocky coastline, deeply indented on the western side by fjord-like inlets, but less indented along the northern coast. Galicia is Spain's most un-typical region. Comparisons with Ireland, Wales, or Bretagne are inevitable, for these four Atlantic-rim territories are the islands of Celtic culture in a European mainstream. Galicia, Bretagne, Wales and Ireland share certain cultural and culinary traditions.

Food Economics: Inland from the coast, Galicia remains a relatively poor agricultural region, with a lot of small farms. The terrain is hilly and rocky, and in many parts densely forested. Galicia's food is also far from Mediterranean. Potatoes are very popular and pork is the meat of choice, while beef from the native Rubia Gallega cattle is highly prized.

It is not surprising, given the long Atlantic coastline of the region, that seafood of all kinds plays an important part in the diet and the economy. The seafood selection in Galicia is quite spectacular - from scallops (*vieiras*), to lobsters and langoustines (Dublin Bay prawns), spider crabs and squid, to all kinds of midwater and deepwater fish. The region's fishing fleet is the largest in Spain and one of the largest in Europe. Galicia is also Spain's centre for aquaculture, especially mussels, oysters, and clams. Today, Galicia is the second largest producer of mussels in the world

History and Culture: Galicia is also a very historical and cultural place. The magnificent capital, Santiago de Compostela, with its great cathedral, has been an important destination for pilgrims from all over

Europe since the 1400s. Pilgrims still trek across northern Spain to worship at the shrine of Santiago (St. James) in Santiago's cathedral.

Typical Food Products: Galicia is a producer of some fine traditional foods and wines. Albariño is a deliciously aromatic, crisp, dry white wine which goes well with seafood. It is produced from a native grape of the same name in the Rías Baixas in the southern coastal region of Galicia. Other notable wines from Galicia include Ribeiro, a fresh, fruity white, and Valdeorras, both whites and reds. Galicia also produces some excellent cheeses, mostly from cow's milk. Notable examples include the "tetilla", named for its curious shape like a woman's breast, a soft, supple, mild cheese, and San Simón, a smoked cheese that can develop a sharper tang. Less easy to find is Cebreiro, an aged cow's milk cheese with a slightly bitter flavour and a buttery aroma that develops with age.

Typical ingredients and dishes: Here are some of the most emblematic ingredients and dishes of Galicia:

> **Lacón con grelos**: This is sometimes considered the Galician national dish - turnip leaves stewed with chunks of potato, chorizo, and salted pork shoulder. Despite the humble ingredients, the result is spicy and delicious.
>
> **Pulpo a feira**: Translated, this means "Fair styled octopus". It is a staple in Galician markets, fairs, and festivals, where people buy it from mobile carts called pulpeiras to eat on the spot from wooden plates or to take home. It is simply boiled and tenderized octopus, cut in chunks and mixed with olive oil, salt and sweet paprika (paprika dulce).
>
> **Percebes (goose barnacles)**: This one of the world's most expensive seafoods; percebes are as expensive as caviar. They are highly prized for their sweet, succulent, briny flavour. They grow only on rocks with very heavy surf and are difficult and dangerous to harvest. They are boiled briefly in salty water and then eaten as they are, with no sauces, no salt, usually as a tapa.
>
> **Caldeirada de pescado**: This is a typical Galician fish stew made with onions, potatoes, and a variety of fish and shellfish and cooked in a garlic and vinegar sauce with hot and sweet paprika.
>
> **Pimientos de Padrón**: These are small green chilli peppers, renowned for their sweetness. They are simply grilled ("a la

plancha") and served with a little salt. Often eaten as a tapa, sometimes they can be quite hot.

Empanadas and empanadillas: These are small pasties of Arabic origin, shaped like squares or wedges. They are filled with tasty, savoury mixtures based on pork, mussels, octopus, or other combinations, often mixed with pickles ("en escabeche") or plain vegetables.

Christmas in Galicia: Galician Christmas cuisine has some dishes which are very typical of the Galician style of cooking.

In more traditional families, cod occupies an important place, especially in the Christmas Eve dinner. Typically, this would be baked cod with cauliflower, coated with olive oil and eaten with a bottle of Ribeiro wine from the region. The origin of this tradition lies in the (now abolished) ban by the Catholic Church on eating meat on Christmas Eve. This ban gave rise to the tradition of eating fish on Christmas Eve and obviously this is especially true in Galicia, where the consumption of fish is customary. Christmas Eve dinner may include cod or other deepwater fish, crabs, prawns, scallops, lobsters, clams and mussels. Sea bream is a popular Christmas dish and octopus is often served as a starter.

Christmas fish courses are often accompanied by the famous Galician white wine called Albariño.

Non-fish favourites in Galicia include lamb, suckling pig, and capons, including the famous "Capón de Villalba con castañas" - stuffed capon of Villalba, with Galician chestnuts.

The most typical Christmas sweets include the "Tarta de Santiago" and various sweet pancakes or crepes called "filloas".

---o0o---

1.3.13 Madrid

Geography: Capital: Madrid. Historically part of Castilla, Madrid today is its own autonomous region, and the most densely populated area in Spain. The Spanish metropolitan area is home to about 6 million people, and is a bustling and prosperous area, with a strong service economy. The area has seen much large scale development in the past decades. Old Madrid is famous for its urban architecture, its ornate churches and its world-famous museum and art-gallery the Prado. Like the rest of central Spain, Madrid enjoys a continental climate, hot and dry in summer, cold and largely dry in winter. The city lies at an altitude of almost 650 metres above sea level, making it the highest capital in the EU.

Food Economics: The rural parts of the region of Madrid tend to have the same culinary traditions as the "two Castillas", but the city of Madrid is quite different. It is such a melting pot of different peoples, that it is almost impossible to say that it has any unique culinary traditions of its own. Rather, it has everyone's culinary traditions all in one place. Every region in Spain is represented in Madrid and a stroll through the restaurant districts will reveal restaurants from every region in Spain. Even more interestingly, Madrid has many immigrants from Latin America who bring not only their own indigenous culinary traditions with them, but they also have their own national interpretations of Spanish Christmas recipes and traditions that were exported to South and Central America several centuries ago. Some of these are quite interesting and often combine very old Hispano-Arabic dishes with the "new" ingredients of the "New World".

History and Culture: Madrid is a "new" capital and its development only really began in the 1560s when King Phillip II moved his court from Toledo to Madrid.

Typical ingredients and dishes: Despite the fact that Madrid is basically filled with people who are not from Madrid, there are still a number of dishes that are considered to be special to the province of Madrid; most of them rather humble, home-style recipes, often originating from a working-class environment. These dishes include "cocido madrileño", the hearty winter stews of chickpeas cooked with chicken, beef, pork, and a whole range of tasty vegetables. There is also "callos a la madrileña", a veal tripe and knuckle stew cooked with spiced chorizo, black pudding (morcilla), onion, and hot and sweet paprika powder.

A typical madrileño food experience also deserves a mention: the tapas custom which, although it exists practically throughout the country, is very well developed in the capital where "ir a tapear" (to go for tapas) in the many tascas, as tapa bars are called in Madrid, is an evening tradition, a way of keeping going until the very late madrileño dinner hour. A popular local drink is chinchón, an anise-flavoured digestif that is distilled in the town of Chinchón.

For the typical madrileño, breakfast means chocolate and churros: thick, dark chocolate into which sticks of unsweetened fried dough, called churros, are dipped.

Christmas in Madrid: Madrid draws much from the countryside around it, such as the famous sopa de ajo (savoury garlic soup, thickened with bread and often flavoured with saffron) and the tradition of grilled meats, especially succulent baby lamb, kid goat and suckling pig (cordero, cabrito, and cochinillo asado), roasted in wood-fired ovens. A long-established festive custom is for madrileños to drive out to the countryside for a meaty lunch in one of the many asadores or smoky chuletascas, where the speciality is tiny one-bite lamb chops, called chuletas, grilled over wood embers.

---oOo---

1.3.14 Murcia

Geography: Capital: Murcia. Murcia is a small region in the south-eastern corner of Spain. The region is located in the eastern part of the Cordilleras Béticas mountains with the highest point (2,027 m) in the Region of Murcia. 27% of the Murcian territory can be described as mountainous, 38% as intramountainous depressions and valleys, and the remaining 35% as flat lands and plateaux. The Region of Murcia has a semi-arid Mediterranean climate with mild winters and warm summers (where the daily maximum regularly exceeds 40 C). With rainfall of only 300 - 350 mm per year, the region has between 120 - 150 days in the year when the sky is totally clear. The region is, however, prone to very heavy downpours. The distance to the sea and the relief causes a big thermal difference between the coast and the interior, especially in the winter, when coastal temperatures are notably higher than those in the interior.

The main river system in the region is the Segura river. This river is rarely able to supply the demand for water from the region and frequently needs to be topped up from the river Tajo.

History and Culture: Murcia's recorded history begins when the Carthaginians established a permanent port there. The Romans referred to the area as Hispania Carthaginensis and it was not until the Moors' arrival that the region began to develop agriculturally. The Moors developed a sophisticated irrigation system and developed the city of Murcia as capital of the Moorish Kingdom of Murcia. This lasted until 1243 when the Moors surrendered to the invading Christian armies of Ferdinand III of Castilla.

Food Economics: Today, Murcia's food production and cuisine is renowned for the high-quality vegetables grown in the "Vega murciana", Murcia's market gardens. Murcia also has some of the best short-grain rice in the world. Mild winters and year-round sunshine, coupled with modern methods of irrigation, have made the region a vegetable supplier for much of Europe, with exports including artichokes, peppers, fava beans, melons, tomatoes, apricots, and lemons.

However, much of this depends on the water supply in the Segura river which rarely carries enough water to supply the agriculture of the region. Indeed, apart from the irrigated areas, the rest of this extremely arid tract of south-eastern Spain often looks decidedly Saharan. Global warming already appears to be having an effect on local climate and there is a very real threat that available water supplies may dry up, sooner rather than later. If so, Murcia may have to return to producing the un-irrigated arid-land crops, like olives, figs, and date palms that it was noted for in its earlier history.

Calasparra is the rice-growing region, high up on the banks of the Segura river, where rich alluvial soil and a steady supply of cold, clean, mountain water combine to produce superior rice in two varieties, Sollana (also called Calasparra) and Arroz Bomba, which was nearly extinct until rescued by chefs and growers just a few years ago. This is a D.O. rice that is grown for quality not quantity - the region produces just 0.05% of all Spanish rice - but the slow-growing grain is highly absorbent, which makes it perfect for Spanish rice favourites from paella to soup-like arroz caldoso.

One Murcian rice favourite is "caldero murciano", similar to arroz abanda from Valencia to the north. Calasparra or Bomba rice is cooked in a colourful fish stock, with garlic and Ñora peppers (also produced in the region). The fish used in the stock is served separately from the rice, which itself is accompanied by a strongly garlic alioli, often thickened with bread.

With a long stretch of coastline, Murcia has a strong seafood tradition, producing shrimps from the Mar Menor, a highly saline lagoon north of Cartagena that is Europe's largest salt-water lake. Recent years have seen an upsurge in the lucrative, but highly controversial practice of raising captive bluefin tuna in huge floating net-pens until they reach the required size for the Japanese market. This practice has led, marine biologists say, to further decimation of the already precarious stocks of bluefin, since the great fish are trapped before they can reproduce. In recent years, responsible chefs and consumers have turned away from bluefin, substituting yellowfin and albacore, less threatened species.

Typical Food Products: Let us take a closer look at the ingredients and traditional dishes of Murcia:

> **Cordero segureño con gurullos**: This is a lamb dish served with pasta. Gurullos are simple, hand-made flour-and-water pastas, shaped into short thin strips.
>
> **Pescado a la Sal**: This is a whole fish coated in a thick salt crust and baked in the oven. The recipe is now popular throughout Spain.
>
> **Cheeses of Murcia**: The Queso de Murcia al Vino and Queso de Murcia are two very similar cheeses, made from pasteurized goat's milk and aged for a brief period to give them a creamy texture. The first is marinated in the strong red wine of the region, which gives it a deep purple-red rind.
>
> **Al ajo cabañil**: Ajo cabañil is a very simple but tasty sauce, made with crushed garlic and vinegar, sometimes with a little cumin added. It is often served with lamb chops and roasted or fried potatoes.
>
> **Mojama**: Salt-preserved tuna is an ancient treat, often called the ham of the sea, served shaved very thin, dressed with a thread of olive oil and a few drops of lemon. Sadly, overfishing has made this a dish we cannot ethically eat any more.
>
> **Michirones**: These are dried fava beans cooked in a stew with chorizo sausage and hot and sweet dried peppers.
>
> **Olive oil from Jumilla:** A classical olive oil of Murcia.
>
> **Zarangollo**: This is a combination of two great Murcian vegetables, courgettes and sweet onions, cooked in olive oil, sometimes with a little finely chopped tomato added. Eggs are broken over the top or stirred in to poach.
>
> **Murcia wines**: Many of the wines of Murcia are made from the "Monastrell" grape, a variety of Mourvedre. The wines of

the region are considered to be "improving" and some are excellent.

Pastel murciano: This is a substantial tart or pie, made with a crust and filled with meats-jamón serrano, chorizo, veal, bacon and hardboiled eggs, peppers, and tomatoes.

Christmas in Murcia: Christmas is generally celebrated with seafood, roasted turkey, lamb, or goat, especially with roasted leg of kid goat. Other popular Christmas main courses include rice with turkey for Christmas day, and combinations of beans with ham, chorizos and blood sausages. Murcia is also well known for its shortbreads and the sweets known as "Cordiales de Murcia" made with sugar, almonds and eggs.

---oOo---

1.3.15 Navarra

Geography: Capital: Pamplona. Navarra is a region covering the foothills and central western section of the Pyrenees, bordering France and the Basque country. But, like Castilla y Leon, it is a region that is very dry in parts, and even barren and inhospitable. The Bardenas Reales natural park even has some spectacular semi-desert landscapes. Navarra is the leading region in Europe in terms of renewable energy.

History and Culture: Navarra is somewhat cramped in against the western Pyrenees. It is land-locked and is another of Spain's historic Basque regions that were never fully conquered by the Romans, Visigoths or Arabs. Navarra today is still a proudly independent region that was never quite fully integrated into the rest of modern Spain.

In its heyday, the region rose to become quite a large kingdom in the 11th century AD, but it was then divided up again by its royal family and Navarra went into something of a decline. Navarra joined the Christian invasions against the Moorish caliphates of Al-Andalus along with the other Christian kingdoms of Northern Spain.

The Pyrenean pass of Roncesvalles is the beginning of the Spanish part of the road to Santiago de Compostela, one of Europe's most ancient Christian pilgrim trails, traversed by pilgrims and hikers to this day.

Food Economics: Navarra's varied terrain gives it an extremely varied cuisine and viticulture. The forested slopes of the Pyrenees in the north are full of wild game, mushrooms, and trout streams. There are market gardens on the sunny banks of the Ebro in the south of the region. Navarra has several fine wine growing districts known especially for their lovely rosados (rosés), many made from the old, native "garnacha" grapes. But Navarra is really best known for its vegetables. It has several varieties renowned enough to have their own controlled denominations of origin. These include "pimientos de piquillo" from Lodosa on the banks of the Ebro, fleshy, sweet red peppers that are roasted, peeled, and then bottled or canned. And, of course, one of the most treasured vegetables of Navarra is the fat blanched white asparagus from that same region. Artichokes from Tudela are equally highly valued. Many a traditional dish of the region incorporates these vegetables. For example, the "menestra de verduras", uses a simple but popular combination of seasonal vegetables with shreds of jamón serrano.

Typical Food Products: Here we will explore in a little more detail the traditional ingredients and dishes of Navarra before focusing on their Christmas specialities:

> **Cogollos de Tudela**: These are the crisp, tender hearts of lettuces raised in the rich lands of the Ebro valley.
>
> **Esparragos blancos**: These are very cherished in Spain and abroad. These fat, white, blanched asparagus are a real regional speciality, often served with home-made mayonnaise.
>
> **Pimientos de piquillo**: This is a small, fleshy, sweet red pepper from Lodosa. These are mostly preserved in tins or jars and are usually whole. They are widely used in Spain and are sometimes stuffed with a puree of bacalao (salted cod).
>
> **Truchas a la navarrese**: These trout come from fast-running mountain spate streams. They are sometimes cooked with a slice of jamón serrano as a filling.
>
> **Pochas (beans)**: These are a pale greenish-white bean, eaten fresh (not dried). They are usually served alone, cooked with a little tomato and onion, or as an accompaniment to braised quail.
>
> **Pacharán/patxarán**: This is a Navarran digestif drink made by steeping sloe berries (from the blackthorn bush) in a strong spirit. This is a traditional after-dinner drink in Navarra, but has become popular all over Spain.

Cheeses: Navarra produces only two important types of cheese: Idiazábal is from the milk of Lacha sheep. It is a firm, lightly smoked, shepherd's cheese. It is often associated with the Basque Country, but Idiazábal is also made in Navarra. The second cheese is Roncal, which is made in the Valle de Roncal (in north-eastern Navarra) from the milk of Lacha and Aragónesa sheep which graze the high mountain pastures. This is a cheese with an ancient history. It is aged for at least four months.

Menestra de verduras: This is a dish of mixed fresh vegetables from the Ebro valley and elsewhere in Navarra, and served with strips of jamón serrano.

Bacalao al ajoarriero: This is made with salty cod, fried with medium-hot choricero peppers. It is then finished with a sauce of tomatoes-onions-garlic, and served with fried potatoes.

Cordero al chilindrón is a rich lamb stew made with fresh and dried red peppers, both sweet and hot. This is a very popular dish in Navarra.

Christmas in Navarra: The Christmas cuisine of Navarra includes "intxaursalsa", a sweet soup of walnuts or almonds typical to many villages in Navarra. A starter might include Bacalao al ajoarriero or a small Cardo (thistle) stew. A popular Christmas main course is "Cordero al chilindrón" - Lamb in Red Pepper sauce.

Navarra is also well known for its "almendras garrapiñadas"- nougat and "turrón royo", typical of Artajona and made with almonds, sugar, honey and wafer. Another unique sweet Christmas dish of Navarra is the candied fruit compote - "compotas de frutas escarchadas".

---oOo---

1.3.16 La Rioja

Geography: Capital: Logroño. To the south of Aragón is La Rioja, on the southern banks of the Ebro River. It is the smallest autonomous region in Spain, and notably famous for its wines. It is a mountainous, largely rural and agricultural region. The Ebro forms La Rioja's northern border, and it flows from the Pyrenees to the Mediterranean south of Barcelona. It is one of Spain's most important rivers, accounting for the region's legendary fertility.

Food Economics: La Rioja is famous for two things: red wine and red peppers. But it has much more to offer then "just" sweet peppers and one of Spain's, and indeed the world's, greatest wines. The Ebro River, the geography of the region and its very fertile land help to explain the exceptional quality of its famous wine and peppers. But the region also produces many other fruits and vegetables including asparagus, artichokes, potatoes, cauliflower, etc.

History and Culture: La Rioja is a stunning region, of rolling vineyards, dramatic mountain ranges (steep and often snow-capped even in early summer), hilltops crowned by medieval castles and walled villages like Fuenmayor and Navarrete, historic monasteries, both ruined and flourishing, like medieval Suso and its Baroque sister Yuso along the Camino de Santiago, the ancient pilgrim route that cuts through La Rioja on its way to Galicia.

La Rioja shares a similar history with its neighbours. It was occupied in pre-Roman times by several tribes and then by the Romans and Visigoths and finally the Moors in 711. It was invaded by Christian forces from Navarra in 923 and thereafter was controlled by either the kingdoms of Castilla or Aragón. It was divided until 1822 and finally in 1980 changed its name to La Rioja and became an autonomous region.

Typical Food Products: Here we take a look at the most emblematic products and dishes of this small but important region:

> **Wine:** For centuries, the region has been synonymous with the most impressive Spanish red wines, based on the "tempranillo" and "garnacha" grapes. However, the region also produces some excellent white wines, made primarily from the native viura grape.
>
> **Red Peppers:** "Pimientos riojanos" (Rioja peppers) are little piquillo peppers, which are sweet and fleshy. They are perfect fresh, but also delicious gently roasted and preserved in their own juices. Red peppers, both fresh and preserved, are in much evidence in the traditional kitchens of La Rioja. They are sometimes stuffed with salted cod (bacalao) or lamb, then dipped in batter and fried (pimientos rellenos). They sometimes form part of a stew, like the "pochas a la riojana"; the winter bean-and-chorizo stews. Such country fare is typical of this region.

Chorizos: La Rioja is famed throughout Spain for the best spicy chorizos (sausages flavoured with choricero chillies).

Lamb chops: Another one of La Rioja's well known delicacies are the tiny chops of milk-fed baby lamb (lechal) or young kid goat (cabrito). These chops are no more than a bite or two on each little bone. They are traditionally grilled over fires of vine cuttings.

Other dishes and ingredients from La Rioja: White asparagus is a regional speciality from Rioja Baja. Then there is "cameros" cheese, a fresh goat's milk cheese. Another favourite game dish is partridge with pears ("perdiz con peras"), cooked with pears in red wine. Another local dish is "patatas a la riojana", which are potatoes roasted with chorizo and smoky paprika. There are many salty cod (bacalao) dishes, often featuring the local pimientos riojanos.

Christmas in La Rioja: Traditional Christmas dishes from La Rioja include Bream in sauce on Christmas Eve. Around the festive period and in the cold Northern winters, there will be "pochas a la riojana" - the hearty winter bean-and-chorizo stews. Such country fare is very typical of this region at Christmas time. The area also has a well-known traditional meatball recipe known as "albóndigas matahambre (riojanas)".

On a sweeter note La Rioja is also quite famous for its marzipan, undoubtedly as the result of influences from the many monasteries in the area. The quality of the region's wines is legendary and there will be few households in Spain that don't have a Rioja on the Christmas dinner table.

---oOo---

1.3.17 Valencia

Geography: Capital: Valencia. The region of Valencia looks out to sea. In this dry, central-eastern part of Spain, the majority of the population is concentrated on the over-developed coastal strip. Thankfully, like most of Spain's tourist areas, this overdevelopment is mostly confined to a very narrow strip along the coast. Generally speaking, this is a dry region, and the hills away from the coast are arid and rocky, like much of Spain. Small villages and towns cling to hillsides, or stand beside rivers or streams. This inland area is sparsely populated, and a world apart from the thronging crowds of Benidorm or La Manga.

Today, the three provinces of the region - Valencia in de centre, Alicante in the south, and Castellón in the north, rising into the Maestrazgo Mountains on the borders with Aragon - are still known for their lush agriculture. Valencia City has become one of Spain's most important ports. The city has now the third largest population in the country after Barcelona and Madrid.

History and Culture: Culturally, the region is very interesting with many pre-Roman, Roman and Moorish connections which it shares with much of Southern Spain. The origins of present day Valencia date back to the former Kingdom of Valencia (Regne de València), which came into existence in the 13th century. James I of Aragon led the Christian conquest and colonization of the existing Islamic taifas with Aragonese and Catalan people in 1208 and founded the Kingdom of Valencia as a third independent country within the Crown of Aragon in 1238. Despite several attempts to become more autonomous over the centuries, the region finally gained the status of "Comunitat Valenciana" in 1982.

Food Economics: Much of the region is agricultural and large areas are given over to the production of fruit and vegetables. Valencia is the capital of the Spanish orange and citrus industry. The Moors introduced the cultivation of palm trees into this area, and the city of Elche, near Alicante, boasts Europe's only extensive palm groves. The region of Valencia is one of Spain's great garden districts, with a rich alluvial soil that has been intensively cultivated since the beginning of time. Arab farmers arrived in Valencia in the early middle ages and introduced an irrigation system for the intensive cultivation of rice, citrus (lemons and sweet oranges), almonds, and dates in Alicante.

Valencia is one of the centres of Spanish rice cultivation, though this crop is not quite as dominant as it was in the past. Centuries of rice growing, mainly around the fresh-water Albufera lagoon south of the city, has made Valencia the centre of Spanish rice cookery.

There are many different ways of preparing short-grain varieties of rice. Obviously the most famous one is "paella valenciana", which is actually a rather modern invention. It started its life as a peasant dish with very simple ingredients - chicken, rabbit, snails, and big green beans called garofons, and it can still be found in this original form throughout Valencia. The Valencianos also don't call it paella either.

Generally they refer to it as "arros de verdures" rice with vegetables, or "arros abanda" in which the rice is served as a separate course from the fish that has been cooked with it, or "arros negre" made with squid and its ink, or "arros marinera" made with seafood.

The seafood is a very important ingredient in many traditional regional recipes. This includes the giant shrimps from Vinarós with their own Denomination of Origin.

The most important juice orange in the world is the "Valencia", named after the place where it originated, and the citrus production is enormously important for the economy of the area.

Other important agricultural products include artichokes from Benicarló in Castellón province, cherries from the Vall de la Gallinera in Alicante province, and cured hams and cheeses from the Maestrazgo.

Typical Food Products: Let us take a more detailed look at the ingredients and dishes which originate in Valencia:

> **All i pebre**: This is a sauce made with almonds ground together with garlic and pimentón in olive oil.
>
> Note: This name also refers to eels from the Albufera lagoon, which are cooked with potatoes in a garlic and paprika sauce.
>
> **Horchata**: Horchata is a refreshing drink that has now become popular all over Spain. It is made from chufas, variously called tiger nuts or earth nuts. Horchata is made like almond milk, by steeping the crushed nuts in water. It is served cold, accompanied by crisp, hot fartons, (fried pastry strips), to dip in the cold drink.
>
> **La pericana**: Here is another famous dish from Alicante, made with salted cod, dried peppers, and garlic.
>
> **Arroz con costra**: This is a baked rice dish that is finished with a crust of egg.
>
> **Cocido de pelotas**: a typical cocido, but with the addition of meat-stuffed cabbage leaves.
>
> **Turrón**: Alicante is famous for its turrones. "Turrón alicantina" is like a nougat with almonds in a baked honey paste. Turrón from Jijona is softer, and made from almonds crushed into a paste and mixed with honey. Originally these were exclusively Christmas sweets, though they are now available all year round.

Arroz rosetxat: This is an oven-baked rice dish, with lamb, pork, sausages (Valencian black pudding), and chickpeas.

Bajoques farcides: These are sweet peppers stuffed with rice, pork, tomatoes and pimentón, from Alicante.

Arroz empedrado: This a dish from Castellón, made with white beans, salted cod, and garlic.

Christmas in Valencia: As in many other regions of Spain, Christmas Eve dinner consists of roast lamb, turkey or chicken with various stuffing. The most traditional Christmas meal is a stew called "Puchero", with meat balls, beef, potatoes and vegetables.

In terms of sweet dishes at Christmas, the most famous of Spanish nougats come from Valencia: Alicante Jijona (soft texture) or Alicante (hard). Nougat is an important industry in the region and carries its own Denomination of Origin (D.O.). Other sweet Christmas desserts include the "Toña", which is a round cake made with flour, eggs, sugar and lemon. Also famous is the "Alcoy"-sugared almonds. These are now produced industrially and home recipes for this old sweet don't exist any longer.

Finally, Valencia is known as the producer of those all-important grapes used throughout Spain for the New Year's Eve celebration of the "Twelve Grapes". These Vinalopó grapes (Aledo grapes) are eaten by almost everyone in Spain during the 12 strokes of midnight on New Year's Eve to bring good luck for the New Year.

---oOo---

1.4 Traditional ingredients

Here is a list of the basic ingredients which you will need in order to prepare many of the recipes in this book. The list excludes products which you need to buy fresh, like vegetables, meats, and fish.

Almonds - Keep some in the shell at all times. Shelled almonds tend to go soft, whereas almonds in the shell stay fresh for years. You can skin almonds (if necessary) by blanching them in boiling water for a few seconds.

Angel hair - This is a kind of fibrous jam made from pumpkin pulp and sugar. It originated in Mallorca, but is used everywhere in Spain now for making confectionary. It is made by caramelising the pulpy meat of pumpkin in strong syrup of sugar and water.

Broad beans - Many dishes use broad beans because they grow very well in the region. They are often dried for use outside of their fresh season (April-May).

Cheeses - Normally, recipes of the area which use cheese require fresh goat's cheese; however, this can be substituted with a young or semi-mature goat's cheese if necessary.

Chick peas - A traditional staple, make sure you keep a good supply of dried chick peas in stock.

Cooking wines - Many dishes call for red or white wines, some require a Muscatel wine. Generally, for cooking it's not necessary to use the best wines. Nonetheless, the wine should be good. If it is palatable as a wine to drink, then it is also suitable for cooking.

Chorizo, blood pudding and cured ham - Many recipes add a few slices of chorizo, blood pudding or cured ham to a dish. These all have a good shelf life.

Dried fruit - Raisins, dried figs, prunes, apricots and muscatel raisins are the most popular dried fruits used in Spain.

Dried herbs and spices - The main herbs and spices used in traditional dishes are: parsley, rosemary, thyme, chilli peppers, black and white pepper, sweet paprika powder, cinnamon powder and stick, cumin, vanilla, garden mint, fennel, saffron, cloves.

Dried Peppers - Pimiento choricero: The choricero pepper is a type of red pepper of the species Capsicum annuum. They are preserved by air drying them on strings. In the kitchen the pepper is re-hydrated before use.

In every traditional Spanish kitchen you will find a string of this type of pepper. The drying of peppers is common in Spain and greatly extends their usable life. Drying also intensifies both colour and taste. To use such peppers requires that they are soaked for several hours before they are needed and generally only the flesh of the pepper is used. These peppers are not to be confused with the Ñora pepper - mixing up the varieties of peppers can ruin a dish - they have a very different flavour. This type of pepper is particularly typical of dishes in the País Vasco and other Northern regions of Spain.

Dried Peppers - Pimiento Ñora: The Ñora is another cultivar of the Capsicum annuum, called a "ball pepper" in Murcia and Alicante, where it is considered native. In fact the peppers originate in the Americas.

The Ñora pepper is small, round and red when ripe and it is mostly allowed to dry in the sun to preserve the fruit. It has a sweet taste and is often used in the regions of Murcia, Valencia and Cataluña. It is used in the manufacture of paprika powder for seasoning of various dishes. It is very common as an accompaniment to fried eggs and some salad dressings, and in the north of Alicante it is part of a delicious dish called Ñora Pericana.

Figs - Dried figs are a traditional ingredient at Christmas time in many European countries, but especially so in Spain where figs grow in such profusion. They are used in stuffing for meats and fowl and also in several sweet Christmas dishes, the most famous of which is Pan de Higo - Fig bread, which is a loaf made of figs.

Flour - When we refer to flour in these recipes we mean white, plain wheat flour, unless we specify otherwise. However, this does not mean that other flour types will not work.

Garlic - Almost all of Spain's savoury dishes use garlic in quite large quantities. Don't skimp on it!

Goat's milk - Some recipes require goat's milk. Most supermarkets in Spain stock this.

Honey: Spain is both a big producer and consumer of honey. The country has a lot of wild flowers and produces many mono-floral honeys. Honey is used in a lot of sweet bakery as well as savoury cooking. The modern popularity of honey derives from the widespread practice of keeping bees that was introduced into Moorish agriculture.

Lard - Pork - Certain traditional recipes in Spain use pork lard - "Manteca". Generally these are roasted meat dishes but lard is still used in the baking of sweet traditional biscuits like the famous "Mantecados". Very often pork lard can be substituted for butter and in some cases olive oil.

Miscellaneous - Bakers yeast, gelatine, baking soda, saffron and (plant-based) food colouring.

Olives - Most recipes using olives will assume the use of green olives, but you can also add some black olives for variety - although black olives are rarely seen in Southern Spain, there are black olives in Spain

- notably from Aragón. Generally it is more convenient to use olives that are already stoned.

Olive Oil - You will probably need two types: One for cooking and one for dressing. Generally, people prefer a sweeter, fruitier olive oil for dressing and a bitterer olive oil for cooking. Try several oils and then select a couple that suit your taste. Like wine, only you can really decide which olive oil is "good" for you.

Pan Cateto - Many recipes call for stale bread and specify "pan cateto". Cateto actually just means a traditionally baked bread. It usually is a round loaf, hand-made. Such bread is readily available in any country baker's in Spain. Similar breads can be found in most rural communities in Europe.

Pasta - Normally macaroni, a flat ribbon pasta like tagliatelle or vermicelli of various thicknesses.

Pine Kernels - Arabic cuisine has left its mark on Spanish traditional cookery and fruit and nuts are often part of both sweet and savoury dishes. Pine kernels, both raw and cooked, are a popular and healthy ingredient in many dishes.

Rice - Many recipes call for the use of rice. We haven't specified which rice you should use, but in general in Spain, the most commonly used rice is round white rice (grown in Spain). However, all types of rice will work but cooking times and conditions may need to be adjusted accordingly.

Stale bread - Never again throw yesterday's bread away. Many recipes use yesterday's hard bread to prepare a delicious dish today! Traditional country bread in Spain is best eaten fresh, because within a few hours the lovely fresh bread is usually rock solid and so bakeries generally bake at least twice per day. But when the bread is hard it just gets used for a different purpose.

Sugar and Syrup - Brown, White and Demerara sugars, icing sugar and caster sugar. Molasses and golden sugar cane syrups are used in many sweet and savoury recipes.

Vinegar - Buy one basic white wine vinegar and one basic red wine vinegar. It's used in many recipes. Also buy some "vinagre de Jerez" for special purposes.

---oOo---

1.5 Christmas in Spain

For many visitors to Spain in the month or two before Christmas, one of the most noticeable features is the absence of commercialism surrounding the whole Christmas celebration. In many Northern European countries the Christmas marketing operation starts up in late September and is in full swing by November, with shelves lined with pre-Christmas junk and the PA systems of every large shop playing the strangely out of season sounds of "All our Christmas Hits" a full month before Advent has even been declared. You won't find this in Spain! In Spain, Christmas is still pretty much a traditional affair.

Yes, supermarkets will have a good few shelves of sweets and cakes aimed at the Christmas market starting in late November, but all in all, it is a much less commercial time of the year in Spain than it is in, for example, Britain. The shops start stocking up on toys in November to give families a chance to buy their children's presents but the giving of presents is mostly confined to the children.

Also, in Spain it is not usual for the streets to be decorated with bright lights until the first week of December, and people will decorate their homes for the second half of the month. This may involve a Christmas tree and probably a "belén", a small nativity scene, which will always include Mary, Joseph and Jesus, as well as the three kings. Many different belén characters can be purchased at this time of year to decorate the domestic belén - some very intricate and beautiful and some very bizarre! When the Christmas lights do arrive on the streets they are often of really spectacular proportions in the cities. Even the smallest village will have some public Christmas lights.

There are a number of holidays and festivals during the Christmas period, which means that there is plenty of time to spend eating and drinking with family and friends. The first of these is December 8th, which is the public holiday called Immaculada - The Feast of the Immaculate Conception. This basically marks the start of the Spanish Christmas celebrations.

Another big day in the pre-Christmas period is the draw for the lottery, "El Gordo", or "The Fat One". Pretty much everyone in Spain buys a ticket for this, and if a winner comes up from a particular town, it is very likely that there will be many winners from the same place. The draw takes place on December 22nd, and whole families gather around the television to see if they have won.

Then, of course, come Christmas Eve and Christmas Day, and this is where a "Spanish Christmas" becomes a little different from Christmas in Britain, for example.

Christmas Eve is called Nochebuena. It is the time for a family gathering for a large and often long meal which may be temporarily interrupted by midnight mass. Midnight Mass is often referred to as "La Misa Del Gallo" (The Mass of the Rooster), because tradition says that a rooster crowed during the night that Jesus was born.

Generally, Spanish children receive only a small simple present from Santa Claus on the night of Nochebuena. The main event in terms of presents takes place when the gifts are brought to the children by the three kings in January. Generally, on Christmas Day, the time will be spent quietly, maybe taking a walk, and having another long leisurely lunch with family.

On December 26th (St. Stephen's Day) one may be surprised to see that work and Christmas shopping has resumed again (except in Cataluña where it is a holiday) after the short interruption of Christmas day - this is because of course the main present giving day still lays ahead!

December 31st is New Year's Eve, known as Noche Vieja, and is a really big night of celebration in Spain. This can be a rather confusing evening for the uninitiated foreigner, because a casual observer walking around a town or city at 9pm would come to the conclusion that the city was completely closed for the night. You will find it hard to find a bar or restaurant open. The reason for this is that they are either closed for dinner or are hosting private or family dinners behind closed doors. Most people will have a meal with their family and friends during the evening, and stay at home until just before midnight. Suddenly, the closed city is wide open again; the party begins and will continue all night!

At midnight, the tradition is to eat 12 grapes, one on each of the ringing bells of midnight. After this, people flood out onto the streets and into the bars for yet another night of drinking, eating, dancing and celebration. The following day is a public holiday, and can be spent sleeping off the partying of the previous night, although the really brave party-goers stay up all night and have their chocolate and churros whilst watching the sun rise.

January 5th is the day all Spanish children are waiting for: the night when the three kings visit and bring them their presents. You may see decorations outside people's houses, with ladders and effigies of the three kings climbing through the windows.

This is also the night of the Cabalgata parade, and the "Reyes Magos" arrive on a float, and throw sweets to the crowds of children. Every child will have his or her favourite king, and the most popular seems to be Balthazar. Before going to bed, the children clean a pair of shoes, in which their gifts can be left, and they leave a snack for the camels and leave out a nightcap for the Kings.

On January 6 the children wake to find the presents left to them. Gradually the month-long Christmas celebrations draw to a close.

---oOo---

1.5.1 The Run-Up to Christmas in Spain

The whole month of December is a kind of preparation for Christmas in Spain. To give a flavour of the season, here are just a few examples of the landmark dates, though there are many, many more provincial and village traditions (the subject of another book at a later date):

December 7th - 8th - Inmaculada: Christmas starts here. Inmaculada is the Patron Saint of Seville, where musical groups from the university, known as 'los tunos', gather around the statue of the Virgin Immaculada in the Plaza del Triunfo (behind the cathedral) in traditional dress and sing songs. On the morning of the 8th children dance the Danza de los Seises (Dance of the Sixes) in the square.

December 13 - El Día de Santa Lucia: Patron saint of the blind. Traditionally the blind sing Christmas carols in the streets, although this is less common in modern times. In the village of Zújar near Granada, bonfires are lit to celebrate the event.

December 21 - The shortest day of the year: This is celebrated in Granada and in neighbouring Jaén by jumping through bonfires for the fiesta of Hogueras. The activity is said to keep illness away.

December 22 - El Gordo: This is when the huge Spanish lottery is drawn. This lottery is so big, they start selling tickets in August.

---oOo---

1.5.2 The Timetable of Christmas Festivities and Meals

There are three main meals in the normal Spanish culinary celebration of Christmas. They are held on Christmas Eve (dinner), New Year's Eve (dinner) and on the Día del Reyes (eating of the Roscón and other sweets). In some regions, like Cataluña, there are also important meals on Christmas Day and St. Stephen's Day (26th December):

Christmas Eve: This is a half-day for most businesses in Spain and people hurry home to prepare for the evening's celebrations. Most bars and restaurants will close and it is very much a family affair. Many people go to midnight mass or 'La Misa Del Gallo' (The Mass of the Rooster). Most families will eat their main Christmas meal on Christmas Eve before this service (and may continue afterwards!). Adults exchange gifts on Christmas Eve and the children receive one or two simple presents.

After the midnight service, people walk through the streets carrying torches, playing guitars and beating on tambourines and drums. One Spanish saying is "Esta noche es Nochebuena, y no es noche de dormir" which means 'Tonight is the good night and it is not meant for sleeping!'

Christmas Day: Most families take a quiet day on Christmas day with a leisurely lunch. The main objective is to relax and enjoy the company of family and friends. Most couples will visit one set of parents on Christmas Eve and the other set on Christmas Day. Many people will have lunch or dinner with their family at a restaurant.

St. Stephen's Day: This is a holiday in Cataluña (and another chance to eat up the Christmas leftovers) but most people in the rest of the country are back to work.

28th December: This is the "Día de Santos Inocentes" - "The Day of the Holy Innocents". It is very much like April Fools Day. People try to trick each other into believing silly stories and jokes. Newspapers and TV stations run fantastic stories. If you trick someone, you can call them "Inocente, inocente". The 28th December commemorates the babies that were killed on the orders of King Herod when he was trying to kill the baby Jesus.

31st December: New Year's Eve: Rather than starting early and building to a crescendo at midnight, the Spanish begin the New Year celebrations after a leisurely private dinner with friends or family, and then go out just before midnight to the bars. The party then continues until about 6am or so.

Dinner is generally a private family affair; often in a restaurant, but behind closed doors. When midnight arrives, the party begins with the traditional eating of twelve grapes at the rate of the twelve strokes of the clock, and once you enter into the New Year, these are washed down with Cava! The eating of the "twelve grapes of luck" is a tradition that dates back from at least 1895, but became established in 1909. In December of that year, some Alicantese vine growers popularized this custom to better sell huge amounts of grapes from an excellent harvest.

New Year's Day: At dawn or in the morning of January 1st, it is usual to take chocolate and churros, either at home with the family or at a café or bar, etc. And then to bed for a few hours!

Día de los Reyes Magos (January 6th): January 6th is virtually as important as Christmas itself, especially for the children, as this is the day when they get their presents. The fun starts the evening before, when the three kings lead their procession through the streets, throwing sweets to the children. Children believe that the Kings bring presents to them at Epiphany. They write letters to the Kings on St. Stephen's Day, December 26th, asking for toys and presents. And then on Epiphany Eve (January 5th) they leave their shoes on windowsills or balconies or under the Christmas tree to be filled with presents. Gifts for the Kings are often left by the children, such as a glass of brandy for each King, a mandarin orange or some walnuts. Sometimes a bucket of water is left for the Kings' camels! If the children have been "bad", the Kings might leave pieces of "coal", made out of sugar, in their presents!

Some big towns and cities have Epiphany Parades with each King having a big float, often shaped like a camel. The main thing is that large amounts of sweets are thrown to the crowds of following children. Everyone also eats Roscón, a sweet, large doughnut-shaped bread covered in glacéed fruit and sugar, and usually filled with cream or chocolate. Inside the bread is buried a small figurine of baby Jesus or of one of the Kings. Watch out! If you find it you have good luck for a year!

---o0o---

2.0 The Recipes - An Introduction

Notes about these recipes

Traditional recipes can be difficult to define very clearly, because they tend to be less exact, less prescriptive than modern recipes. Traditional cooks work using an instinct for their ingredients which is somewhat *above* the need to weigh or measure all the ingredients exactly. Therefore, they often make assumptions about how a dish should be prepared. We have tried to eliminate this ambiguity as much as possible by providing different recipes for the same dish when available. This choice of recipes allows the reader to get a feeling for the way the dish is prepared in reality and for the local variations that exist.

Optional ingredients: Because of the flexibility within a recipe, this means that some of these recipes often refer to an ingredient or seasoning as "optional" or "to taste", meaning that you should add the ingredient at your own discretion. These can very often be quite big decisions for a cook to make, so it's worth thinking in advance about these options and reading the alternative recipes we provide. Cooks in Spain tend to use less salt (in general) than the amounts used in Northern European cuisine, but ultimately it comes down to personal choice and taste.

Undefined number of servings: Not all of our collected recipes specify the number of "servings" as would be normal in a modern recipe book. One reason for this is that many traditional dishes are quite often shared between several people dining together. To make matters more complicated, many traditional dishes can be equally served either as tapas, starters or main courses - there are no rules about what can be served when! That means that many recipes are interchangeable within a meal and the cook needs to develop an understanding of the recipe in order to be able to gauge the ingredient quantities needed in accordance to how it will be served. In other words, you will sometimes need to judge for yourself the ingredient amounts that you will need to use for a particular number of diners. Obviously making a "tapas version" of a dish requires smaller quantities of ingredients per serving than making the "main course version". In Spain, nothing is quite fixed with regards to which dish can be served at which time.

Alternative recipes: To help with the problem we have tried to provide alternative recipes when possible for each dish and we suggest that you read all alternative recipes for a dish before beginning.

Local variants: For most recipes very many local variations exist and these can be quite different from one village to another. We have generally documented the most popular versions of each dish, but bear in mind that there will certainly be more quite different variants in existence.

Traditional techniques

NOTE: As in all culinary traditions, there are certain techniques which are commonly used in the kitchens of Spain. To avoid having to repeat the details of these techniques, we define them here for you. Sometimes they have different names according to the region.

A sofrito: This is a warm sauce made from very finely chopped ingredients (that may vary according to the dish it will be added to) cooked in olive oil until soft. Usually it contains onions, tomatoes, garlic, parsley, paprika powder, salt, but the ingredients may vary slightly according to a particular recipe.

A majaillo (or majadillo, majado, or mojado): This is made by grinding a number of ingredients together into a paste, usually with a mortar and pestle (or in a blender). This paste is then added to a dish during its preparation.

Use of herbs and spices: In many dishes involving pulses, the addition of spices like mustard, cumin and star anise are not just a matter of adding flavour, or serving as a reminder of our Arabic past, but also a good way to aid digestion - especially with some of the more heavy dishes.

A la plancha: This is a cooking technique where a food is grilled on a hot plate with a little olive oil. Vegetables, fish or meat are often prepared in this way. It is a healthy way to prepare food, using very little else than the natural juices to cook the food.

Tools and utensils you will need

Apart from the usual kitchen tools and utensils you may find that you need the following additional tools to make these recipes:

- A blender with several speed settings.

- One small and one large mortar and pestle to make the *majaillo* pastes which many recipes use.

- A purée mill. This is a hand turned utensil for making purées like potato or tomato purée.

- A spice bag to hang in certain dishes when you don't want to mix the herbs and spices directly into the dish. These are usually reusable open cotton pouches with a string tie.

- Roscos (doughnuts) of various flavours are a popular traditional sweet. If you are planning to make a lot of roscos, it may be worth buying a doughnut cutter; it is a simple hand tool that makes for easier and more consistent cutting out of dough to make a rosco.

---oOo---

2.1 Starters, Salads, Vegetables, Gazpachos

AJOBLANCO DE ALMÁCHAR
Garlic Soup of Almáchar

Despite being best known as a cooling summer soup, gazpachos of Almonds are also a typically Christmas dish especially in rural areas of southern Spain where there is often a good supply of almonds at this time of year.

Here is a little history of the dish. Ajoblanco was first created in Almáchar by the Moors. The combination of fresh fruit and dried fruit was classical Moorish culinary practice and this became one of the most popular dishes of the time. Ajoblanco remains one of only two white soups worldwide in which no dairy product is used.

Cold soups are particularly popular in Andalucía because they are quite refreshing during the long hot summers and they are also very simple and easy to make. They are the basic sustenance of the workers out in the field, tending the vineyards or harvesting the grapes. Ajoblanco taken together with a few fresh grapes or apple makes a delicious, refreshing and nutritious dish.

The popularity of this particular cold soup, so the story goes, spread during the late nineteenth century. It became popular outside of the area when an engineer, who was working in rural Málaga province, asked a local woman for some water. Instead, she made the man some Ajoblanco. He was so impressed by the taste and simplicity of the dish that when he returned to Madrid he publicised the dish in glowing reports.

Ingredients (serves 6):

      90 g blanched almonds
      3 cloves garlic, peeled
      0.5 teaspoon salt
      4 slices stale white bread, crusts removed
      1 l of ice water
      7 tablespoons olive oil
      3 tablespoons white wine vinegar
      2 tablespoons sherry vinegar

1 tablespoon butter
6 slices white bread, crusts removed, cut in cubes
225 g seedless green grapes or slices of apple

Preparation:

1. Grind almonds, 2 garlic cloves and salt to a fine consistency in a blender.

2. Soak stale bread in 1 cup of iced water then squeeze to extract moisture. Add the bread to the blender.

3. With the blender running, add 6 tablespoons of olive oil and one cup of iced water slowly in a steady stream.

4. Add vinegars and mix on high speed for 2 minutes.

5. Pour into a bowl. Add the remaining water and mix well. Adjust seasonings with salt and vinegar. Chill for up to 6 hours.

Optional - croutons:

6. Heat butter and remaining oil in a pan.

7. Crush remaining garlic clove and add to pan with bread cubes, tossing to coat.

8. Cook over very low heat, stirring occasionally, 20-30 minutes or until cubes are golden.

9. Serve soup ice cold, garnished with the croutons and fresh grapes or apple slices.

CARDO CON BÉCHAMEL DE ARAGÓN
Aragónese Cardos in Béchamel sauce

This is a well-loved Christmas Eve recipe, especially in Aragón and Navarra.

Ingredients:

>500 g of Cardo thistle stems, cleaned and chopped in approx. 5cm lengths
>250 g fresh button mushrooms
>Béchamel sauce (prepared in advance)
>30 pine kernels
>Grated cheese to taste (pick a cheese you like and which browns well)
>Olive oil
>Salt
>Pepper

Preparation:

1. Wash the cardos and clean the mushrooms.

2. Sauté the mushrooms in a large frying pan with a little olive oil until slightly browned.

3. Add the pine nuts to the pan and sauté.

4. Add the cardo stems, season and then fry everything together for a few minutes.

5. Once the cardo is cooked, place the whole mixture in a casserole dish and put aside.

6. Prepare a béchamel sauce and pour this over the cardo mix in the casserole dish.

7. Sprinkle grated cheese on top and season with pepper to taste.

8. Grill the dish for about 10 minutes. As soon as the top begins to turn golden brown, it is ready to serve. Garnish with fresh parsley.

ENSALADA EL REMOJÓN
Salad "El Remojón"

This is a simple but very complete traditional salad, found in some villages of the eastern coastal zones of Andalucía. It is a variation on the so-called "Málaga Salad" but with more ingredients. The salted cod is roasted before being soaked to remove the excess salt. The use of seasonal fruits like orange livens up the salad and the use of salt cod made the salad a favourite for meatless Christmas Eve dinners.

Ingredients (serves 6):

    0.5 kg potatoes
    2 large tomatoes
    4 onions
    3 oranges
    3 cloves of garlic
    400 g of salty dried cod
    3 radishes
    0.25 kg of marinated olives
    1 sprig of parsley
    Vinegar (to taste)
    Olive oil
    Salt (to taste)

Preparation:

1. Roast the cod directly on the fire, shake off the salt and then put to soak in water.

2. Boil the potatoes and cut them into slices.

3. Peel the tomatoes, remove the seeds and cut them into cubes.

4. Add olives (without stones), sliced radishes, diced orange and then the cod in small pieces.

5. All this is mixed and seasoned with parsley, salt and finely chopped garlic.

6. Add a generous splash of olive oil and vinegar to taste.

GAZPACHO DE ALMENDRAS Y PASAS

Almond and Raisin gazpacho

Almond Gazpacho is often taken as a Christmas delicacy. Here is a very simple recipe that combines sweet and savoury tastes in this delicious light almond gazpacho.

Ingredients:

>150 g of almonds
>1 egg
>1 clove of garlic
>Some good quality vinegar
>Olive oil
>Salt
>An apple and some raisins, for garnish

Preparation:

1. Blend the almonds with the egg, garlic, a dash of vinegar, a dash of oil and salt.

2. Add cold water and ice cubes, until you obtain the required consistency. Add salt, oil and vinegar to taste.

3. Serve cold (add some ice-cubes, if necessary) with thinly sliced or diced apple and some raisins.

PARPUCHAS DE MÁLAGA
Cod Pancakes of Málaga

Here is another salt cod recipe often used on religious festivals when meat is not permitted. It makes a delicious and tasty starter for Christmas Eve dinner. It's a little time consuming but definitely worth the wait.

Ingredients:

>3 eggs
>One and a half cup of water
>Cod desalted and crumbled
>Parsley
>Garlic
>Saffron
>Yeast
>Flour - enough to thicken the dough

Preparation:

1. Put warm water and yeast in the blender and mix.

2. Add the eggs, parsley, garlic, saffron and blend again. Pour into a bowl.

3. Now, gradually add the flour and crumbled cod, stirring all the while to create a soft dough.

4. Leave the mixture to stand overnight.

5. Gently heat some olive oil in a frying pan and add the dough with a spoon and fry. Try to make the "parpuchas" (pancakes) quite thin - they will expand.

PATATAS AL ROMERO

Potatoes with Rosemary

This is a simple way of making roasted potatoes a little bit special for the Christmas season when they are served to accompany delicacies like, for example, leg of lamb in honey.

Ingredients:

    Potatoes
    Garlic
    Several sprigs of fresh rosemary
    Onions (About 50% of the potatoes in weight)

Preparation:

1. Peel the potatoes and cut them into slices (about 1cm thick) or dice them into cubes. (Small new potatoes can be used whole). Peel and slice the onions and peel and crush the garlic.

2. Put all ingredients in a baking dish, sprinkle with salt, add several sprigs of rosemary, a little water with oil and mix well. Bake at 180°C until the potatoes start to brown. Make sure the rosemary and potatoes are well mixed, so as to pass the herb's flavour to the potatoes.

3. After the baking, remove the rosemary sprigs and use them as decoration.

PATATAS A LA SIDRA DE ASTURIAS

Potatoes in Cider from Asturias

The Cider of Asturias is an important local product and its high quality is protected by its own D.O. (Designation of Origin). It is used in various recipes. Here it is used to prepare this delicious potato dish, which accompanies many a Christmas dinner in the North of Spain.

Ingredients:

    6 medium potatoes
    25 g of butter
    2 tablespoons of olive oil
    2 cloves of garlic
    Thyme
    Salt
    300 ml of cider
    300 ml of stew broth ("caldo de puchero")

Preparation:

1. Peel the potatoes and cut them lengthwise into flat pieces.

2. Put the butter with the olive oil in a frying pan, and fry the potatoes on all sides until golden brown. At that moment add the sliced garlic and fry until evenly browned.

3. Add the cider and the broth, ensuring that the potatoes are half covered.

4. Sprinkle with thyme, and add salt to taste.

5. Leave to cook for about fifteen minutes over a medium heat. After this time turn the potatoes and cook them for another fifteen minutes. If they become dry, add a little more liquid.

6. In the meantime, preheat the oven to 180°C and bake the potatoes for about ten minutes until well done inside and the required amount of liquid has evaporated.

7. Serve hot. They are ideal to accompany meats.

TORTILLITAS DE COLIFLOR
Cauliflower Fritters

This recipe almost certainly uses cauliflower as a substitute for cod. Even though cod was long considered food for the poor, many couldn't even afford cod, but they still made the same tortillas, substituting the cod for chunks of cauliflower with extraordinary and delicious results.

Ingredients (serves 4):

    0.5 kg cauliflower
    2 eggs
    2 cloves of garlic
    1 sprig of parsley
    Flour
    Olive oil
    Salt (to taste)

Preparation:

1. Boil the cauliflower in salted water until it is tender. Drain it and allow it to cool.

2. In a bowl beat the eggs and crumbled pieces of cauliflower. Finely chop and add the parsley and garlic. Add salt to taste. Add the flour little by little, stirring with a wooden spoon until the mix thickens slightly.

3. Put plenty of oil in a pan and when it is hot, use a spoon to put portions of the mixture into the hot oil.

4. When the tortillas are golden brown take them out and lay on kitchen paper to absorb the excess oil.

5. Note that the dish can also be made by separating the cauliflower into florets, coating them in batter and deep frying them.

---oOo---

2.2 Soups

SOPA DE AJO - SOPA CASTELLANA
Garlic Soup of Castilla

Traditionally this is a very economic but very warming and tasty winter soup, very prevalent in rural areas. Despite its humble background it is a popular Easter dish, but has also become a Christmas favourite especially in Castilla.

Ingredients (serves 6):

    150 g of Serrano ham
    10 cloves of garlic
    6 eggs (1 per person)
    12 slices of stale bread
    2.5 litres of beef stock
    Salt to taste
    Pepper to taste
    2 tablespoons of paprika powder
    50 ml of olive oil

Preparation:

1. Peel and coarsely slice the garlic. Put aside.

2. Choose a large fireproof dish, heat the olive oil in it and add the garlic. Sauté the garlic until it begins to brown and then add the finely chopped ham. Stir with a wooden spoon.

3. When the garlic is honey coloured, add 6 slices of bread and turn them over a few times. Remove the pan from the heat and sprinkle in the paprika. Stir well. Return the saucepan to the heat and sauté everything for 2-3 minutes. Remove from the heat and add the beef stock. Leave to boil on a medium heat for about 20 minutes.

4. After these 20 minutes, add the rest of the bread, previously toasted with a little olive oil. Place them on the surface of the soup and let them float until soft. Add salt and freshly ground black pepper to your taste.

5. Break the eggs and drop them into the soup. Let the eggs curdle for 2-3 minutes. Serve very hot in earthenware bowls. You can also add ham, chorizo, fried bacon etc., according to your taste.

CREMA DE ANDARICAS (NÉCORAS) DE ASTURIAS
Crab Cream Soup of Asturias

This is a hot winter soup and a very traditional Christmas soup in coastal areas of Asturias. The "andarica" (crab) is very popular seafood in Asturias. Here is one typical recipe for a creamed crab soup based on a fish and crab broth.

Ingredients:

    1 kg of crabs
    300 g hake
    1/4 cup cider brandy
    0.5 cup cider
    2 egg yolks
    1 tablespoon of butter
    100 ml. of cooking cream
    2 carrots
    1 tomato
    1 onion
    1 bunch of parsley
    3 cloves of garlic
    Salt
    Pepper

Preparation:

1. Boil the crabs for 10 minutes in water together with half an onion, a peeled clove of garlic and half the bunch of parsley.

2. Meanwhile, in another saucepan, gently simmer the hake in 0.5 litre of water with half an onion, two peeled cloves of garlic, the tomato, the peeled carrots and the remaining parsley.

3. Once the crabs are cooked, cut out the meat and put aside. Keep the broth.

4. When the fish is cooked, strain the broth, add the cider and cider brandy to it, along with the crabmeat, the crab broth, the hake and the carrots and blend the whole mixture together. Put the resulting puree to boil in a saucepan, adding the butter, the cream and the beaten egg yolks. Stir well, add salt to taste and quickly bring to the boil just before serving hot.

6. Serve the crab soup in a bowl with croutons and parsley garnish.

SOPA CACHORREÑA DE MÁLAGA

Cod and Orange Soup of Málaga

These tasty soups are part of the popular cuisine of Andalusia and often served at fiestas where abstinence from meat was required. They all have in common the use of pepper, garlic and bread, but it is only in Málaga that the soup uses the peels or the juice of bitter oranges as part of the recipe. This is what distinguishes this recipe from others in Andalucía.

Ingredients (serves 4):

    4 pieces of salt cod (desalted)
    4 eggs
    3 or 4 cloves of garlic
    1 orange peel (dry or fresh)
    1 slice of old bread
    Black peppercorns (to taste)
    Vinegar (to taste)
    Olive oil
    Salt (to taste)

Preparation:

1. Hard boil the eggs, leave them to cool, remove the shells, and put aside.

2. Put one and a half litre of water in a saucepan, add the orange peel and bring to the boil. After 5 minutes, add the pieces of cod, letting them cook for another 5 minutes (depending on the thickness of the cod).

3. While this is boiling, make a majado in a mortar with the peppercorns, the garlic, a dash of vinegar, some breadcrumbs and paprika. Once crushed, add a ladle of broth to make the paste thinner and then pour the mixture into the saucepan with the cod. Add salt to taste whilst stirring. Remove the orange peel and the four pieces of cod. Put aside.

4. The soup is served in two parts: First serve the hot broth with small pieces of the remaining bread on top. Then in a second course, serve the pieces of cod with the hardboiled egg. The traditional way of eating this is to crumble the cod, cut up the eggs, mix them together and add a dash of olive oil.

SOPA DE CEBOLLA
Onion Soup

Onion Soup "au gratin" originated in France and has been venerated as a traditional peasant dish there for at least 200 years. It was mentioned by the author Dumas as one of his favourite meals, though generally it was considered to be "poor man's food", being made, as it was, with pieces of old bread and old cheese and basically containing no meat.

Nonetheless, onion soup became very popular in France and very quickly spread to Northern Spain where it also became a well-liked traditional winter-time soup. These days it tends to be served only at special occasions, because it is a little time-consuming to make. For this reason it is usually served during fiestas and large family meals where there is time to spend in the kitchen. Prior to the changes in the rules on fasting and abstinence in the Catholic Church, it became a popular dish for Christmas Eve in its meatless form.

Here we give a recipe for a Catalan version of the soup, with beef stock, but the beef stock can also be omitted, or replaced by vegetable stock, without much alteration to the taste of this delicious soup.

Ingredients:

>6 large mild onions
>30 ml Olive oil
>60 g butter
>3 tablespoons flour
>1 clove of garlic
>2 litres of beef stock (or, alternatively, a vegetable or other broth)
>12 slices baguette bread
>1 teaspoon of sugar
>Salt to taste
>Freshly ground black pepper to taste
>20 ml of brandy or cognac
>100 g of grated cheese (a type that melts easily)

Preparation:

1. Peel and cut the onions into very thin "half moons". Put aside. Peel and finely chop the garlic.

2. Put the olive oil and the butter in a large saucepan and gently cook the onions and garlic with a little salt and black pepper. Stir with a wooden spoon until the onions are translucent, they should not darken or burn. On a low heat this will take about 20-25 minutes. Slowly add a tablespoon of sugar.

3. Sprinkle the flour into the pan and stir gently to mix well. Add the brandy and leave 1-2 minutes for the alcohol to evaporate. Add the broth. Season with salt and pepper, if necessary, and bring to the boil. Leave the soup for 15-20 minutes over a very low heat - taking care that it does not to burn.

4. Cut the bread into thin slices and toast them lightly. Spread them with some crushed garlic. Pour the soup into individual earthenware bowls and place the toast on top of the soup in each bowl. Sprinkle the grated cheese over the soup and bread.

5. Put the bowls into an oven preheated at 200°C. Gratinate at 220°C for 5-6 minutes and serve immediately.

SOPA DE GALETS O CALDO DE NAVIDAD DE CATALUÑA

Pasta broth of Cataluña

This pasta soup is a traditional Christmas soup of Cataluña. Many types of pasta shells are sold, but the best known are those of Christmas, which are considered the largest. They are believed to be either Catalan or Italian originally, but the giant shell version is totally traditional to the Catalan Christmas.

Ingredients:

>Half a Chicken
>Bones to make a broth
>2 leeks
>2 sticks of celery
>1 turnip
>1 parsnip
>4 carrots
>1 potato
>0.25 kg of large pasta shells
>Salt to taste

Preparation:

1. Clean and remove all the fat from the chicken and chop the meat.

2. Clean and chop the vegetables.

3. Add the meat and vegetables with the broth bones to a large pan filled with water to cover the ingredients, and boil for 2 hours.

4. Remove from the heat. Take out all the ingredients and strain the broth.

5. Bring the broth back to the boil.

6. When it is boiling, add in the pasta shells. Cook the pasta until it is done.

7. Serve pasta and broth together.

---oOo---

2.3 Main Dishes

Main dishes have been divided into several types of traditional plate:

    Goat's meat
    Lamb
    Pork
    Poultry
    Stews and Fricassees
    Casseroles
    Fish

2.3.1 Goat's Meat

CABRITO A LA MIEL
Kid Goat in Honey

Young goat is a treasured meat in the mountainous regions of Spain where goats are farmed for both milk and meat. Traditionally, young male goats are "sacrificed" before they are 3 months old and their tender meat is highly prized in Spanish cuisine.

Here is a traditional recipe from the Alpujarras in the province of Granada, where goat in honey is a popular Christmas dish. This is a recipe that descends directly from Moorish cuisine, combining savoury and sweet flavours.

This particular recipe comes from the village of Beires, situated in an area where many of the last Moorish families hid during their expulsion from Granada when the invading Christians finally overcame the Moorish kingdom. You may use lamb or goat, but the important thing is that you use a young (suckling) animal.

This recipe is for kid goat but later we also later provide a variant of this recipe using sucking lamb.

Ingredients (serves 6):

> Two legs of Kid goat
> 3 onions
> 6 cloves garlic
> 2 bay leaves
> 0.5 teaspoon white pepper
> 0.5 teaspoon cayenne pepper
> 1 glass of white wine
> 1 small glass of wine vinegar
> 4-5 strands of saffron
> 150 g of Rosemary honey
> Olive oil
> Salt

Preparation:

1. Put some olive oil into an earthenware casserole dish and heat it up. When it is hot, add the very finely chopped onions and garlic.

2. When everything is well fried, add the meat, turning it over a few times to brown on all sides. Let it fry for some minutes.

3. Next, add the saffron, white pepper, cayenne pepper, the bay leaves, salt and wine. Stir in well. Reduce the heat and leave to cook until the sauce is reduced slightly. Add more salt if necessary.

4. Place the casserole dish in a pre-heated oven at 180°C, and leave it to roast for 35-40 minutes. During this time, regularly baste the meat with the sauce. If necessary, add some hot water to make sure the sauce does not become too thick.

5. A few minutes before removing the meat from the oven, mix the honey with the vinegar in a saucepan and put it on a medium heat, stirring constantly. Allow it to reduce slightly until it is well blended and has a syrupy consistency.

4. Pour the honey sauce over the meat and leave it in the oven for about another 10 minutes.

5. Serve in the casserole dish.

CABRITU A LA SIDRA DE ASTURIAS
Kid Goat in Cider from Asturias

Asturias is famous for its ciders and also for its excellent goat meat. Here the two come together in a recipe combining Kid goat with a cider sauce. The dish is a favourite in the region for a Christmas Eve or New Years Eve dinner. This recipe calls for the use of a wood-burning oven, but a similar result can be achieved by roasting the meat in a conventional oven; with shorter cooking times and at a temperature of about 180°C.

Ingredients:

>Half a kid goat
>1 head of garlic (peeled and chopped finely)
>Laurel
>Thyme
>Romero
>Pepper
>Natural cider
>Salt
>Olive oil

Preparation:

1. This dish has to be prepared the day before it is to be eaten. The kid should be steeped in its sauce for 24 hours.

2. Cut the meat into pieces and sprinkle them with salt and pepper. Put the meat in a roasting tray and add rosemary, thyme, bay leaf and chopped garlic. Then add a splash of oil and stir. Put the tray in the fridge. It is important to cover the tray with plastic film to concentrate the flavours better during the overnight seasoning.

4. The next day, the goat's meat is baked very slowly in a wood oven for 4 hours. Every half hour turn the pieces and baste the meat with its own juices. After 3 hours add about 1 litre of cider, put the dish back into the oven for the last hour of cooking.

CHOTO AL AJILLO DE ALCAUCÍN
Kid Goat in garlic from Alcaucin

This dish originates in the mountainous border lands between the provinces of Granada and Málaga where the keeping of goats has gone on for millennia. This dish is made with a lot of garlic and is best taken with some of the local mosto (immature wine) of the area. It can be eaten as a starter or main course and is a favourite for New Year's dinner.

Ingredients:

- 1.5 kg of kid goat meat
- 1 head of garlic
- 40 ml olive oil
- 300 ml dry white wine
- 1 bay leaf
- 1 chilli pepper
- Peppercorns
- Salt and pepper

Preparation:

1. Season the meat with salt and pepper and sauté in the oil, along with the garlic, over a high heat.

2. When they start to turn brown, add 2 glasses of wine, the chilli, pepper and bay leaf. Leave to simmer, stirring occasionally with a wooden spoon, until all the wine has reduced (about 35-40 minutes).

3. Remove the meat and place in a dish to serve. Put the pan onto a high heat again. Add another glass of wine whilst stirring with the wooden spoon to dissolve the juices from the meat to make a sauce.

4. Pour this sauce over the meat and it is ready to serve.

CHOTO A LA NERJEÑA O CABRITO EN SALSA DE ALMENDRAS

Kid Goat in Almond Sauce from Andalucía

Often eaten during the festive season when there is a good supply of both almonds, Málaga wine and young goat's meat to be had. The killing of a kid goat or lamb at times of religious feasts has many resonances in Middle Eastern cuisine and is often mentioned in biblical texts. This recipe is typical of Nerja in the province of Málaga.

Ingredients:

>   3.5 kg kid goat
>   Offal from kid goat
>   200 g of almonds
>   200 g of Cateto bread
>   A head of garlic
>   1.5 litre of white Málaga wine
>   1 teaspoon of food colouring (saffron)
>   1 teaspoon of paprika powder
>   2 large bay leaves
>   1 branch of fresh thyme
>   300 ml of olive oil
>   Salt
>   Two chilli peppers
>   A dash of vinegar
>   1.5 litre of water

Preparation:

1. Cut up the goat meat.

2. Fry the goat meat with the garlic until brown. Just before the garlic is browned add the wine, water and salt. When this starts to boil, add the bay leaves, the thyme, paprika, saffron and chilli.

3. Make a majado: Fry the almonds until brown and put aside. Fry the garlic and the bread, and mix them with the almonds.

4. Fry the offal with a little salt. When this is cooked, add the majado.

5. Add 2 cloves of raw garlic to the majado mix with a little stock from the goat's meat.

6. Shortly before the goat's meat is tender, put the majado through a blender (or grind it in a mortar) to make it into a smooth paste. Add this paste to the pan with the goat's meat.

7. Serve as soon as the meat is tender.

---oOo---

2.3.2 Lamb

Lamb is a popular Christmas dish in many parts of Spain. Generally the main stipulation is that the lamb should be three or less months old and still taking its mother's milk. This improves the quality of the meat. Here is a basic recipe for roast shoulder of lamb.

CORDERO ASADO AL HORNO
Roast Marinated Lamb

Ingredients (serves 4):

    1.5 kg leg of lamb
    3-4 garlic cloves, peeled
    10 ml salt
    40 ml parsley, chopped
    10 ml dried oregano
    60 ml olive oil
    100 ml brandy

Preparation:

1. Grind the garlic with the salt into a paste in a mortar. Add the parsley and oregano and grind into a thick paste.

2. Spread the mixture over the lamb and leave the meat to absorb the flavours for 3 to 4 hours.

3. Place the lamb in a roasting tray and pour the olive oil over the meat.

4. Roast in an oven that is preheated to 200°C until cooked to your taste, basting frequently.

5. The usual cooking time is 20 minutes per half kilo. Add an extra half an hour to have the meat "well-done". Add the brandy to the juices 15 minutes before the lamb is ready.

4. Let the lamb rest for 10 minutes before carving. Serve with all the juices.

CORDERO AL CHILINDRÓN
Lamb in Red Pepper sauce

This is a typical dish of the north-eastern regions of Spain, like Navarra - Aragón - Basque Country. In the past this was a traditional Sunday lunch dish, but it is now more typical as a main course of the Christmas Eve dinner.

"A Chilindrón" basically means that a red pepper and tomato sauce with plenty of garlic is added to a piece of meat, generally roasted. It is suitable for lamb, chicken, and rabbit. The mixture of meat and vegetables is then left for a while and the whole dish takes on a characteristic dark red colour, due to the natural red pigment of the peppers and tomatoes.

Ingredients (serves 6):

    1.5 kg lamb
    3 red peppers
    2 dried red peppers
    5 cloves of garlic
    5 ripe tomatoes
    Rind of 1 lemon
    150 g serrano ham
    Olive oil
    1 sprig of parsley
    White wine
    Salt
    Pepper

Preparation:

1. Prepare the lamb, cut to pieces and season with salt and pepper.

2. Soak the dried peppers for 30 minutes.

3. Dice the ham.

4. Finely chop the tomatoes and put aside.

5. Cut the onions into very thin strips. Peel the garlic but leave the cloves whole.

6. Clean the peppers and cut them into very small cubes.

7. Chop the parsley and put aside.

8. Grind one clove of garlic with the parsley. Remove the flesh from the dried peppers and grind this into the mix. Put aside.

9. Put some olive oil in a frying pan and fry the pieces of lamb.

10. Subsequently, add the cloves of garlic and the lemon rind and cover with a mixture of white wine and water (half of each). Quickly bring to the boil.

11. Make a sofrito: In a separate pan make the sauce by stir-frying the onions, peppers, salt and pepper. When the mix starts to brown, add the ham and then the tomato. Leave to simmer until the vegetables are tender.

12. When the sofrito sauce is ready, add it to the meat, together with the paste of ground parsley, garlic and peppers.

13. Continue simmering until the lamb is tender. Serve hot.

CORDERO DE NAVIDAD A LA MIEL
Christmas Lamb with Honey

The origins of this dish (apart from the wine and the beef stock) are firmly fixed in the Arab culinary tradition of Southern Spain, before the arrival of the Northern Christians in the 15th century. There are many remaining versions of "Cordero a la Miel" throughout Andalucía and other parts of Spain even to this day, and similar recipes are considered a delicacy in many Arabic countries, where lamb is still one of the favoured meats.

This dish is considered such a delicacy, that it now graces many a Christmas dinner table in Andalucía and other parts of Spain and there are numerous variations using different herbs and spices, including thyme, rosemary, ginger and other traditional Arabic digestive herbs and spices.

In our recipe, the lamb is generally served with some slices of potato oven baked in olive oil with rosemary and garlic. The same recipe will work for either leg or shoulder of lamb.

Ingredients (serves 4):

    2 legs of lamb
    Meat stock
    150 g rosemary honey
    4-5 strands of saffron
    1 small glass wine vinegar
    1 glass white wine
    0.5 teaspoon hot red paprika powder
    0.5 teaspoon white pepper
    2 bay leaves
    6 cloves of garlic
    4 onions
    Olive oil

Preparation:

1. Put a fireproof casserole dish with some olive oil on a moderate heat. Add the chopped onions and sliced garlic and fry.

2. Once fried, add the meat and keep turning it to brown the pieces of lamb for a few minutes.

3. Add the saffron, paprika, bay leaf, wine and beef stock to cover. Stir well and reduce the heat. Simmer until the sauce begins to thicken.

4. Pre-heat the oven to 180°C and place the casserole dish in the oven for about 35 minutes. Baste the lamb frequently with the sauce, making sure that it is not reduced too much. If it starts to dry, add some hot water, or a little of the stock to the casserole dish and keep the lamb moist.

5. Put the honey with the vinegar in a saucepan and mix well. Heat the mixture until the sauce begins to thicken. Add this mixture to the lamb, and leave it in the oven for another 10 minutes.

6. Serve immediately, for example with oven-baked slices of potato with olive oil, garlic and rosemary.

CORDERO AL ROMERO CON PURÉ DE AJOS

Lamb and Rosemary with garlic purée

Ingredients:

    16 lamb chops
    16 sprigs of rosemary
    50 ml extra virgin olive oil
    1 tablespoon ground black pepper
    Zest of 1 lemon
    1 glass of white wine
    20 g grain mustard
    Salt
    Pepper

For the puree:

    2 heads of garlic
    200 ml extra virgin olive oil
    4 boiled potatoes
    120 ml of milk
    Salt
    Pepper

Preparation:

For the lamb chops:

1. Mix the ground pepper together with the mustard, the lemon zest, the oil and wine. Brush each chop with a little of this mixture.

2. Take a sprig of rosemary, wrap it around each lamb chop and tie with thin meat string. Put aside.

For the puree and serving:

1. Toast the whole garlic heads in olive oil for 30 minutes over a low heat. Then peel them and place the garlic cloves with the potatoes and the milk in a blender and blend well. Whilst blending, add a drop of the oil from the frying of the garlic to the mix.

2. Fry the lamb chops in a frying pan with a little of the garlic olive oil. Serve with the garlic purée.

PALETILLA DE CORDERO
Shoulder of Lamb

Ingredients:

    1 shoulder of lamb (lamb's weight 6-7 kg)
    1 head of garlic
    3 Bay leaves
    1 onion
    Cayenne pepper
    Salt (to taste)
    Freshly ground black pepper (to taste)
    Olive oil (Verdial)
    1 glass white wine
    Thyme
    Cognac 1 measure

Preparation:

1. Season the meat.

2. Put in an ovenproof casserole dish, adding the whole cloves of garlic, the pepper, cayenne powder, thyme and the thinly-sliced onion.

3. Add the glass of wine, the cognac and fill up with water until half of the meat is covered.

5. Put the dish in the oven at 200°C for about 45 minutes. Keep an eye on the meat and baste it regularly with its own sauce.

6. Serve when the meat is tender.

---oOo---

2.3.3 Rabbit

CONEJO ESTOFADO DE NAVIDAD
Rabbit Stew

This is a typical wintertime stew often eaten around the days of Christmas when game is quite plentiful.

Ingredients:

>   1 rabbit
>   150 g of carrots
>   100 g onion
>   100 g green pepper
>   150 g leek
>   300 g ripe Tomatoes
>   3 cloves garlic
>   200 ml white wine
>   0.5 litre water
>   Oregano
>   Bay leaves
>   Paprika powder
>   Black pepper corns
>   Dried red peppers
>   Salt

Preparation:

1. Cut up the rabbit. Chop the carrot, leek, pepper and tomato into small pieces.

2. Briefly fry the rabbit meat in olive oil, and when it begins to brown, add the paprika powder along with the chopped vegetables and the herbs and spices.

3. Then add the wine and fill up with water to cover the meat, season and leave to stew on a low heat for about 30 minutes.

4. After this, remove the meat, take out the bay leaf, and blend the remaining ingredients into a smooth sauce. Put the meat in an earthenware bowl and cover the meat with the sauce.

5. Serve hot.

CONEJO GUISADO AL MUSCATEL DE EL BORGE
Rabbit Stew with Muscatel from El Borge, Málaga

Here is a local dish that combines rabbit with Muscatel raisins in a popular stew often served in the winter and particularly during the days of Christmas.

Ingredients:

>1 kg of rabbit (in pieces)
>50 ml olive oil
>1 onion
>1 carrot
>2 cloves of garlic
>100 g of prunes
>30 g Muscatel raisins
>600 ml beef stock
>150 ml Muscat Wine
>100 g of spring onions
>A pinch of fresh thyme
>Salt
>Pepper

Preparation:

1. Fry the meat with a little olive oil until it is a light golden colour. Put aside.

2. Meanwhile, chop the onion, carrot and garlic and fry these in olive oil in an earthenware casserole dish until the carrot is tender.

3. Add the meat, the muscatel wine, beef stock, raisins and prunes. Cook over a low heat for 20 minutes.

4. Add the spring onions and cook for a further 15 minutes.

5. Check to see if the meat is tender and add salt and pepper to taste. Serve together with the vegetables and dried fruits.

CONEJO EN SALSA DE NUECES

Rabbit in Walnut Sauce

Not all Christmas meals in Spain call for expensive ingredients or sophisticated menus. Indeed, some of the most favoured dishes are simple traditional country recipes that have been enjoyed for centuries.

Dried fruits and nuts provide a good compliment to all kinds of meats and make for a delicious sauce. This dish is even tastier if it is prepared the day before and allowed to rest for a day before serving. Here we present a recipe for a simple rabbit dish in a rich walnut game-sauce.

Ingredients (serves 2):

- Half a rabbit
- 50 g peeled walnuts
- 2 cloves of garlic
- 1 slice of bread
- 1 dash of white wine
- Vegetable stock (or water)
- Olive oil
- Salt & Pepper

Preparation:

1. Cut the rabbit into pieces and season with salt and pepper.

2. Heat a little olive oil in a low casserole dish and brown the rabbit meat on both sides.

3. Remove the meat and use the same oil to fry the garlic and bread, both chopped up. When these start to brown, put the meat back in the casserole, mix with the bread and garlic, and add the walnuts and wine. Let the wine evaporate and then pour in the stock (or water) to almost cover the meat. Add salt to taste.

4. Cover the casserole and cook over a low heat for about 45 minutes until the rabbit is tender.

5. Optionally, we can blend the sauce to make it smooth by passing it through a purée mill. In this case put aside some of the walnuts, purée the rest of the sauce and then reduce it for a few minutes if necessary.

6. Serve the rabbit hot on a bed of sauce, garnished with the walnuts.

---o0o---

2.3.4 Pork

LOMBARDA NAVIDENA
Christmas Red Cabbage with Bacon

This is a very typical winter and Christmas time dish in Málaga province of Andalucía. It is typical of the region because it uses some fairly mundane ingredients but produces a delicious and exotic festive dish.

Ingredients (serves 4-6):

>900 g red cabbage, shredded
>40 ml olive oil
>3-4 garlic cloves, sliced
>1 chorizo, skinned and chopped
>Toasted pine kernels to decorate
>115 g salty bacon, diced small
>40 ml wine vinegar

Preparation:

1. Cook the cabbage in salted water for 10 minutes. Drain and discard the water.

2. Heat the oil in a large frying pan and gently fry the garlic, chorizo and bacon until the garlic and bacon start to brown. Add the cabbage and stir well. Simmer for 15 minutes, stirring frequently. Do **not** add salt.

3. Add the vinegar and simmer for 5 more minutes. The cabbage should be creamy and very tender.

4. Serve hot decorated with toasted pine kernels.

FILETES DE LOMO AL VINO (ANDALUCÍA)
Loin fillets in a wine sauce (Andalucía)

A popular Christmas and wintertime treat using Málaga Dulce wine or similar and dressed with Muscatel raisins.

Ingredients:

    300 g Lean filets of pork
    75 g Málaga (Muscatel) raisins
    1 medium glass of the local sweet Málaga wine
    Olive oil (Nevadillo if possible)
    Salt (to taste)
    Pepper (to taste)

Preparation:

1. Season the meat with salt and pepper and fry in olive oil.

2. When the meat is cooked, add the raisins and the Málaga wine.

3. Continue cooking on a medium heat until the liquid is reduced by at least half (or to taste). Then serve.

LOMO RELLENO AL HORNO
Baked Stuffed Loin

This is a really popular traditional festive dish throughout Spain, and has a delicious contrast of flavours. There are many variations in the fillings that are used, but most are based on the traditional Arabic penchant for creating a contrast of sweet and savoury tastes which has permeated Spanish cuisine. The variations also depend on the locally available ingredients during the festive season in the different parts of Spain. For example, this dish is also baked using apples and nuts other than almonds in the stuffing in Northern regions of the country.

Ingredients (serves 4):

>4 tablespoons olive oil
>1 onion, finely chopped
>2 garlic cloves, chopped
>1.5 cups breadcrumbs
>4 dried figs, chopped
>8 green olives, stoned and chopped
>0.25 cup flaked almonds
>1 tablespoon lemon juice
>1 tablespoon fresh parsley, chopped
>1 egg yolk
>1-1.2 kg boneless pork loin (preferably with the side flap attached)
>Salt to taste
>Pepper to taste
>Paprika powder to taste
>Cooking twine

Preparation:

1. Preheat the oven to 200°C

2. Sauté the onion with the garlic in olive oil (put aside 1 tbsp of oil for later) until soft.

3. Remove from the heat and stir in the breadcrumbs, figs, olives, almonds, lemon juice, parsley, and egg yolk to make the stuffing.

4. Unroll belly flap from pork loin to open the loin up. Spread half the stuffing over the flat piece, roll it up, and tie the joint at intervals with the twine.

5. Pour the remaining oil into a small roasting pan -- add the pork loin. Roast for about 1 hour 20 minutes.

6. Take the remaining stuffing mix and form into little balls. Add them to the pan some 15-20 minutes before the end of the cooking time.

7. Leave the pork loin to rest for 10 minutes after removing from the oven. Take off the twine before slicing to serve.

---o0o---

2.3.5 Poultry

CAPÓN RELLENO (FRUTOS SECOS) PARA NAVIDAD
Stuffed Capon - Fruit and Nuts

In Britain a capon is just a large chicken, but in fact a capon is a Roman invention, developed at a time of acute grain shortages, when fattening chickens was forbidden. The farmers realised that a young male "rooster" that was castrated, gained weight without being fed large amounts of valuable wheat. Thus the process of "caponisation" came into being.

A stuffed capon is still a highly esteemed mainstay of a Christmas lunch in Spain, with ordinary chickens being seen traditionally as low quality "peasant food".

In this typical capon recipe the traditional Arabic influences are clear: sweet dried fruits and nuts being mixed with savoury ingredients to make a delicious stuffing mixture. The use of dried fruit to produce a sweet/savoury dish is very popular in the Arab / Moorish cuisine, even to this day. It is not only a delicious combination, but it is also an exceptionally healthy one.

The amount of dried fruits you use can be varied according to availability and your taste and the pork sausages as part of the stuffing can be entirely substituted for more fruit. You can also add diced apple, onion and a small amount of black truffle to enhance the flavour even further. Dried breadcrumbs can be used as a stuffing ingredient if you wish to reduce the dried fruit content.

Ingredients (serves 6):

> 1 large capon - 3.5 kg
> 100 g pine kernels
> 300 g prunes (without stones)
> 300 g dried apricots
> 300 g dried figs
> 500 g Pork sausages
> 0.25 kg pig lard for basting
> 0.75 ml bottle medium dry cava (semi-seco)
> Optional for the stuffing: diced onion, apple, dried bread crumbs

Black truffle - to taste
Pepper - to taste
Salt - to taste

Preparation:

1. Put the figs, apricots, prunes and pine nuts to soak in half of the bottle of cava for about four hours to marinate. Keep the other half of the cava for later.

2. Cut the sausages into very small pieces and sauté them in a frying pan with a little lard.

3. When they are almost cooked, add the marinated dried fruits. Let this stuffing mix simmer on a very low heat for about half an hour.

4. Fill the capon with the cooked mixture, pushing firmly to ensure it is fully stuffed.

5. When the stuffing is finished, stitch up the capon with cooking twine and a thick needle. With the help of a plastic syringe, inject some of the remaining cava into the capon, taking care to leave some cava for basting during cooking.

6. Grease the capon with some lard, season it with salt and pepper and put it into the oven at 200°C for one hour. After that, continue at 170°C for an hour and a half more, during which time we will need to baste the capon with the remaining cava and a little water, if necessary.

7. When the capon is cooked, cut fillets to serve and use the rest by finely chopping it and serve it accompanied with the stuffing.

CAPÓN RELLENO DE HIGOS Y TRUFAS AL OLOROSO DE JEREZ

Stuffed Capon - Figs, Truffles and Oloroso Sherry

This is a popular recipe in the province of Cádiz in Andalucía. Cádiz has an abundance of excellent (dried) figs and, of course, is famous for its Jerez wines (Sherry). The recipe calls for 150 g of black truffles. This quantity can of course be reduced to make the dish a little less expensive and according to individual tastes.

Ingredients:

>1 capon of approx. 3 kg
>1.5 kg dried figs
>0.25 kg of lard
>Pepper to taste
>Salt to taste
>150 g of black truffles
>1 bottle of sherry - variety Oloroso

Preparation:

1. Clean the capon inside and out and singe if necessary to remove any residual feathers.

2. Soak the figs for at least twenty-four hours in the Oloroso sherry to soften them. Bring them to the boil and then drain the sherry and set aside. Add the chopped truffles to the figs.

3. Melt the lard and pour it over the figs and truffles.

4. Add salt and pepper to your taste and let it cool.

5. Once cool, fill the capon with the stuffing, sew it up and leave to stand in a cool place for twenty-four hours.

6. Place the capon in a greased roasting tray and coat the capon with lard. Put it in a medium oven for 2 - 3 hours together with a sauce of stock and oloroso sherry, seasoned to your taste. Regularly baste with the sauce to keep the meat moist during roasting.

7. Roast until browned and cooked through, garnish and serve.

PATO AL HORNO CON PERAS CARAMELIZADAS DE CATALUÑA

Roasted Duck with caramelised Pears of Cataluña

This is a traditional recipe for festive days in Girona in Cataluña. The same recipe is used with goose instead of duck, and apparently was a favourite of Salvador Dalí.

Duck is often cooked with fruit, such as peaches, apples, figs or cherries. Duck with orange is a classic that is supposed to have originated in the French cuisine, and the dish was already to be found in medieval and Renaissance kitchens. Other examples of duck prepared with fruit: in the Penedès region of Cataluña there is a famous recipe made with prunes and pine nuts which was mentioned in 1487 in a contemporary cookery book. In Menorca, the nuns of Mahón, make an exquisite duck with quince at Christmas time, based on a recipe published in 1763. The combination of duck, fatty meats, fruit and dates goes back a very long time and originates in ancient Rome, but was enthusiastically adopted during the Moorish era of Spain.

Ingredients (serves 4):

> To estimate the size of duck needed, allow 250 g of meat per guest, but assume that 20% is fat. So in this case we need a 1.2 kg duck
> 2 carrots
> 2 young onions (large spring onions)
> 2 cloves of garlic
> 4 small hard pears
> 4 lumps of brown sugar
> Half a glass of red wine
> Half a glass of water
> Salt
> Ground black pepper

Preparation:

1. Clean the duck inside and outside. Make some cuts in the breast of the bird and insert slices of garlic. Season the duck with salt and pepper inside and outside.

2. Clean and cut the carrots into strips and thinly slice the onion. Cover the bottom of a deep roasting dish with the sliced onions and the carrot. Place the duck on top of the vegetables. Add the red wine and water.

3. Preheat the oven to 180°C and put the duck in to roast for approximately 1.5 hours.

4. During the roasting keep the duck moist by basting it with its juices every 15 minutes, using a ladle. The meat should not be allowed to dry out and should become a golden brown. Turn the duck at least once during roasting.

5. Clean and peel the pears.

6. When the duck is fully cooked, remove it from the oven and let it rest for about twenty minutes.

7. Blend the broth that remains in the roasting tray and put it into a saucepan or frying pan (depending on the amount of broth left). If it is a frying pan, cut the peeled pears in half, but if there is enough broth, use a saucepan and add the pears whole.

8. Put the pan on a medium heat and add the four lumps of sugar and half a teaspoon of salt. In half an hour the pears will be caramelized. Serve the duck and pears together, covered with the sauce. This is nice served with roast potatoes.

PAVO CON TRUFAS
Roast Turkey with Truffles

There are many recipes for roast turkey, but one of the Christmas favourites uses truffles. This is a variation especially favoured in Aragón.

Aragón is a region famous for its black truffles, found especially in the eastern areas of Huesca and the mountainous zones of Maestrazgo, Gúdar and Javalambre in Teruel. Teruel is the leading province in truffle production and sets the price and quality for the whole of Spain. The truffles are highly prized internationally and most are exported to France and Italy. However, there should be enough left in Spain for you to prepare this delicious Christmas Turkey with truffles.

Ingredients:

    1 turkey of about 3 kg
    400 g of pork tenderloin
    1 tomato
    1 small onion
    100 g of ham
    150 g of truffles
    1 tablespoon flour
    1 cup Olive oil
    1 cup water
    1 clove of garlic
    Lard
    Ground pepper
    Parsley
    1 bay leaf
    Sal

Preparation:

1. Clean the turkey and season with salt and pepper, inside and out. Leave it somewhere cool to rest until the next day.

2. Next day, prepare a stuffing with the pork tenderloin. First, fry the finely chopped onion and add the also finely chopped, peeled tomato. Add the minced pork (seasoned with salt and pepper) and the crushed garlic with the parsley.

3. When the meat is tender, add the ham diced into very small pieces. Remove the pan from the heat and stir the mixture briefly. It is important not to overdo the cooking of the ham otherwise it will make the dish too salty. In a separate pan, roast a tablespoon of flour with a little olive oil and mix this with the stuffing.

4. Let the stuffing cool slightly and then start to stuff the turkey whilst adding approx. 50 g of the Aragón truffles, cut up into very small pieces. Sew up the turkey to stop the stuffing from falling out and let it stand in a cool place until ready to roast.

5. Pre-heat the oven to 160°C. Pour the cup of olive oil and the water in a roasting tray. Add the bay leaf. Coat the turkey with lard and place it in the tray.

6. The turkey must remain moist during roasting. During cooking it is important to turn the turkey once or twice so that it browns on all sides.

7. When the turkey meat becomes tender (1.5 to 2 hours depending on the oven), shake on the remaining 100 g of truffles cut into medium pieces. Leave to roast for 10 minutes more and serve.

PECHUGA DE PAVO CON SALSA DE ALMENDRAS
Turkey Breast with Almond Sauce

This is a popular main coarse dish wherever almonds are plentiful, mostly in Andalucía, where almonds form a central part in many traditional Christmas dishes, both savoury and sweet.

Ingredients (serves 4):

    1 kg turkey breast
    1 onion
    3 cloves of garlic
    150 g peeled almonds
    180 ml white wine
    Salt
    Pepper
    Few strands of saffron
    2 bay leaves
    Olive oil

Preparation:

1. Dice the onion and slice the garlic. Fry them in olive oil over a low heat. When browned, remove from the heat, take out the onions and garlic and put them aside. Use the same oil to fry the almonds. When browned, put the almonds aside.

2. Cut the turkey into conveniently sized pieces and then use the same oil to brown the meat.

3. Now transfer the turkey to another pan, add a little of the olive oil used earlier to fry and then add the wine. Leave it to cook on high heat until the wine is reduced and the alcohol evaporated.

4. Crush the fried onion and garlic in a mortar until it becomes a paste (or add a little water and use a blender).

5. Add the onion and garlic paste to the meat. Crush the almonds (not too finely) in a mortar and add to the meat.

6. Season the meat and add the bay leaves and some toasted strands of saffron, cover with water and cook until the meat is tender and the sauce has thickened.

7. Serve with the sauce.

PERDICES AL VINO MUSCATEL DE SEDELLA, MÁLAGA

Partridge in Muscatel wine from Sedella, Málaga

This was a traditional Christmas dish in areas where partridge were plentiful. It provided a welcome source of protein and variety in remote rural areas during the Spanish winter. Alas, over-hunting has reduced partridge numbers severely in many areas and it will be many years before they recover. However, farmed partridge is also available and this makes a perfect substitute for the wild variety. Here is a traditional recipe from Sedella in the Montes de Málaga.

Ingredients:

>Partridges
0.50 kg Leeks
Half cup olive oil
4 cloves garlic
1 large red pepper
1 glass of sweet Muscatel wine
Chicken stock
Salt (to taste)
Pepper (to taste)
Ground thyme (to taste)

Preparation:

1. Clean and open the partridges. Season with salt and pepper

2. Stir-fry the leeks, garlic and red pepper in a frying pan with some olive oil.

3. When they start to brown, add the partridge and fry until golden brown.

4. Place the partridge and stir-fried vegetables in a heat-proof casserole dish, add the ground thyme and wine, and cover all of this with chicken stock. Cook until the meat is tender (about 30 minutes) and the sauce has thickened.

5. Serve together with the sauce.

POLLO RELLENO DE NAVIDAD

Christmas stuffed Chicken

This is a classic Christmas dish throughout Spain with dozens of variations in the stuffing recipe. This particular stuffing recipe is one with a Mediterranean twist, using dried fruit and almonds in the style of the traditional Arabic cuisine of Andalucía, but with the optional addition of a little (non-Arabic) bacon.

Ingredients (serves 4)

    1 large chicken

For the filling:

    1 large aubergine
    1 tomato
    1 onion
    1 green pepper
    100 g of bacon
    150 g pine kernels
    150 g almonds
    150 g of prunes
    150 g of raisins
    500 ml chicken broth
    Olive oil
    Salt
    Ground black pepper

Preparation:

1. Preheat the oven to 220° C for twenty minutes. Prepare the chicken for stuffing ensuring that it is completely cleaned.

2. Heat a little olive oil in a frying pan. Peel and finely chop the onion. Add the onion to the pan with a pinch of salt.

3. When the onion begins to fry, add the chopped tomato, the aubergine (peeled and diced) and the green pepper (chopped). Fry everything together for five minutes.

4. Add the chopped bacon, the dried fruit and the nuts and stir-fry the whole mixture.

5. Add half of the chicken broth to the mixture. Season to taste with salt and pepper and cook over high heat for about ten minutes. Then allow it to cool enough that it can be handled for stuffing the chicken.

6. Fill the chicken with the mixture. Place the stuffed chicken in a baking tin and pour the remaining chicken broth over the chicken.

7. Put the chicken in the oven and roast for 80 minutes at 160 °C, making sure to keep the chicken moist and that the top doesn't burn.

8. Serve immediately.

---o0o---

2.3.6 Stews and Fricassees

CARDO DE NAVIDAD DE NAVARRA
Christmas Cardo Stew of Navarra

The "Cardo" is a type of large thistle and it is a typical winter vegetable, very popular in Aragón, Navarra and La Rioja. For many Navarros, no Christmas dinner would be complete without it!

Ingredients:

    Cardos
    Flour
    Milk
    Garlic
    Olive oil
    Salt

Preparation:

1. Clean the cardos (removing any fibrous parts), leaving them in a bowl of water with a splash of lemon juice.

2. Cut them into pieces, and boil them in plenty of salted water until tender.

3. Heat some olive oil in a frying pan and stir-fry a couple of cloves of garlic in slices. Add a tablespoon of flour and before it browns, add a splash of milk.

4. Let this cook for a few minutes until it becomes a light béchamel sauce. Dilute the sauce with a little bit of the liquid from the cooking of the cardos and, if necessary, add salt to taste.

5. Add this sauce to the cardos and serve hot. Optionally, sprinkle some pine kernels (piñones) on top.

CARDO DE NOCHEBUENA DE ARAGÓN
Cardos in Almond sauce of Aragón

Here is another variant of the Christmas cardo tradition, this time served with an almond, garlic and onion sauce. This recipe is a very traditional Christmas Eve dish in many villages in the Aragón region.

Ingredients (serves 4):

    2 kg of cardos (thistles), cleaned and with the stringy fibres removed
    100 g of blanched almonds
    50 g of flour
    1 small onion
    500 ml milk
    Olive oil
    Water
    Salt
    Lemon

Preparation:

1. Clean the cardo stems very well (removing all fibrous / stringy parts) and then soak them in a large bowl with water and a splash of lemon juice for an hour. Chop the cardos into short pieces (about 4 cm long).

2. Place the cardos into a saucepan of boiling water and salt. Let them cook for about 1 hour 30 minutes.

3. In the meantime, make the sauce: Fry the onion, very finely chopped, in the olive oil, until it turns golden brown. Add the flour to the onions whilst stirring. Then add the milk (pre-heated) and continue to stir the mixture.

4. Chop the almonds and crush them in a mortar until obtaining an almond paste. Add this paste with a little salt (to your taste) to the sauce mixture and cook for a further five minutes.

5. Finally, add the sauce mixture to the cardo thistles and then let all simmer together for about another ten minutes.

6. Serve hot.

COCIDO DE TAGARNINAS Y CARDOS DE MÁLAGA
Thistle and Chickpea stew of Málaga

This winter stew, often served during the Christmas season originates in Eastern Andalucía on the border between Málaga and Granada. It starts to be eaten from the beginning of November and is like many traditional stews, i.e. it is really two courses in one. The first course is the cabbage and vegetable broth, served in a bowl. The second course is the meats, eaten with bread, which is used to soak up the sauce.

Ingredients (serves 6):

> 0.5 kg of chickpeas (soaked in water overnight)
> 0.25 kg of potatoes
> 0.5 kg of cabbage (green beans)
> 150 g of cardo thistles
> 150 g of tagarninas (golden thistles)
> 1 carrot
> 0.25 kg veal shank
> Half a chicken
> 1 piece of fresh bacon
> 1 piece of raw bacon
> One marrowbone (for stock)
> 1 piece of blood sausage
> 1 piece of fresh chorizo
> Salt (to taste)

Preparation:

1. Pierce the black pudding and the chorizo with a fork. Boil them both for a few minutes in a pan. When done, put them aside.

2. Put the chickpeas to the boil in a pan, together with the broth bone, bacon, chicken and veal and simmer on a low heat for an hour and a half until the broth is white, skimming every so often. Put aside.

3. Take all the cooked ingredients out of the broth and replace with the vegetables (cabbage, potatoes, carrots, cardo thistles and tagarninas thistles). Let them cook for about twenty minutes, and add salt to taste.

4. After that, put the meats and chickpeas back in the pan with the vegetables. Boil for a moment and at the last minute add the black pudding and the chorizo. Serve hot.

FABADA ASTURIANA

Asturian Bean and Chorizo Stew

This dish is a very popular winter stew and it is uniquely traditional to Asturias. In fact "Fabada" could be called the Asturian national dish, because it is so emblematic of the regional cuisine. It is not particularly a Christmas dish, but it is eaten in the days around Christmas because it is so warming, filling and delicious, and also because many Asturians returning to their family homes for the festivities want to eat their national dish whilst at home. This dish is slow to prepare, but in Asturias they say that the best fabadas get better overnight!

Ingredients:

>500 g of Asturian "fabas" beans
>2 chorizos
>3 black pudding sausages
>250 g pork shoulder
>250 g bacon
>3 tablespoons olive oil
>1 bay leaf
>Saffron
>Half an onion
>2 cloves of garlic
>Fresh parsley, tied in a bunch
>Salt

Preparation:

1. The day before preparing this dish, wash the beans and put them to soak overnight in plenty of water so that they won't be dry the next day.

2. The next day, strain the beans and put them into a saucepan covered with fresh, cold water. Add the bay leaf, parsley, oil, peeled onion and whole cloves of garlic. Also add in all the meat.

3. Bring to the boil and leave to cook very slowly. Remove any foam as it forms.

4. In the meantime, toast the saffron (this can be done in a microwave for about 90 seconds) and then crumble it. Add it to the dish after about 30 minutes.

5. During the cooking, the beans must remain covered with liquid. So this may mean that you need to add cold water as required.

6. Stir the pot occasionally to prevent sticking.

7. When the beans are almost cooked, remove the bay leaf, parsley, onion and garlic cloves, add salt to taste and serve.

GACHAS MANCHEGAS
Savoury Porridge of La Mancha

This is a typical winter recipe for a savoury porridge of La Mancha. It is a meal with many calories and traditionally it was eaten during the times of the grape or olive harvest to sustain the workers during the cold days in the field. Now it has become one of the region's most typical dishes and is often eaten during the Christmas festivities. The recipe uses vetch flour, which is flour made from the beans of the vetch, which grows wild in many parts of Spain. The flour is used in many rural Spanish recipes.

Ingredients:

    2 strips of bacon
    2 chorizos
    2 black pudding sausages
    1 head of garlic
    1 tablespoon sweet paprika powder to taste
    Salt to taste
    Vetch flour (the flour made from vetch beans)

Preparation:

1. Chop and fry the chorizos, the bacon and the black pudding. Put aside.

2. Fry the garlic and put aside.

3. Add 4 - 6 tablespoons of vetch flour to the pan and toast it along with a tablespoon of sweet paprika powder.

4. Gradually add some hot water and stir until it starts to boil.

5. Stir until obtaining a smooth flour mixture, and then add all the previously fried ingredients.

6. Serve the gacha in the same pot, accompanied by wine and bread.

MARMITAKO

Fresh Bonito fish and Potato stew

This dish originally was cooked on board Basque fishing boats when tuna was plentiful and it soon became a favourite stew on dry land. Marmita translates as 'pot' or 'casserole' in Basque so that marmitako literally means 'from the pot'.

The decline of tuna fish means that the more plentiful bonito is now used by the ethical cook. The stew can be partly made in advance and then reheated (for up to a day) and then adding the bonito fish before serving.

The dish is a great Christmas Eve favourite in the Basque country. This recipe uses bonito fish (not tuna!) but other types of fish can also be used including salmon.

Ingredients (serves 6):

  2 dried choricero peppers
  0.5 kg fresh bonito fish (fillet)
  Coarse salt
  1 kg potatoes
  0.33 cup olive oil
  1 onion, finely chopped
  2 cloves garlic, chopped
  0.5 green pepper cut into narrow strips
  1 tablespoon sweet paprika powder (pimentón)

Preparation:

1. In a dish, cover the dried choricero peppers with boiling water and let them stand until soft (ca. 30 min.). Drain the peppers, slit them open, and scrape off the flesh with a knife, discarding the seeds, skins, and stems. Put the flesh aside.

2. Cut the bonito fish into small pieces. Sprinkle with coarse salt and put aside.

3. Peel the potatoes. Cut into pieces about the size of a chestnut and put aside.

4. In a saucepan, heat the olive oil over a medium heat. Add the onion, garlic, and green pepper, and the flesh from the choricero peppers, stir well, and cook, stirring occasionally, until the onion and green pepper

have begun to soften and all the ingredients: are well blended (about 5 min.).

5. Add the chopped potatoes and pimentón and mix well. Season with a little salt and add water to cover by about 4 cm. Bring to a boil, then cover, decrease the heat to medium and cook until the potatoes are tender.

6. Now, add the pieces of bonito to the pot and simmer until the bonito is opaque (about 5 min.).

7. Remove the pot from the heat and let it stand for about 30 minutes before serving.

8. If the soup is very clear, mash a piece or two of potato against the side of the pot with the back of a spoon and stir the pot a little.

9. Reheat gently to serving temperature. Ladle the stew into warmed bowls and serve at once.

POTE ASTURIANO DE BERZA
Asturian Leaf Kale Stew

This is one of the most typical winter dishes of Asturias, even though the best known is probably the Fabada - the bean stew. It is made using leaf kale which is a "year round" green and is a most welcome fresh vegetable in the cold winters of Asturias. It can also be substituted with chard or green cabbage - though it isn't quite the same. This traditional recipe is quite flexible about quantities; some people preferring more or less beans or more or less meat.

Often, traditionally, this dish was made the day after a fiesta to use up the expensive leftovers from the day before - hence the addition of chorizo, black pudding, bacon and ham. So even if it doesn't actually make it to the Christmas Eve dinner, the "Asturian Pot" is an important and traditional dish around the festive period.

Ingredients:

    2 bunches of leaf kale or chard
    2 chorizos
    2 black pudding sausages
    2 slices of bacon
    2 pieces of ham
    Potatoes
    Sweet paprika powder
    Onion
    Olive oil
    White beans - fabada of Asturias
    Salt

Preparation:

1. Soak the beans overnight. The next day, rinse and drain them.

2. Clean the kale and cut up very finely. Clean, peel and dice the potatoes.

3. Boil the black pudding and chorizos in a saucepan with water to remove some of the fat and then drain.

4. Stir the beans into a deep pan with the olive oil to coat them and then cover them with water. Add the black puddings, chorizos, ham and bacon and put the pan onto the heat.

5. When the pot starts to boil, add the chopped kale and let it simmer for 45 minutes.

6. Add the diced potatoes and cook for another 15 minutes, add salt to taste and let the pot rest for at least half an hour before serving. (It is said that the Asturian Pote improves if left for a day).

7. Serve in individual earthenware bowls.

---oOo---

2.3.7 Casseroles

CARDO DE NAVIDAD DE CATALUÑA
Christmas Cardo casserole of Cataluña

The "cardo" thistle, also called the cardoon in English (Cynara cardunculus), is a typical wild ingredient in many peasant dishes in rural Spain. It has been cultivated by Greeks and Romans and is especially used in soups and stews. It is related to the artichoke, but generally only the stems are eaten.

In recent years, the cardo has become less popular, because cardo dishes require quite a lot of work to prepare, but they are very tasty. However, in the Christmas season, when there is more time for cooking, the cardo is often prepared as a special treat. The cardo thistle is a typical winter vegetable, very popular in Navarra, Aragón, Cataluña and La Rioja, where it is an essential dish for dinner on Christmas Eve. We will also describe several cardo Christmas recipe variations from various regions in Spain. Here is a casserole of cardo with cheese and eggs from Cataluña:

Ingredients (serves 4):

>A bunch of thistles
>2 tablespoons flour
>Salt and pepper to taste
>1 tablespoon butter or lard to grease the baking dish
>Bread crumbs soaked in milk
>2 handfuls grated cheese
>1 tablespoon olive oil
>Parsley, chopped garlic and oregano
>3 or 4 eggs

Preparation:

1. Scrape the cardo stems with a knife, removing the stringy fibres. Cut the stems into small pieces and put them into water mixed with flour (this is to stop them going black). Then put the cardos into a pot with boiling water and salt and bring to the boil.

2. Once cooked, drain the cardos, let them cool down, and put them into a greased baking dish. Prepare the covering by mixing the bread

crumbs (previously soaked in milk), salt, and pepper, adding the grated cheese, olive oil, garlic, chopped parsley and oregano, together with the 3 or 4 beaten eggs.

3. Cover the cardos with this mixture and place the dish in a moderate oven until the topping is golden brown. Once cooled, cut into squares and keep in the refrigerator until serving time.

4. Tip: If you have too many boiled cardos, you can use them in the topping - just chop them up finely or grind them and incorporate into the topping mixture.

CAZUELA DE FIDEOS A LA MARENGA

Pasta and fish casserole "a la marenga"

In several coastal areas in Andalucía is a popular fish and pasta dish. The success of the recipe lies in the broth that is made with various fish including "rock fish". It is often served around the days of Christmas.

Ingredients (serves 4):

>150 g various types of fish (cuttlefish, prawns, squid, clams, and "rock fish")
>4 or 5 anchovies
>1 ripe tomato
>1 pepper
>Half an onion
>3 or 4 cloves of garlic
>100 g of almonds
>1 slice (ca. 100 g) of dry "Cateto" bread (from the day before)
>0.5 teaspoon paprika
>Saffron
>0.5 kg of thick vermicelli
>1 bay leaf
>Half a glass of white wine
>Olive oil
>Salt (to taste)

Preparation:

1. Clean the fish and anchovies. Set aside.

2. Blanch the almonds in hot water for a minute to remove the skin and when they are dry, toast them quickly in a frying pan with olive oil and set aside.

3. In the same oil fry the bread for a moment and then put it aside on a plate with a little bit of water to soak into it.

4. With a mortar and pestle, make a well ground majadillo of the bread, the fried almonds and the paprika. Set this aside.

5. Make a sofrito with the garlic, onion, pepper and tomato and, just before it is ready, pour it in a pan with the wine, the fish (but NOT the anchovies), season to taste and add the saffron, bay leaf, vermicelli and the majadillo, letting it boil for 10-15 minutes.

6. Once it is ready, place the anchovies on top, cover the pan and leave to stand for a few minutes, so that the anchovies are cooked in the steam and the heat of the dish itself. It is then ready to serve.

---oOo---

2.3.8 Fish

BACALAO AJOARRIERO DE ARAGÓN
Cod Ajoarriero of Aragón

Salt cod or salted cod is a staple throughout Spain. For many centuries it was necessary to salt fish in order to preserve it. Even after the invention of refrigeration eliminated that need, salt cod continues to be especially popular in Spain. Traditionally (until into the 20th century), meat was not eaten on Christmas Eve and so there are many festive fish dishes for the dinner of Nochebuena.

In this traditional cod dish from Aragón and Navarra, a mixture of onions, garlic, pepper and tomato sauce is cooked with salt cod to make a sweet and salty main course. It is a classic dish, often served with fried potatoes.

Ingredients (serves 4):

>800 g salted cod
>2 dried sweet peppers (pimientos choriceros)
>1 large onion
>2 large cloves of garlic
>0.5 green pepper
>0.25 cup olive oil
>3 roasted piquillo peppers or 2 roasted red peppers
>200-250 ml sofrito (sauce) of tomato made in advance
>2-3 sprigs of parsley (chopped) for garnish

Preparation:

1. The salted cod must be soaked in water to leach out the salt. Usually this takes several hours (even overnight, depending on how heavily salted it is). Rinse the salted cod under cold running water and gently rub off salt. Cut the fish into pieces of approximately 8 cm. Place them in a (glass) dish, cover them with cold water and refrigerate. Change the water every 8 hours or so for between 24 to 36 hours. This allows time for the salt to leach out of the fish.

2. Finally, rinse the salted cod again under cold running water. Allow to drain on paper towels and pat dry. Cut the fish into pieces of 2-3 cm. and set aside.

3. The sweet dried peppers, called "pimientos choriceros", should be soaked in warm water for about 30 minutes. Once hydrated, drain the peppers. Cut them open, scrape out the pulp and discard the skin, as it is too tough to eat.

4. Peel and chop the onion and the garlic. Remove the seeds from the green pepper and chop. Chop the roasted peppers.

5. Pour olive oil into a heavy-bottom frying pan and put on a medium heat. Sauté the onion, garlic and green pepper until the onion is translucent. Add the roasted peppers and the tomato sofrito (sauce) and simmer for about 5 minutes.

6. Add the desalted cod to the pan and mix well to coat the fish. Simmer for about 15 minutes, stirring occasionally. The fish will release water, making more sauce. Garnish with chopped parsley.

BACALAO CON COLIFLOR A LA GALLEGA

Cod and Cauliflower of Galicia

This is a very traditional dish in Galicia and is eaten on the night of Christmas Eve - Nochebuena. In the past, in the area north of Lugo, the dish was considered "almost obligatory" at Christmas time, and today it is still typical for Christmas Eve dinner.

The origin of this tradition is religious. Christmas Eve appeared for centuries in the church calendar of mandatory "vigils". The calendar of vigils meant that, as recently as the nineteenth century, there were some 150 days of observance a year, which called for compliance to various religious duties and the abstinence from meat. Christmas Eve being one of these, the fishing communities of Galicia created a simple dish of cod and cauliflower which, despite the abolition of these religious obligations, has remained a favourite to this day.

Ingredients (serves 4):

> 1.2 kg Salt cod fillets
> 1.5 kg potato
> 600 g Cauliflower
> 100 g onion
> 1 head of garlic
> 50 g paprika
> 1 glass of olive oil
> Salt

Preparation:

1. Put the salt cod fillets in water for 2 days, changing the water every 8 hours.

2. Cut the potatoes into thick slices and boil in salt water with the cauliflower and onions. When the potatoes are about half cooked, add the pieces of cod and cook until the potatoes are fully cooked.

3. Make a sauce by browning the chopped garlic in a frying pan with the olive oil. Remove from the heat; add the paprika powder and a ladle of cooking liquid from the cod.

4. Serve the dish by putting the potatoes on a plate, top with the cod and place the cauliflower around the sides. Cover with the sauce.

BACALAO A LA VIZCAÍNA
Cod Stew of Biscay

This recipe is very traditional and well known and it can be a very good first course at a Christmas Eve dinner:

Ingredients (serves 4-6):

    8 fillets of salted cod fillet (desalted in fresh water overnight)
    300 ml Olive oil
    5 cloves of garlic
    700 g red onions
    700 g of tomatoes
    3 red peppers
    3 dried red peppers (choriceros)
    Two slices of toast
    Flaked almonds
    1 Bunch of fresh parsley finely chopped

Preparation:

1. De-scale and de-bone the previously desalted fish and dry with a clean cloth.

2. Pour 100 ml of olive oil in a heat proof casserole dish and fry 2 cloves of garlic, peeled and cut in half. When the garlic starts to turn brown, take it out and put aside. Use the same oil to fry all the onions except one, peeled and cut into "half moons". Once the onions are done (about 20 minutes over a low heat), add half of the tomatoes, peeled, deseeded and dried. Leave the mix to fry slowly.

3. In the meantime, in a separate pan, fry 1 small onion finely chopped and the remaining tomatoes, cut into large chunks, the red peppers, the dried red peppers (previously soaked in water) and the slices of toast. Leave to simmer until tender and then grind the mixture in a blender. The resulting sauce is then added to the tomato and onion we previously prepared, and mixed together.

4. Place a large frying pan on a medium heat and add 250 ml of olive oil and 3 cloves of garlic, cut in slices. When the garlic starts to brown, remove the garlic and place the cod fillets in the oil with the skin facing upwards. The cod should be thoroughly dried (to avoid "spitting"). If necessary, you can flour the fillets slightly. When the fish begins to colour, turn it over and keep in mind that it should be lightly cooked

but not fried. Remember that the actual final cooking will be done together with the sauce.

5. Put a layer of sauce in the bottom of a fireproof earthenware dish, place the cod fillets on the sauce and then cover them with the remaining sauce.

6. Cook the cod for 5 to 8 minutes in the sauce on medium heat.

7. Before serving, leave to stand for about 10 minutes. Add chopped parsley and almond flakes to taste.

LANGOSTINOS DE SANLÚCAR
Prawns from Sanlúcar in Cadiz

Prawns from Sanlúcar

In Andalucía, especially in coastal areas, it is very common to have seafood for the Christmas Eve dinner. This is a tradition that dates back to the previous canon laws which made Christmas Eve a "vigil" and a day of abstinence from meat.

These days the old tradition continues, because it is an opportunity to eat some of the area's local delicacies. One of the most favourite and traditional dishes is Prawns of Sanlúcar de Barrameda or Huelva and Cádiz. The prawns that are caught in Sanlúcar de Barrameda at the mouth of the River Guadalquivir are considered to be some of the best in Spain.

Ingredients (serves 6):

    1 kg prawns
    Coarse salt

Preparation:

1. Fill a saucepan with enough water to boil the prawns, and add some salt. Put it on a full heat.

2. In the meantime, prepare a large container with cold water, a handful of salt and plenty of ice cubes.

3. When the water in the pan is boiling, add the prawns. You will see that the boiling stops. When the water starts to boil again, remove the pan from the heat, remove the shrimps and drain. Put the prawns into the container with the iced water and leave them there for 1 - 2 minutes.

4. Remove the prawns from the cold water, drain them well and layer them in a dish. Cover them with a damp cloth and place them in the lowest part of the fridge until serving time.

5. Serve with a mayonnaise, or a cocktail sauce (salsa rosa) of your choice.

MEJILLONES A LA ASTURIANA

Mussels in the Asturian style

Mussels are a popular winter dish in Asturias and Cantabria and are often served as a starter for dinner on Christmas Eve. Here we bring you a simple traditional recipe which a delicious wine sauce.

Ingredients:

    2 kg of mussels
    10 tablespoons of butter
    Bouquet of parsley
    4 cloves garlic
    Olive oil
    6 tablespoons white wine
    Salt

Preparation:

1. Finely chop the parsley and the garlic.

2. Put the mussels in a little water with some salt, boil them and then strain off the broth. Put the mussels and broth aside.

3. Melt the butter slowly in a large frying pan; add the olive oil, the garlic and parsley. Stir in the mussel broth.

5. After two minutes, add the wine and after another two minutes add the mussels. Mix well and then leave to cook for a few more minutes.

6. Serve hot on a platter.

MERLUZA Y ALMEJAS EN SALSA VERDE

Hake Fillets with Clams in Salsa Verde

This is one of the most popular traditional Basque dishes and a special favourite for Christmas Eve in that region:

Ingredients (serves 4):

>1 tablespoon coarse salt
>1.5 teaspoons salt
>24 small clams
>0.33 cup olive oil
>0.5 cup dry white wine
>1 tablespoon flour
>2 tablespoons chopped fresh parsley
>2 cloves garlic, finely chopped
>Fresh parsley for garnish
>0.5 teaspoon dried chilli pepper in flakes
>2 hard-boiled eggs, peeled, quartered lengthwise, for garnish
>1 kg hake fillet, cut into 16 pieces
>4 cups water
>Salt to season
>4 white asparagus sliced across
>1 cup green peas (pre-cooked)

Preparation:

1. Scrub the clams under cold running water, discarding any that stay open.

2. In a large bowl, cover the clams with water and add the coarse salt. Let this stand for 2 hours to clean the sand from the clams, then drain.

3. In a large saucepan, bring the clams to the boil with 4 cups of water over a medium heat. Cover the pan and cook for about 5 minutes, or until the clams open.

4. As the clams cook, occasionally stir them with a wooden spoon to help them to open.

5. Drain the clams, but keep aside the cooking stock for later. Discard any clams that have not opened.

6. Heat the olive oil in a large casserole dish. Add the garlic and chilli flakes and fry until the garlic begins to brown

7. Sprinkle the flour over the garlic and stir with a wooden spoon until the mixture is well blended

8. Add 3 cups of the clam cooking stock and the salt, parsley, peas and wine.

9. Decrease the heat to medium and boil, stirring occasionally, for 5 minutes, or until the sauce thickens slightly. You can add more stock if you prefer a thinner sauce.

10. Mix all the ingredients, and boil gently for 2 minutes, or until the sauce is blended and looks whitish green.

11. Sprinkle the hake pieces with salt and place in a single layer in the sauce.

12. Cook, turning the fish once, for 2 minutes on each side, or until opaque at the centre when tested with a end of a knife.

13. Add the clams and asparagus whilst shaking the pan gently to prevent sticking, and simmer for 2 more minutes to ensure that everything is heated.

14. Serve hot, garnished with the pieces of egg and sprinkled with parsley.

SALMÓN AL CAVA

Salmon with Cava

The addition of Cava to the salmon makes for a delicious, traditional, and very refined dish; ideal for the festive season.

Ingredients (serves 4):

    4 salmon steaks
    1 onion
    1 glass Cava Brut
    A few sprigs of rosemary
    30 g butter
    2 tablespoons cream
    Salt
    Pepper

Preparation:

1. Peel and cut the onion into slices, sauté with the butter over low heat in a frying pan. Add the cava and rosemary and simmer for 5 minutes.

2. Clean the salmon and place the steaks in a baking dish. Sprinkle with some salt and pepper to taste and pour the Cava sauce over the fish. (Remove the rosemary).

3. Put the baking dish in a preheated oven at 200°C for 12 minutes. Just before the end of the baking, add the cream to bind the sauce.

4. Serve immediately, together with, for example, baked or boiled potatoes, green beans, and some boiled slices of carrot.

---oOo---

2.4 Sweets and Confectionary

ALFAJORES ANDALUCES DE MEDINA-SIDONIA
Spicebread of Medina-Sidonia

This is a sweet with a very clear history and has descended more or less untouched from the Hispano-Arabic era.

The alfajor or alajú is a traditional sweet from Andalucía, but the most popular producers come from the old town of Medina Sidonia in the province of Cádiz. The word alfajor is believed to derive from the Arabic for "excellent," or from the word alfahua meaning "honeycomb", or from the Arabic 'al-hasú' meaning "filled". The anonymous Arabic cookbook "tabīkh Kitāb al-Maghreb" mentions a very similar spicey sweet bread and in the twelfth century Raimundo Martin describes the Hispano-Arabic 'fasur' which means 'nectar'. The presence of this sweet is evident in the area of southern Spain during the twelfth and thirteenth centuries and mentioned again after the Christian invasion of the area. The ingredients described then are pretty much the same ingredients that are still in use today.

Today, the town of Medina Sedonia is considered to be the authentic source of this sweet and has a regulating council to protect the name and excellent quality of the "Alfajor de Medina Sidonia".

This is very much a Christmas sweet and, despite its origins in deepest Andalucía, it is known and loved throughout Spain.

Ingredients (40 pieces):

    120 g sugar
    120 ml water
    400 g bread crumbs
    200 g raw whole hazelnuts
    300 g whole, blanched, peeled almonds
    20 g whole anise seed
    75 g sesame seed
    1 g ground coriander seed (optional)
    10 g ground cinnamon
    0.5 tsp ground cloves
    450 g honey

Syrup for coating:

> 200 ml water
> 200 g sugar

Sugar for coating:

> 1 cup icing sugar

Preparation:

1. To make a syrup: Pour the water into a small saucepan and add the sugar. Put the pan on medium-high heat. Stir until the sugar is completely dissolved. Bring to the boil and then reduce to a simmer. Cook until the mixture is thickened into a syrup. Remove from heat and allow it to cool.

2. Toast the almonds and hazelnuts. Grind the nuts, anise, sesame and coriander seeds in a blender until the nuts are finely ground. Place in a medium-sized bowl. Add cinnamon and cloves and mix with a wooden spoon.

3. Measure the honey into an ovenproof measuring cup and heat in a water bath until almost boiling.

4. Pour the syrup into the bowl with the nuts and spices mixture and stir well. Whilst mixing, gradually add the warm honey. Mix all the ingredients thoroughly.

5. Whilst the mixture is still warm, form the mixture into small sausage-shaped rolls by hand and place them on greaseproof paper to cool.

6. Make another syrup in a saucepan. Remove from the heat and leave to cool for 5-10 minutes. Roll the alfajores in this syrup and then roll them in icing sugar. Cool on greaseproof paper.

7. When they are cool, wrap them in absorbent paper.

ALMONDS GARRAPIÑADAS
Sugared Roasted Almonds

This is a delicious and simple way to turn raw almonds into an instant, exotic delicacy by caramelising them in hot sugar. This sweet turns up in many regions of Spain, but is particularly popular in Murcia and often prepared in large copper pans and sold on the street at Christmas time and during other festivals. They can be preserved in airtight containers or jars for several months.

Ingredients (serves 4):

150 g almonds (with skin)
200 g sugar
240 ml water

Preparation:

1. Rinse the almonds and place them in a bowl with the sugar and water. Stir to mix and leave to stand for 24 hours.

2. When you are ready to make them, place them in a heavy-bottomed (preferably copper) saucepan and put on a medium heat.

3. Stir the almonds occasionally with a wooden spoon. When they start absorbing the water and the foam begins to turn white, stir them continuously, scraping the sides of the pan with the spoon, until the almonds are drying.

4. When they are almost dry, remove them from the heat and finish stirring them until they are loose.

5. Empty the pan into a marble or similar bowl or surface, separate them and let them cool. Serve or preserve in airtight containers (a kilner jar or similar).

BIZCOCHO DE NAVIDAD CON FRUTA ESCARCHADA
Christmas cake with candied fruit

The following is a recipe for a generic Christmas cake with candied fruit as made in many parts of Spain. This recipe can be adapted to use all kinds of flavourings like vanilla, cinnamon and different fruit contents and coverings, according to your taste.

Ingredients (serves 6):

    1.5 cup condensed milk
    1 cup butter
    2 tablespoons brown sugar
    4 eggs
    2 cups flour
    1 tablespoon baking powder
    1 cup chopped candied or crystallized fruit
    1 cup raisins

Preparation:

1. Beat the butter with the brown sugar until creamy.

2. While beating, add the egg yolks and mix well.

3. Add the condensed milk to the mixture and stir in the flour with the baking powder gradually. Mix with a wooden spatula.

4. Add the candied fruits and the raisins and fold in the egg whites, beaten until stiff.

5. Put the mixture in a baking tin and bake at 200°C for 40 minutes.

6. When baked, leave to cool and decorate with a single, simple covering and some candied fruit before serving.

BORRACHINOS DE ASTURIAS

Bread dumplings in syrup of Asturias

This dish is also known as "Miñuelos" in Asturias. It is an ancient dessert that originated in the villages of Asturias and was made to bring with you to be eaten when working on the land. It has a high energy value and is also a good way to use up old bread. Today it has become a typical Christmas dish in Asturias.

Ingredients:

For the dough:

>200 g of old, hard bread
>100 g of sugar
>3 eggs

For the syrup:

>250 g of sugar
>0.25 litre water
>0.5 litre white wine (young muscatel works well)
>1 stick of cinnamon

To fry:

>0.25 litre of olive oil

Preparation:

1. Trim off the bread's crust and crumble the bread very finely.

2. Beat the egg whites until stiff, mix them with the bread crumbs in a bowl, adding in the egg yolks and the sugar until obtaining a consistent mixture. If the dough is too soft, add more bread crumbs.

3. Heat the olive oil in a frying pan.

4. Spoon the dough into the hot oil and let it fry slowly until brown.

5. In the meantime, make the syrup by boiling the wine, water, sugar and cinnamon together for 10 minutes. Then add the fried borrachinos, leaving them to cook for 15 minutes.

6. The borrachinos can be served hot, although it is more common to serve them cold.

BORRACHUELOS DE NAVIDAD DE MÁLAGA
Sweet Christmas fritters of Málaga

Here is a sweet Christmas recipe typical of Málaga province. It's a slightly complicated and time-consuming dish, but it's definitely worth the effort. Borrachuelos are a very typical breakfast treat taken together with a glass of anise liquor on Christmas morning.

Ingredients:

    2 kg of flour (1kg bread flour and 1 kg plain flour)
    600 g sugar
    4.5 glasses Sweet wine
    2 litres of olive oil (half to make the dough and half to fry the fritters)
    Juice of 2 oranges and the peel of 1 orange
    30 g of aniseed
    75 g sesame seed
    5 g cinnamon powder
    1 dash sweet anise liquor
    Honey
    Water
    Sugar to coat the fritters

Preparation:

1. Heat the 2 litres of olive oil. When it is hot add the orange peel and leave to fry until it is browned, then remove the peel. This gives the oil an aroma of orange.

2. Then use a fine colander and fry the seeds in the hot oil. When toasted, put them aside.

3. Form a heap with the 2 types of flour on a smooth work surface. Add the orange juice and the cinnamon and mix together.

4. Begin to incorporate the wine and oil alternately and add the fried sesame seeds and the anise, whilst working the dough until it is smooth and easy to manipulate.

5. When it is completely workable, roll out the dough, cut out the fritters in little circles or ovals and fold them over, ready for frying. It is wise to seal the edges of each fritter with a little water.

6. Fry in plenty of oil (not too hot) until they are golden brown.

7. Whilst still hot, sprinkle the fritters with sugar. Alternatively, you can coat them in honey, for which the fritters should be cold. In this case, put the honey in a small saucepan together with a little water, warm gently and then baste the fritters with the mix.

8. Serve the fritters cold with a glass of sweet anise liquor. Feliz Navidad!

BUDÍN DE NAVIDAD

Spanish Christmas pudding

One of the first preparations for the Christmas table is this traditional Spanish Christmas pudding recipe.

Ingredients:

    0.25 cup of butter
    0.5 tsp. of ground cloves
    1 tsp. of ground cinnamon
    1 tsp. of nutmeg
    1 tsp. of grated orange zest
    0.5 tsp. of grated lemon zest
    0.5 tsp. of salt
    0.5 cup of brown sugar
    1 egg (beaten)
    1 cup of grated carrot
    1 tbsp. of lemon juice
    1.75 cups flour
    1 tsp. of baking powder
    1 tsp. of sodium bicarbonate
    1 cup of raisins
    0.5 cup of chopped walnuts

Preparation:

1. Beat the butter until creamy, then add the cloves, cinnamon, nutmeg, grated orange and lemon zest, salt and sugar, stir well and subsequently add the beaten egg, the grated carrot and the lemon juice.

2. In a separate bowl, mix together the sifted flour with the baking powder and the sodium bicarbonate. Gradually fold this into the butter mixture and mix well.

3. Once it is all mixed thoroughly, add the raisins and nuts.

4. Grease a baking tin and pour in the mixture, cover well and steam cook for two hours.

BUÑUELOS DE MANZANA A LA CANELA

Apple and cinnamon doughnuts

The origin of doughnuts is believed to be Arabic. In Moorish Granada they produced fritters made with honey water and flour and then dipped into boiling honey. The first written recipes for donuts originated in 16th century Spain. The recipes were for both sweet and savoury doughnuts, filled or unfilled.

Doughnuts are traditionally eaten during celebrations: For example, in Cataluña they are eaten during lent, in Madrid and Andalucía during holy week, and in Valencia during the "Fiesta de Fallas". There are many more examples. In many Northern areas, apple doughnuts are a favourite snack during the Christmas festivities.

Here we have a very simple and quick-to-prepare recipe. The original recipe calls for the addition of cognac, but you can also use muscatel wine. It depends on your taste.

Ingredients:

  2 rennet apples (for example, Golden Reinette)
  Muscatel Wine (or cognac)
  160 g flour
  160 g sugar
  200 ml water
  Olive oil for frying
  A mixture of cinnamon powder and icing sugar to serve

Preparation:

1. Core and peel the apples. Cut into slices of no more than 1cm thick.

2. Place the apple slices in a tall glass or in a jar. Cover with muscatel wine (or brandy if you choose this option) and marinate for 4-5 hours.

3. Prepare the batter by mixing the flour, sugar and water until it is a creamy paste that will serve to coat the apple slices.

4. Dip the apple slices into the batter and fry them in hot olive oil.

5. Once they are golden coloured, remove them from the oil, put them on a plate with absorbent kitchen paper and sprinkle them with the cinnamon and sugar mixture.

6. Serve hot.

CASADIELLES DE ASTURIAS (I)
Walnut Pasties of Asturias (I)

Casadielles is a sweet dish that is very typical of Christmas and carnival celebrations in Asturias. Also called "galletielles", this is yet another variation on the "empanadilla" (filled pastry), which is very similar indeed to the "samosa", which has its origins in India, East and North Africa and the Arab world. The only difference in concept is that samosas tend to be savoury, whereas this is a sweet. Also known as "bollinas", these walnut filled pasties can be fried or baked. Here we give the more traditional fried recipe, followed by the much simpler baked version.

Ingredients (for 10 casadielles):

For the pastry

>200 ml wine
>100 ml olive oil
>1 egg yolk
>100 g butter
>1 tablespoon baking powder
>Flour
>5 g of salt

For the filling

>100 g ground walnuts
>100 g white sugar
>120 ml of anis liquor
>120 ml water

Preparation:

1. Flavour the frying oil by slowly warming it up with a lemon peel and a stick of cinnamon. After a few minutes remove the oil from the heat and allow to cool again. Just before the casadielles are ready to be fried, remember to remove the lemon peel and the cinnamon from the oil.

2. Mix the olive oil, the wine and the salt in a bowl, beat it vigorously with a whisk until it is emulsified slightly and becomes white.

3. Then add the baking powder, the egg yolk and the butter and continue beating.

4. Gradually add the flour to make a soft dough that does not stick to your hands.

5. Roll out the dough with a rolling pin and then fold it up again, repeat this operation 4 times.

6. Make a ball with the dough, put it in a bowl and cover it with a damp cloth. Let the dough rest in a cool place for about 2 hours.

7. In the meantime, make the filling: Mix the walnuts, sugar and anis liquor together and gradually stir in the water. Set aside.

8. After the dough has rested, roll it out again with a rolling pin and cut out squares. This quantity should make 10 casadielles, so this should help you determine the exact size.

9. Spread some of the filling in the middle of each square of pastry and fold the edges toward the centre, like a little package. Seal the edges with some water and close the joint by pressing with a fork.

10. Fry the casadielles in the scented oil. When browned, take them out and put them to drain on some kitchen paper for a few seconds. Serve them hot, sprinkled with a little icing sugar.

CASADIELLES DE ASTURIAS (II)
Walnut Pasties of Asturias (II)

This is the alternative recipe for Casadielles, but this time baked rather than fried. It uses pre-prepared pastry, but of course you can also make your own.

Ingredients:

    0.5 kg of puff pastry
    400 g of walnuts
    400 g of sugar
    Cinnamon powder
    Icing sugar
    1 measure of anise liquor
    2 egg whites

Preparation:

1. Grind the walnuts in a mortar or blender and mix together with the sugar, anise liquor and the egg whites.

2. Roll out the pastry and cut into rectangles. Place some filling on each piece of pastry, roll it up and bake in a pre-heated oven for 8 to 10 min. at 200°C.

3. When browned, remove them from the oven and sprinkle them with icing sugar, or icing sugar mixed with a little cinnamon.

CHURROS

Churros

On New Years morning when the festivities of the night are coming to an end, the tradition is to adjourn to a café for breakfast. And taking churros with coffee or chocolate is one of the time-honoured breakfasts for this occasion.

Churros are a simple form of fritters, popular in all of Spain but especially in Andalucía. They are eaten for breakfast or merienda with milky coffee or thick hot chocolate. If you feel up to making them on New Year's day, here is a recipe!

Ingredients for approx. 32 churros:

    275 g plain flour
    2.5 g salt
    550 ml water
    Olive Oil

Preparation:

1. Sift the flour and salt together.

2. Bring the water to the boil and add the flour. Stir briskly over the heat until the flour has been incorporated into stiff, sticky dough. Leave it to cool a little.

3. While still warm use a strong piping bag with a narrow, fluted nozzle. Pipe out into 10cm lengths.

4. Fry in batches in very hot oil until brown and crisp.

5. Drain on kitchen paper and eat warm (they can also be slightly sugared).

CORDIALES DE MURCIA

Filled Almond Sweet of Murcia

These are almond sweets, typical of Christmas time in Murcia, and made in most homes in the region. Their origin is believed to be the town of Pacheco in Murcia.

Ingredients:

    0.5 kg of ground almonds
    350 g of sugar
    6 eggs
    Grated zest of 1 lemon
    "Angel hair"
    Wafers

Preparation:

1. Put all the ingredients in a bowl, (except for the "angel hair" and the wafers), mix and knead into a consistent dough.

2. Pre-heat the oven to about 150 °C.

3. In the meantime, place pieces of wafer (large enough to take a piece of dough 6-8cm wide) on a baking tray.

4. Use the dough to form small balls and fill each with a small portion of "angel hair" and close up the dough ball again. Place each cordial on a piece of wafer on the baking tray.

5. When the tray is filled, place it in the oven for 15 to 20 minutes until the cordiales are golden coloured.

6. Remove from the oven and allow them to cool completely.

CRESPILLOS DE BARBASTRO

Borage fritters of Barbastro

The origin of the crespillo lies in the traditional rural practice of using the best leaves of the borage, chard or spinach for a main course and using the normally discarded parts for a sweet dessert. The women of Aragón developed this delicious dish in order to make use of the entire plant rather than just cooking the tender heart of the plant.

The eating of crespillos has become linked with a well-known local Aragónese fertility festival held every year in late March celebrating the fertilisation of the flowers of the olive trees in the area. It is similar to the dish of "paparajotes" in Murcia where lemon leaves are used. Crespillos can be taken as an appetizer or dessert. If eaten as a dessert, add sugar and/or honey. Despite the association with spring, crespillos are also a popular dish at Christmas time, to celebrate the end of the old year and the start of the new one.

Ingredients:

>2 bunches of borage
>1 glass of brandy or (more traditionally) anis liquor
>2 eggs
>3 tbsp. flour
>1 small glass of milk
>Sugar
>Honey (optional)
>Olive oil

Preparation:

1. Clean and separate the borage leaves, selecting only the smaller and tender inside leaves. Wash these thoroughly with water and dry them.

2. Cover the leaves with the brandy and leave them to stand for a couple of hours.

3. When the leaves are marinated in cognac, make a soft batter with beaten egg white, salt, flour and milk (optionally add a tablespoon of honey). Prepare a frying pan with enough olive oil to fry the fritters.

4. Dip the borage leaves into the batter. They need to be well coated.

5. Fry them in the hot oil until golden brown. Serve sprinkled with sugar if eaten as a sweet, and leave them as they are if eaten as a starter.

DULCE DE MANZANA
Sweet Apple Preserve

Apples are often used in cooking and especially in sweet bakery and sauces. In Spain it is common to preserve apples for future use as a kind of jelly made with apples and sugar ("dulce de manzana"). This has the advantage that it remains preserved for months and is very handy for adding into a recipe that calls for apples. It is very easy to make, but it is time consuming. To make this work you need to use rather unripe apples in order to take advantage of the natural pectin in the fruits. The amount of sugar to use is a little bit a matter of taste. It should be between 550 - 700g /kg of cleaned apples.

Ingredients:

> Slightly unripe apples
> Sugar

Preparation:

1. Clean the apples by cutting them into quarters and removing the seeds. Cut them into small pieces, weight them and put them into a heavy-bottomed saucepan.

2. Calculate the amount of sugar required based on the weight of the apples (see above) and then add this amount of sugar to the apples in the saucepan. Put the pan on a low heat.

3. Stir for a few minutes, using a wooden spoon, to coat the apple pieces evenly with the sugar. There is no need to add water.

4. When the sugar is fully dissolved and begins to form a syrup with the apple juices, stir frequently until the apple is cooked and begins to turn golden. Take the pan off the heat.

5. Crush the apples in the pan until you have a smooth, homogeneous paste. Put the pan back on the heat for a few minutes until the apple mix is shiny and caramel-coloured.

7. Use plastic or other rectangular boxes for the storage of the apple preserve. The tops should be wide, so that the apple can be removed when set. Pour the apple mix into the boxes.

8. Let the apple jelly cool and solidify, and store it in a cool, dark place (there is no need to keep it in the fridge).

ESCALDAO DE ASTURIAS

Bread Pudding of Asturias

This is a typical rural Asturian Christmas dessert, which can be kept for several days. It is somewhat reminiscent of bread and butter pudding, but uses caramelised sugar and slices of sweet bread instead. In some Asturian homes it replaces the traditional marzipan.

Ingredients:

>A loaf of sweetened maize bread (known as boroña)
>Sugar
>Water
>Butter
>Honey, to taste

Preparation:

1. Cut the bread into slices.

2. Make a caramel with the sugar in a pan. Add the water to the caramel, allow it to dissolve and then add the butter. Let it melt.

3. Put a layer of slices of bread in a heatproof dish and allow them to soak in the caramel mixture. Top with another layer of bread and soak again, and so on till all the bread and caramel mix is used.

4. Cook for 30-45 min., stirring frequently to prevent burning, until obtaining a golden brown paste. Serve hot, with honey to taste.

GALLETAS DE ANÍS

Anis Biscuits

Anis is one of the typical Christmas flavours in Spanish seasonal confectionary. It's use originated in Arabic times, when anis was added to various heavy dishes to aid digestion.

Ingredients:

>100 g flour
>150 g sugar
>40 g butter at room temperature
>A teaspoon of bicarbonate
>Two tablespoons of anise liquor
>One tablespoon of milk
>Icing Sugar

Preparation:

1. Put all the ingredients into a bowl, mix well and then knead until you have a ball of consistent dough.

2. Preheat the oven to 170°C. Roll out the dough to about 1 cm thick and cut out the biscuits with star-shaped or round biscuit cutters. Place each biscuit on an oven tray lined with baking paper.

3. Put the tray in the middle of the oven and bake for about 15 minutes until the biscuits are golden brown and crispy.

4. Allow them to cool on a rack, lightly sprinkle them with icing sugar and serve.

GALLETITAS DE VAINILLA
Vanilla biscuits

Vanilla biscuits are a Christmas favourite in many European countries, but especially in Spain (and in most of Latin America). No Christmas is complete without vanilla biscuits. In parts of Spain they are often baked using lard rather than butter.

Ingredients:

    100 g butter
    350 g. White flour
    1 tsp. Vanilla Essence
    1 tsp. Baking Powder
    150 g sugar
    2 Eggs

Preparation:

1. Slowly melt the butter in a saucepan or just leave it out of the refrigerator for a while.

2. Mix the butter with the sugar. Add the eggs and the vanilla essence. Mix until blended.

3. Add the flour sifted together with the baking powder. Mix well until it becomes a dough.

4. Leave the dough to rest in the refrigerator for about 30 minutes.

5. Remove from the refrigerator, roll-out, cut the biscuits and bake in a moderate oven for about 10 to 15 minutes (Moderate oven = 180°C).

6. Let them cool on a rack and serve with coffee or tea.

GALETTE DE PÉROUGES DE CATALUÑA
Catalan Sugar Cake of Pérouges

This is actually a sweet that originates in Pérouges, a mediaeval town near Lyon in France, but which has been adopted by Cataluña and is sometimes eaten as a Christmas sweet.

Ingredients:

    220 g flour
    125 g butter
    30 g sugar
    Grated zest of half a lemon
    Pinch of salt
    100 ml water
    1 egg
    7 g yeast
    100 g butter
    70 g sugar

Preparation:

1. Mix the flour, the 125 g butter (in pieces), the 30 g sugar and the pinch of salt in a bowl. Crumble the ingredients together.

2. Add the egg and the yeast (dissolved in water) and knead the mix to form a dough. Add more flour if you think it is needed to make a good dough.

3. Put the dough aside and let it rise until it has doubled in volume. Pre-heat the oven to 220°C.

4. Roll out the dough into a very thin circle. Put this on a greased ovenproof plate and mark an edge with your finger all around the circle.

5. Place some small pieces of butter on the surface and sprinkle the surface with sugar. Bake immediately at 220°C for about 15 minutes.

6. Remove the cake from the oven, coat the surface with the remaining butter and then place it under a hot grill for a final quick caramelisation of the surface sugar, taking care not to burn it.

7. Finally, remove and set aside to cool before serving.

GUIRLACHE DE ARAGÓN
Nougat of Aragón

This nougat is simply made with almonds and caramelised sugar - solidified. It is a recipe which is very typical of many areas of the former Kingdom of Aragón (Aragón, Cataluña and Valencia) but similar recipes can be found in many parts of Spain and it has Arabic origins. This nougat was popularized by the French in Aragón during the nineteenth century and its name Guirlache is derived from the French word "grillage" (toasted).

Nougat is popular as a Christmas sweet by itself, but it is also used as an ingredient for cakes or desserts. This recipe for the Aragónese nougat is quite basic and easy to make. Some regional recipe variations add a little honey or substitute the sugar for honey.

Ingredients:

    0.5 kg of sugar
    0.5 kg raw whole almonds
    1 small lemon
    Anis seed (to taste)
    Olive oil

Preparation:

1. Put the sugar in a frying pan with the juice of just under half of the lemon.

2. Over a medium heat, continuously stir the sugar and lemon juice with a wooden spoon to prevent burning. The caramel is formed when the sugar has melted (at 160°C) and turns into a slightly thick, light coloured liquid. It should not be dark. Manage the caramelisation by taking the pan from the heat if necessary and gently swirling the melting sugar around.

3. When the sugar has started to caramelise, add the almonds to the pan, continuously stirring the mixture. Keep stirring until the mixture changes colour and begins to brown. It is very important at this point to prevent the caramel from burning.

4. When you see that the mixture has acquired this nougat's typical brown colour, remove the pan from the heat and pour everything on a sheet of baking paper on which we have previously rubbed a little olive oil to avoid the nougat sticking.

5. Spread out the hot mass, and shake a small amount of anise seeds over the surface, according to your taste.

6. Let the nougat cool for 15 minutes before cutting it up and serve.

HOJALDRINAS

Wine and Orange Christmas cakes

This is another popular Christmas sweet similar to the mantecados, but based on wine and orange zest and juice - thus giving them a completely different flavour. This recipe uses butter, but more traditionally the recipe used pig lard.

Ingredients:

    600 g flour
    400 g butter
    50 ml orange juice
    50 ml white wine
    Grated orange peel (3 oranges)
    Icing sugar

Preparation:

1. Melt the butter in a bowl. Add the filtered orange juice and the white wine. Mix well until the butter is well dissolved.

2. Add the 600 g of flour through a sieve and then the grated peel of 3 oranges.

3. Stir it all together with a spoon until the ingredients are well mixed. Form the dough into a ball with your hands.

4. Cover the dough and leave it in the refrigerator for one hour.

5. On a smooth surface, roll out the dough with a rolling pin and then cut it into rectangles of about 4x6 cm.

6. Place the pieces of dough in an oven tray lined with baking paper. Put the tray in the fridge for a while. In the meantime, preheat the oven at 180 degrees C. When the dough is cold, place the tray into the preheated oven and bake for 30 minutes.

8. Remove from the oven and leave the cakes to cool on a cake rack.

9. When cool, dust them with icing sugar and serve.

MANTECADOS DE NAVIDAD
Almond Christmas Biscuits

Mantecados are a traditional Christmas confectionary of Andalucía, quite similar to shortcake. A visit to the town of Estepa in Sevilla province during the months leading up to Christmas reveals an entire town busy making a vast array of traditional Christmas confectionary - based usually on the almond - including their famous Mantecados. The area around the town supplies the almonds, olive oil and lard that are the basic ingredients for many Andalucían confectionaries. The mantecado and the aroma of cinnamon are very emblematic of Christmas in Spain and no Christmas would be complete without them.

Ingredients (serves 4):

> 150 g lard
> 200 g sugar
> 100 g ground almonds
> 300 g flour
> 1 tablespoon ground cinnamon

Preparation:

1. Put the flour in a frying pan and toast it over a very low heat, stirring all the time with a wooden spoon.

2. When we see that the flour is starting to brown, remove it from the heat and place in a bowl with the ground almonds. Allow to cool.

3. In another bowl whisk the lard until very smooth and creamy. Then add the cinnamon and sugar and stir well until all is thoroughly mixed.

4. Add the flour and almond mix to the dough, stirring constantly until it is dry enough not to stick to the bowl.

5. Dust a smooth kitchen surface with flour to prevent sticking and place the mix on it. Use a rolling pin to flatten the dough well until you obtain a sheet of about 2 cm thick. Divide the dough into equal parts, forming small balls to get the basic shape of the mantecados.

6. Put these on a baking tray and bake them in a pre-heated oven at 150 °C for about 10 minutes or until golden.

7. Remove from the oven and allow them to cool.

8. You can sprinkle a little icing sugar over them before serving.

MANTECADOS DE ACEITE DE NAVIDAD
Almond and olive oil Christmas Biscuits

This typical Andaluz shortcake has many variations using, for example, cinnamon, almond, and chocolate. But one thing that all of these varieties have in common is calories - because their main ingredient is lard. Here we have suggested a traditional recipe that substitutes the lard for olive oil to make them healthier but just as delicious.

Ingredients:

>0.5 kg wheat flour (wholemeal flour can be used)
>0.25 l Olive oil
>190 g sugar
>2 teaspoons ground cinnamon
>Grated zest of two lemons

Preparation:

1. Place all the ingredients in a bowl and knead until well blended. Roll the dough out on a smooth surface.

2. When rolled use a mould or the rim of a glass to cut out the shortbreads.

3. Preheat the oven to 180 degrees and line an oven tray with baking paper.

4. Put the shortbreads on the tray and into the hot oven.

5. Bake the mantecados for about 10 minutes. Keep an eye on them because it maybe less, depending on your oven.

6. Once they are removed from the oven, let them cool.

7. When they are still warm, they are very soft and crumbly, but when they cool, they become harder. To maintain their freshness, it is best to keep them in a container and cover them with kitchen paper.

MANTECADOS DE ALFARNATE
Christmas biscuits of Alfarnate

This is just one variation on the Mantecado recipe and typical of the many delicious Andalucían Christmas sweet specialities. This one originates in a mountainous part of eastern Málaga province known for its almonds.

Ingredients:

- 1 kg butter
- 1 cup Olive oil toasted
- 2 Egg yolks
- 0.50 kg of sugar
- 3 measures of dry anise liquor
- 15 g Ground cinnamon (according to taste)
- 15 Ground cloves
- 3 kg flour

Preparation:

1. Make a dough with all the ingredients - it should not be sticky; add a little more flour if it is.

2. Roll out the dough and cut out round shapes for the cakes.

3. Baste the tops with beaten egg whites and powdered sugar.

4. Place the cakes on baking paper in an oven tray. Bake in the oven at 180°C for about 15 minutes.

5. Allow to cool - remember that they will be quite delicate and very crumbly.

MANTECADOS MANCHEGOS

Shortbread biscuits of La Mancha

Here is another regional version of mantecados; this time with both wine and anise liquor flavour.

Traditionally, the dough for the mantecados was prepared at home and then brought to the local bakery to bake. Families had large tins with a capacity some four times bigger than what a domestic oven tray could accommodate. These were filled with the uncooked mantecados and brought to the baker to be baked as soon as his ovens were empty. These same tins were also used to carry red peppers for roasting, or for baking other homemade biscuits or cakes in large quantities.

The mantecados of this recipe are very easy to prepare, with very simple ingredients: white wine, flour, lard and sugar. You can then add flavourings to taste, like, for example, anise, or orange/lemon zest and juice.

Ingredients:

    0.5 kg of pig lard (can be substituted for butter/margarine)
    0.6 kg flour
    200 ml white (La Mancha) wine
    1 small glass of Anise liquor
    Ground anise seed to taste
    1 pinch of salt
    Icing sugar to finish the cakes

Preparation:

1. Leave the lard to soften at room temperature a few hours.

2. Beat the lard, the wine and the anise together.

3. Sift the flour and salt into the whipped butter and wine mix. Mix just enough without having to knead.

4. Make a ball of the dough and leave it covered in a bowl to cool overnight (or refrigerate the dough for at least 1 hour to harden).

5. Roll out the dough using a rolling pin until it has a thickness of about 3 cm or a little more. Cut out the shortbread with a diamond-shaped dough cutter about the size of 2 bites.

6. Place the mantecados slightly separated from each other on an oven tray lined with baking paper. Preheat the oven to 180-200°C. Put the tray in the oven and reduce the temperature to 100°C.

7. Bake for about 60 minutes. The mantecados should NOT be very brown, just baked.

8. Remove the tray from the oven and leave the mantecados to cool on the tray (they are very fragile when hot). When cool, shake some icing sugar over them. Serve when completely cold.

MARQUESAS DE NAVIDAD

Marquesa Christmas Almond Cakes

This is one of the most traditional Christmas sweets in Spain and it is also one of the simplest to prepare.

Ingredients:

    100 g of ground raw almonds
    66 g icing sugar
    1 large egg
    20 g cornstarch
    1 teaspoon of yeast
    Grated zest of half a lemon
    50 g almond cream
    15 g butter
    Icing sugar for dusting
    Small paper moulds for baking the marquesa cakes

Preparation:

1. Toast the ground almonds in a frying pan over a medium heat for about 5 minutes, stirring all the time so they do not burn. Remove the pan from the heat and put the almonds into a bowl.

2. In a separate bowl, beat the egg and then add the sugar and the yeast. When all is well blended, add the cornstarch and the lemon zest and beat again.

3. Stir in the melted butter and the almond cream and continue beating.

4. Finally add the roasted almonds and mix until well blended.

5. Place the paper moulds in a baking tray and fill each of them with the cake mix.

6. Place the tray in a preheated oven at 175°C for about 10 minutes, making sure that the cakes do not brown too much.

7. When they are baked, remove the cakes from the oven and carefully remove them from the baking tray. Place them on another baking tray to cool and then cover with a generous "snowfall" of icing sugar.

MAZAPÁN, TRADICIONAL DULCE DE NAVIDAD
Marzipan, the traditional Christmas sweet

Marzipan is the archetypal Christmas confection, beloved throughout Europe. However, let us remember that European marzipan actually came from Moorish Spain. It arrived in "Al-Andalus", which was an area covering much of Spain, at the time of the Arab Kingdoms. Some believe Marzipan originated in China, from where the recipe moved on to the Middle East and then to Europe via the Caliphate of Cordoba and the Kingdom of Granada when almond cultivation was introduced into Spain.

Marzipan is used to make decorations and as fillings for cakes. Because it is so malleable, many towns and villages in Spain have a tradition of using marzipan to make religious and other figures as well as animals and fruits to provide a decorative and delicious sweet treat at Christmas time. Some of these figures and decorations are truly works of art and it may be hard to bring yourself to eat them!

Here is one basic recipe for the making of marzipan.

Ingredients:

    280 g peeled and chopped almonds
    400 g sugar
    240 ml water
    2 egg whites
    4 tablespoons icing sugar
    1 teaspoon vanilla

Preparation:

1. Heat the water in a pan with the sugar until the sugar dissolves and the mixture begins to boil.

2. Leave to boil without stirring until it has a temperature of 110 °C (use a food thermometer to check the temperature).

3. Remove from the heat and stir the mixture very carefully. Add the almonds, beaten egg whites and vanilla. Mix everything thoroughly.

4. Place the saucepan over a moderate heat for a few minutes, just until the mixture starts to pull away from the sides of the saucepan.

5. Put some icing sugar on a smooth surface and add the mixture from the saucepan. Knead well, then make shapes as required or form into a cylinder or cake for later use.

6. Wrap in cling film and put in an airtight container for storage.

FIGURITAS DE MAZAPÁN
Marzipan figures

Marzipan descends from a centuries' old tradition of combining almonds with sugar. The resulting 'dough' is quite pliable, and confectioners use this attribute to create whimsical figures before toasting them in an oven. The result is marzipan 'figuritas', little figures.

During the battle of Navas de Tolosa in the year 1212, it is said that the nuns of the San Clemente convent took care of the wounded soldiers. According to tradition, they ground up their stores of almonds in mortars and pestles, and then kneaded them together with sugar to create emergency rations. This type of bread (pan) produced with a pestle (maza) is supposed to have given rise to the name mazapán in Spanish - marzipan in English. It's a nice story, but the reality is that marzipan was probably introduced into Spain by the Arabs as a super-charged way of preserving high protein foods for their armies when they were on the march, and as a source of protein and sugar during long winters in remote areas.

In later times, marzipan was used to create artistic shapes to celebrate Christmas by making figures and "carving" other religious or domestic objects. This tradition is still alive and well and not just in Spain. The only limit to what can be made in marzipan is your own imagination!

Ingredients (for 3 people):

> 300 g of ground almonds
> 300 g of icing sugar
> 2 tablespoons water
> 1 egg white
> Grated zest of half a lemon (optional)
> Ground cinnamon (optional)

Preparation:

1. Put the almonds, sugar and water into a deep bowl. If you like, you can add half a lemon zest and some cinnamon powder.

2. Knead the mixture with your hands until the marzipan is a uniform smooth dough. Leave the dough to rest in a cool place for at least two hours.

3. Now comes the creative part: making the figurines. This is definitely a task for the children to enjoy and there are no limits to what you can

make. You can buy kits of shaped biscuit cutters to make the cutting out simpler and more professional but its not really necessary - the most important thing is to make some funny and interesting shapes.

4. When your figures are all finished they should be painted with beaten egg white and placed on an oven tray lined with baking paper.

5. Preheat the oven to 200°C. Put the tray in the oven for just 2 minutes. As soon as the marzipan begins to brown, remove it from the oven.

6. Allow to cool, and serve.

MELINDRES DE GALICIA
"Ladyfingers" of Galicia

These small, glazed doughnuts are a typical Galician sweet. They are very popular in winter time and during the Christmas festivities.

Ingredients:

For the dough:

> 3 egg yolks
> 2 egg whites
> 4 tablespoons of melted butter
> 3 tablespoons of sugar
> 250 g flour
> Anise liquor

For the icing:

> 250 g sugar
> 200 ml water
> 1 egg white

Preparation:

1. Mix all the ingredients for the dough in a bowl, but keep some of the flour back, in case it proves to be too much. Knead the dough until it does not stick to your hands. Add more flour as necessary.

2. Let the dough rest for half an hour and then make small dough balls, flatten them slightly and make a small hole in the centre with your finger. Remember to make the hole a bit large because it will close up during baking. When formed, place the doughnuts on an oven tray lined with baking paper. Pre-heat the oven to 170°C.

3. Bake the doughnuts until they begin to brown.

4. In the meantime, make a thick syrup for the icing with the water and sugar. Whisk the egg white until it becomes stiff. Then gradually add the syrup to the beaten egg white until all is well mixed.

5. Dip the melindres in the icing, making sure that they are well coated, and then let them drain on baking paper.

6. When they are dry, they are ready to eat. Store them in an airtight container and they will remain fresh for many days.

NEVADITOS DE CANTABRIA

Snow Cakes of Cantabria

Nevados, also called nevaditos, which means "snow-capped" is the apt name given to a type of small Christmas cake. These traditional, snowy-white cakes are covered in icing sugar, and have now become popular throughout Spain. The recipe is thought to have originated in Cantabria, in the far North of the country.

Ingredients (for approximately 40 cakes):

>200 g of lard (can be substituted for butter or margarine)
>500 g of flour
>125 ml vino blanco (muscatel wine works well)
>0.5 teaspoon of salt
>50 g of sugar
>Icing sugar for coating

Preparation:

1. Preheat the oven to 180ºC.

2. Put the flour in a mixing bowl, make a hollow in the centre and put the lard (at room temperature), wine, salt and sugar in it. Mix everything together. Knead thoroughly for a few minutes until it becomes a workable dough.

3. Roll out the dough with a rolling pin, making it about 1 cm thick. Cut out shapes: stars, circles or other festive shapes with a pastry cutter.

4. Place the nevaditos on a baking tray lined with baking paper, separating them slightly.

5. Bake them for about 30 minutes until they are lightly browned.

6. Take the nevaditos out of the oven and coat them with icing sugar when they are still hot. Leave to cool on a rack.

7. When they are cooled, sprinkle them again with icing sugar and serve.

PAN DE CÁDIZ
Fruit Marzipan of Cadiz

The "Pan de Cadiz" (also called Turrón de Cadiz) has no relationship with bread - except that it is baked in an oven and is often shaped and made to look like a traditional loaf of bread. It is a sweet consisting of a mass of marzipan filled with candied fruit. It is the most famous and typical sweet of the city of the same name, but it is a relatively recent invention. In its present form, its original creation is attributed to baker Antonio Valls Garrido, who created the Vienna patisserie in Cadiz in the early 1950's. However, although the shape of the sweet itself was created at this time, the delicacy itself is thought to be based on the much older marzipan and fruit balls that were first documented in Cadiz in the 18th century, but may have been made there for much longer. Pan de Cádiz is now a very popular sweet on Christmas tables throughout Andalucía and indeed, the whole of Spain.

Ingredients:

    250 g icing sugar
    250 g of ground raw almonds (preferably Marcona)
    1 egg
    1 egg yolk to paint the top of the loaf
    Mixture of candied fruit

Preparation:

1. Make the marzipan as follows: Mix the sugar with the ground almonds and add the beaten egg. Knead the mixture by hand until smooth.

2. Weigh the whole mix and then divide it into three equal portions.

3. Preheat the oven (grill only) to 250°C.

4. Knead each of the portions of marzipan a bit more, and roll them out into an oval shape.

4. Prepare a baking tray with a piece of baking paper and place one of the marzipan ovals on the paper. Cover this with candied fruit, chopped or cut into strips, and then place another marzipan oval on top.

5. Repeat the process adding more candied fruits. Finally, cover this with the last oval layer of marzipan, using your thumbs to press down

the sides and smooth over the point where the three layers meet. Shape carefully into a "loaf".

6. Carefully make a diamond pattern on the top of the "loaf" with a sharp knife, and brush it with egg yolk. Place the tray into the oven to brown.

7. There is no need to bake the "loaf", just to brown the top until it is slightly golden, which does not take very long. As soon as it starts to turn golden, remove the loaf from the oven and place it on a rack to cool.

8. Serve when cool. To store: wrap the loaf in cling film and put in an airtight container so that it does not dry out.

PAN DE HIGO
Fig Loaf

Fig "bread" is a very typical Christmas dessert in Spain and, together with the famous Mantecados these are the richest and most popular Christmas sweets in Spain. Accompanied by a glass of muscatel wine, fig bread is a delight for the palate! Fig bread is also a very complete and nutritious food containing dried fruits and nuts and very welcome in the cold days of winter.

It is traditional in Spain to eat nuts and dried fruits especially during the most important religious festivals, such as Christmas. Historically, the Catholic Church encouraged religious celebrations to be accompanied with plenty of food, it being supposed that the faithful would associate their faith with lots of good food. Similar recipes for this pan de higo are found in Extremadura, Andalucía and Murcia where figs and almonds grow side by side and are harvested at about the same time in September.

Ingredients:

    1 kg dried figs
    0.5 kg of roasted skinned almonds
    1 tablespoon of ground cinnamon
    1 glass of rum
    3 tablespoons of honey
    0.5 teaspoon of ground aniseed
    A pinch ground cloves

Preparation:

1. Remove the tops from the figs and chop them up finely.

2. Roast the almonds and chop finely (leave a few large slices for decoration).

3. Mix the figs and almonds, add the ground cloves, cinnamon powder, ground anise seed, the rum and the honey and mix it all thoroughly until obtaining a consistent and firm dough.

4. Shake flour on a round or square cake tin and fill with the mix. Place a heavy weight on top of the mixture, using greaseproof paper to cover the "loaf". Let it set for a day or two. You can also make rolls of fig "bread", coating them with a little flour and let them dry for a couple of days. To serve, cut the loaf into thin slices.

PASTEL DE GLORIA O TETILLAS DE MONJA
Gloria Cakes - Almond Meringues

The "Gloria cake" is an exquisite sweet, thought to be of Arabic origin, and known in different regions of the southeast of Spain. On account of their shape and colour, they have been given picturesque popular names, like cow's teat or nun's nipple.

It is quite exotic but simple to make and nowadays a Christmas favourite in many parts of Spain with its distinctive almond flavour.

Ingredients: (About 10 cakes):

> 0.5 litres of egg whites
> 850 g of sugar
> 8 egg yolks
> 0.25 kg of ground almonds
> Angel bread (wafers)
> Icing sugar

Preparation:

To make the egg yolk mixture:

1. Put 90 ml. of water with 250 g of sugar in a saucepan and let it boil for a minute. Take the pan off the heat and add in the beaten egg yolks.

2. Return the pan to the heat and let it simmer, stirring continuously. When the mixture has thickened, remove from the heat and leave to cool.

To make the almond paste:

3. Make an almond paste by putting 0.25 kg of sugar in a saucepan with 40 ml of water. Bring to the boil, add the ground almonds and mix together well until obtaining a smooth dough. Take off the heat and set aside.

To make the meringue:

4. Use a large mixing bowl and pour in the egg whites and beat until stiff, adding the remaining sugar gradually, until the mix has a good consistency.

To make the cakes:

5. Preheat the oven to 250°C.

6. Line an oven tray with baking paper and place some pieces of wafer on the paper, leaving some space between wafers.

7. On each piece of wafer, put a circle of almond paste. On top of the almond dough, put a tablespoon full of the egg yolk mixture.

8. On top of the egg yolk mixture, create a little "mountain" of meringue using a spoon and covering the entire base.

9. Once the cakes are prepared, put the tray into the oven for 10 to 15 minutes, until the meringues are "set" and become slightly browned. Take them out of the oven and sprinkle them with some icing sugar.

10. Allow the "Gloria cakes" to cool and serve.

PASTELITO DE GLORIA

Little Glory Cakes

This is a small sweet cake based on almonds that is very typical of traditional Andalucían Christmas baking. This version uses sweet potatoes to create the filling, but other fillings may be used. Like most traditional Andalucían sweets, it has its origins in the era of the Arabic Al-Andalus with its extensive use of almonds in confectionary. These cakes are VERY sweet.

Ingredients:

    300 g finely ground fresh almonds
    300 g Icing Sugar
    3 egg whites

For the filling:

    200 g Sweet Potatoes
    200 g Sugar

Preparation:

1. Cook the scrubbed, unpeeled potatoes in plenty of water until tender.

2. Let the potatoes cool slightly and then peel and purée them.

3. Pour the potato purée into a saucepan with the sugar and cook over medium-low heat until the mix comes away from the bottom of the pan. Put it in a bowl and leave to cool.

4. In the meantime, make the marzipan by mixing the ground almonds with the icing sugar and egg whites.

5. Mix thoroughly and then spread the mixture on a smooth work surface. Use a rolling pin to flatten it until it is about 2 cm thick.

6. Cut out the shapes with a round biscuit cutter.

7. Put a portion of the sweet potato mix on each circle of marzipan and cover with another slice of marzipan.

8. Give the cakes their round shape and seal and coat each cake with egg white. Bake in a medium hot oven for about 15 minutes until slightly firm.

9. Set the cakes aside, let them cool and sprinkle them with icing sugar.

PASTELILLOS DE CABELLO DE ÁNGEL DE MURCIA
Angel hair Pasties of Murcia

These cakes are a traditional Christmas dish from Águilas in Murcia. It is a very old recipe and very popular in that region.

Ingredients:

    1.25 kg flour
    500 g lard
    500 g sugar
    500 g "angel hair"
    3 egg yolks
    250 ml of "mistela" (sweet fortified wine)
    Half a sachet of yeast
    Grated peel of 1 lemon

Preparation:

1. Mix the lard and lemon peel together well in a bowl. Add the sugar and continue mixing by hand.

2. Add the lightly beaten egg yolks and continue working the mixture until it is thoroughly blended.

3. Add the wine and keep mixing.

4. Gradually stir in the flour. Work the dough on a floured surface until smooth.

5. Roll out the dough with a rolling pin and use a pastry cutter (round or star shaped) to cut out the pasties.

6. Place the bases in a greased oven tray. Put a spoonful of the "Angel hair" on each base. Then add the lid and press the edges together well.

7. Finally, seal the pasties with some beaten egg and sprinkle with sugar.

8. Bake in a hot oven (about 200°C) until golden brown.

9. Serve when cooled.

LAS PELADILLAS DE CASINOS
Sugared Almonds of Valencia

This is a typical candied sweet, made from almonds coated with sugar. It originates in Valencia and is often present on the Christmas table throughout Spain, accompanying other almond sweets like nougats, polvorones, marzipans, mantecados, etc. It has been widely exported to other countries in the past as a traditional festive sweet.

The major producers of sugared almonds in Spain are found in the towns of Casinos in Valencia and Alcoy in Alicante, where sugared almonds have been manufactured and exported from, using a traditional manufacturing process for at least two centuries.

Besides the traditional sugared almonds, other variants are made with different types of chocolates. In the town of Casinos, every year on the last weekend of November you can visit the annual Feria of handcrafted sweets and try all of these traditional coated almonds and the famous D.O. nougat of Casinos.

This is not a product that can be easily produced in a domestic kitchen, so we make no attempt to provide a recipe. However, it is such a traditional and well known Christmas sweet that we thought that it deserved a mention. The best option for the reader is to buy some from any of the excellent manufacturers in Casinos.

PERAS AL VINO DE MÁLAGA

Pears in wine from Málaga

Ingredients:

    1 kg of cooking pears
    1 litre of red wine
    A few pieces of cinnamon
    6 or 7 cloves
    A little sugar

Preparation:

1. Wash and peel the pears, leaving the stalk on the pear.

2. Put the pears into a saucepan. Add some water as well as the wine, the cinnamon, cloves and sugar.

3. Boil the pears until they are tender, put them aside and allow them to cool to room temperature. Serve.

PESTIÑOS
Sweet Fritters

A pestiño is a Christmas or Holy Week pastry that is popular in Andalucía and Murcia in Southern Spain. It is a piece of dough, deep fried in olive oil and glazed with honey or sugar. Pestiños are very easy to make and can have a lot of different flavours using, for example, white wine, anise, cinnamon or cloves as optional ingredients. They can be dipped in sugar or honey. Here we give two variations of this recipe just to whet your appetite!

Ingredients:

>1 kg of flour
>Olive oil
>1 glass of white wine
>2 eggs
>Peel of half a lemon
>Peel of half an orange
>Icing sugar or honey to taste

Optional flavourings:

>30 g anise seeds and 60 ml anise liqueur
>>or
>
>2 tsp of cinnamon powder and 6 cloves

Preparation:

1. Fry the lemon and orange peels (and optionally the anise seed) in hot olive oil.

2. In a bowl, whisk the flour, eggs and other ingredients together (optionally adding the anise liquor). Add the oil infused with orange and lemon flavour and stir with a wooden spoon until it becomes a smooth dough.

3. Roll out the dough evenly on a smooth surface into a thin layer. Cut the dough into rectangular pieces. Fold the 2 opposing corners together and fry the pestiños in plenty of hot oil.

4. Once fried, coat the pestiños with icing sugar or honey. Optionally add anise seed and anise liquor.

PESTIÑOS DE MÁLAGA

Pestiños ("Angel Wings") of Málaga

This is the Málaga variant on the previous Pestiño recipe, also a typical Christmas and Easter week dish - along with sweet doughnuts, cod dishes and rice puddings.

Such dishes are especially favoured during religious feasts, because they are sweet and they contain no lard - which was, of course, forbidden during Holy days of abstinence like Lent and Christmas Eve. Thus it was possible to enjoy some really rich and delicious delicacies without breaking the rules on fasting.

Ingredients:

    1 cup of olive oil
    Orange peel
    Lemon peel
    A little less than a glass of white wine
    1 tablespoon sesame seeds
    1 small glass of brandy
    1 pinch of baking soda
    850 g white (bread) flour
    Sugar
    Cinnamon powder

Preparation:

1. Heat some olive oil in a frying pan and brown the orange and lemon peels.

2. Remove the pan from the heat and add a tablespoon of sesame seeds to the oil (so that they don't burn). Pour it into a bowl.

3. To this mixture add the white wine (which should be at room temperature), the glass of brandy, a pinch of baking soda, half a teaspoon of ground cinnamon and the flour. Start to knead the mixture until it becomes a smooth dough.

4. Once the dough is made and is consistent, leave to stand for 1 hour.

5. Take small amounts of the dough and roll them into squares, then fold them over. Place each of these into hot olive oil (not too hot to prevent burning). After taking them from the oil, drain, sprinkle them with sugar and cinnamon and serve.

POLVORONES DE ESTEPA

Shortbreads of Estepa (Seville)

The polvorón is a typical Christmas confectionery in Spain and particularly in Andalucía. The most famous ones are made in Estepa, an old Arabic town in the province of Sevilla. The polvorón is basically shortbread. There are quite a lot of variations on the basic recipe, including one variety - "polvorones de limón" - which is very popular and aromatic. It uses a paste made with whole grated lemons, skin and all. In all cases, the smell of cinnamon and anis from freshly baked polvorones at Christmas is guaranteed to imbue everyone with a festive spirit!

Ingredients (makes 45):

    400 g flour
    225 g of lard (can be substituted with butter)
    150 g icing sugar
    2 tablespoons anise liquor
    0.5 teaspoon ground cinnamon
    Grated lemon rind (or 2 lemons grated into a paste, if making the Polvorones de limón)
    Flour and icing sugar for dusting

Preparation:

1. Pre-heat the oven to 150°C. When it is at temperature, toast the flour. To do this pour the flour in a baking tray and spread it out with a spatula. Put the tray in the oven for 6 minutes to toast slightly. Then remove from the oven, stir it with the spatula and toast it again for another 6 minutes.

2. Sift the flour into a bowl. Add the cinnamon, sugar, and some grated lemon rind (or the lemon paste). Add the lard or butter and anise and knead well.

3. Dust a smooth surface with a little flour, place the dough on the surface, sprinkle with some more flour and then roll out the pastry to a thickness of about 1.5 cm. Use a round biscuit cutter to cut the shortbreads and place them on an oven tray lined with baking paper.

4. Bake at 170 °C for 15 minutes. Allow the polvorones to cool before sprinkling them with icing sugar. Serve on Christmas morning.

POLVORONES DE CHOCOLATE

Chocolate Shortbread

One of the most delicious Christmas biscuits is definitely "polvorones de chocolate" - chocolate shortbread.

Ingredients:

    250 g flour
    80 g icing sugar
    125 g butter
    60 g of ground roasted almonds
    25 g cocoa powder
    0.5 teaspoon cinnamon
    A pinch of salt

Preparation:

1. Preheat the oven to 180°C. Spread the flour on a baking tray lined with baking paper. When the oven is hot, place the tray into the oven to toast the flour for about 15 minutes. Take care not to burn the flour, so stir it occasionally. When the flour is toasted, take it out and let it cool.

2. Mix the flour well with the butter, cocoa, icing sugar, salt and cinnamon. Add the almonds and continue kneading until obtaining homogenous dough.

3. Increase the oven temperature to 220 °C degrees and in the meantime prepare the shortbreads by rolling out the dough to a thickness of about 1.5 cm. Cut out the shortbreads with a circular biscuit cutter and place aside on an oven tray lined with fresh baking paper.

4. Put them in the oven for about five minutes (or until golden).

5. Remove them from the oven and let them cool. Sprinkle with icing sugar and/or cocoa powder to taste.

PRESTINES DE EXTREMADURA
Anis and Honey fritters of Extremadura

This is a sweet Christmas dish, typical of Extremadura. This basic recipe is from the municipality of Villafranca de los Barros in the province of Badajoz and is easy to make and traditional.

Ingredients:

    4 cups of flour
    1 cup of sugar
    1 cup of red wine with aniseed
    Olive oil
    Orange peel
    Honey

Preparation:

1. Boil the wine together with the aniseed.

2. Put the olive oil in a frying pan on a medium heat and add a few pieces of orange peel. Take them out when they are fried.

3. Strain the wine (removing the aniseed) and mix the boiled wine and the warm oil with the flour.

4. Mix well, knead it thoroughly and form about 45 prestines (little balls).

5. Deep-fry the prestines.

6. When the prestines are fried, coat them with honey and serve.

PURÉ DE CASTAÑAS CON QUESO DE AFUEGA'L PITU
Chestnut purée with cottage cheese

Traditionally, this Asturian dish was served on special days, like when the animals were slaughtered, or during Christmas time. It is delicious and is still a very popular sweet, despite the fact that its preparation is a little time consuming. You will need to have something to make the cheese in; a fine nylon sieve will serve for this. Traditionally, the milk was curdled in an earthenware pot and the cheese made in a round woven basket mould.

Ingredients:

For the cheese:

>5 litres of milk
>Some rennet
>Salt

For the puree:

>2 kg chestnuts
>1 tablespoon of flour
>Butter
>Milk

Preparation:

1. To make the cheese, put the milk into a low earthenware dish (like a casserole dish) and add a little salt and rennet. Leave somewhere warm in the kitchen. The next day the milk will have curdled.

2. Prepare a container for the cheese and fill it with the curds from the curdled milk until it is full. Let the cheese stand for two or three days, and when solid, take out the cheese - it is better to use the cheese fresh than to allow it to cure.

3. Boil the chestnuts and purée them together with a little sugar, a little milk and a tablespoon of flour. Cook well and then pour the mix into a buttered bowl.

4. When the purée is cool, serve it accompanied with the cottage cheese.

ROSCÓN DE REYES
Ring of the Three Kings

Roscón de Reyes (the ring of the kings) is a Spanish pastry traditionally eaten to celebrate Epiphany. It is generally 30cms or more in diameter and there are many different recipes, but usually it is decorated with dried cherries, figs, quinces, and other candied fruits. The Roscón de Reyes is traditionally eaten on January 6, during the celebration of the "Día de Reyes" (The "Day of the Kings") which commemorates the arrival of the three Magi or Wise Men to visit the infant Jesus.

In Spain (and in most other parts of the Hispanic world), this is also the day on which Christmas gifts are given (unlike in other countries where gifts are given on Christmas day). The gifts are said to come from the Three Wise Men, hence the connection with the Kings (Reyes). Therefore, there is a great deal of excitement involved for all and especially for the children, who wait eagerly for the Kings to come to bring them gifts.

The tradition of placing a little trinket (often a figure of the Christ Child) in the cake is very old. The baby Jesus, when hidden in the bread, represents the flight of Jesus from King Herod's massacre of the innocents. Tradition says that whoever finds the baby Jesus figurine, is blessed and must take the figurine to the nearest church on February 2, Candlemas Day (Día de la Candelaria). Another tradition includes hiding a dry bean in the Roscon as well as the figurine of the baby Jesus. In this tradition, whoever finds the figurine is crowned and becomes the "king" or "queen" of the banquet, whereas whoever finds the bean has to pay for next year's Roscón.

The history of this dish is, however, much older than Christianity. The traditional Roscón de Reyes dates back to ancient Rome and its Saturnalia festivities which took place between 21st and 23rd December to celebrate the winter solstice. Tradition says that Roman patricians shared round bread containing honey, figs and dates with the slaves and freedmen of their cities as a sign that they would live together in harmony in the New Year and to mutually celebrate the rebirth of the year after the short winter days leading to the solstice.

Over the years, the Roscón has had some powerful enthusiasts. They say the biggest promoter of the cake was Louis XV of France. Apparently, Louis' cook was of Slavic origin, and entertained the Monarch at Epiphany with a traditional Roscón from his own country with a surprise baked inside the cake: a medallion of diamonds purchased with the collaboration of other members of the royal court!

While the tradition was lost in Eastern Europe, Louis XV was so delighted with the invention that he decided to propagate the recipe, with a coin inside as a surprise, when entertaining French and other European aristocracy. So it was that during the eighteenth century, the Roscón came to Spain, where it rapidly became a welcome traditional treat at noble tables. Soon the custom of the Roscón spread to the tables of the common people in Spain and then gradually throughout the Spanish colonies.

It is best served with a cup of hot chocolate whilst waiting the arrival of the 3 Kings and their sacks of presents!

Ingredients:

    650 g flour
    250 ml of warm milk
    25-30 g of fresh yeast
    120 g Sugar
    120 g butter, melted
    2 eggs and 1 egg yolk
    10 g salt
    2.5 tablespoons orange blossom water
    Grated rind of 1 large lemon and 1 orange

To decorate:

    Candied fruits to taste
    Sugar
    1 egg, beaten
    An orange
    Bakeable figurines (not too small)

Preparation:

1. Mix some of the warm milk with 2 or 3 tablespoons of the flour. Add 25-30 g of crumbled fresh yeast and mix well. Cover the mixture and let it ferment for about 15 to 20 minutes in a warm place.

2. Once the starter mixture has fermented, make the dough using a large mixing bowl: add the remaining flour and gradually mix in all the remaining ingredients: sugar, lemon and orange zest, salt, milk, eggs, sugar, the fermenting starter yeast mix, orange blossom water and finally the melted butter. Stir well until it becomes a smooth mix.

3. Put some flour on a smooth surface and knead the dough for a few minutes by hand. If necessary add a little more flour to work the dough.

4. When well mixed, shape the dough into a round cake and place it in a large airtight container or in a container covered with a damp cloth. Leave to rise for a couple of hours in a warm place.

5. After this time the dough should have risen to about twice its size.

6. Take the dough from the container and on a smooth floured surface, knead it again and slowly shape it into a ring. With these quantities we can also make 2 medium sized roscones.

7. When shaping the roscones, remember that the hole in the middle will become smaller during baking, so it is best to make the hole in the middle quite big.

8. When they are shaped, leave them again to rest for about an hour, covered and in a warm place. A useful tip is to heat the oven to 50°C, switch it off and put the roscones in the oven to keep them warm.

9. Finally, coat the roscones with egg, and decorate the top to your liking, for example, with all kinds of candied fruit, candied oranges, sliced almonds, sugar, etc. If you want to hide a figurine in the Roscón, this is the time to do it!

10. Once the roscones are decorated, put them into a preheated oven at 180°C for about 20 minutes.

11. When baked, take them out and leave to cool.

12. Some people like to cut them in half and fill them with cream, chocolate mousse, custard or some other favourite filling, but this is not necessary.

ROSCOS DE ANIS

Anis Doughnuts

Ingredients:

    Half cup olive oil
    50 g ground almonds (without skin)
    Cinnamon powder - a tablespoon
    Anis seeds - a tablespoon
    0.5 kg cake flour
    Half cup sugar
    1 glass of sweet Muscatel wine
    Half a cup olive oil
    Sweet anis liquor (to taste)
    Icing sugar (to coat the doughnuts)

Preparation:

1. Pour a little olive oil into a frying pan and roast 50 g of ground almonds (without the skin), taking care not to burn them.

2. Take a large bowl and put in the almonds, ground cinnamon, anis seeds, the pastry flour, the sugar, olive oil, muscatel wine and a little sweet anise spirit (according to your taste).

3. Knead all the ingredients together until the dough is smooth and compact.

4. Coat your hands with flour and start to make the doughnut rings by rolling and shaping the dough.

5. Fry the doughnuts in hot oil, taking care not to burn them.

6. When golden brown, remove the doughnuts from the hot oil, drain them on kitchen roll and coat them with icing sugar.

ROSCOS CARREROS DE MÁLAGA
Doughnut "volcanoes" of Málaga

This is a type of doughnut which is a favourite in the area around Málaga. These "roscos" are made in the shape of a volcano with a hole in the middle. With their spicy flavour of cloves and cinnamon, they evoke the tastes of the Nasrid past of these two remote Arabic villages which lie on the ancient route between Málaga and Granada.

Ingredients:

    1 dozen eggs
    1 kg of lard (or butter) at room temperature
    1.5 kg pastry flour
    0.25 kg sugar
    Half a glass of brandy
    5 ground cloves
    Cinnamon powder (to taste)

Preparation:

1. Separate the egg yolks and whites.

2. Beat the egg whites.

3. Mix all the ingredients (except the egg yolks) in a large bowl and work the mixture together to become a consistent dough.

4. Tear off small portions of the dough. Roll them out on a smooth work surface, and, with the palm of the hand, shape them into little "volcanoes". Place them on a baking tray and baste with the egg yolks.

5. Bake at 180°C for 10 minutes.

ROSCOS DUROS DE NAVIDAD

Crispy Christmas doughnuts

This is a traditional Asturian recipe for small crispy Christmas doughnuts. They smell and taste delicious. The dough is very easy to make and very manageable to work when making the doughnuts.

Ingredients:

- 550 g flour
- 220 g Sugar
- 200 g of olive oil
- 115 g of white wine
- 15 g of sesame seeds
- 15 g of anise

Preparation:

1. Put the sugar, oil, wine, anise and sesame seeds in a bowl. Mix them all very well and then add the flour. Knead thoroughly into a smooth dough.

2. Let the dough rest for 15 minutes while the oven is preheated to 220°C.

3. Make the doughnuts and place them on a greased oven tray or line the tray with greaseproof paper. Place into the oven.

4. The baking time will depend on the size of the doughnut. A small-ish doughnut takes about 15 minutes, until they start to colour.

5. Take them out of the oven and put them on a rack until cooled.

ROSCOS DE HUEVO

Egg Doughnuts

Ingredients:

    5 Eggs
    25 tablespoons of olive oil (first use the oil to fry the lemon rind)
    25 tablespoons of sugar
    35 tablespoons of orange juice
    Ground cinnamon
    Lemon rind
    1 teaspoon bicarbonate of soda
    1 sachet of dried yeast
    Flour

Preparation:

1. Make the dough by mixing eggs, olive oil, the sugar, orange juice, cinnamon, baking soda, yeast and flour. When the dough has reached the right consistency, let it rest for between 30-60 minutes.

2. Take small amounts of dough and shape the doughnuts. Deep fry them in hot olive oil. When they are golden brown, place on kitchen roll and sprinkle with sugar and cinnamon whilst still hot.

ROSCOS DE MINUTO DE ALFARNATE

One minute Rosco doughnuts from Alfarnate

For when you have unexpected Christmas visitors, here is a recipe from Alfarnate in Málaga province to rustle up some festive doughnuts in a hurry.

Ingredients:

For one egg:

> 8 tablespoons of milk
> 8 tablespoons of sugar
> 6 tablespoons of olive oil
> 1 teaspoon of ground cinnamon
> 1 pinch of aniseed
> 1 glass of brandy
> 0.5 sachet of dried yeast
> Flour as required to make the dough

Preparation:

1. Beat the egg whites until stiff, and then add the yolks, sugar, milk, cinnamon, anise, oil and brandy.

2. Add in the flour and knead well until it becomes consistent dough.

3. Make doughnuts with a diameter of about 8 cm. Fry them in abundant oil. When they are fried, place them on some kitchen paper to drain and coat them with icing sugar.

ROSCOS DE NARANJA

Orange Doughnuts

The Rosco de Naranja (Orange Doughnut) is a traditional Christmas dish in Eastern Málaga. Locally, the recipe is known as the "recipe of ten", because for every kilo of flour, it takes ten oranges, ten tablespoons of oil and ten tablespoons of sugar. They are delicious!

Ingredients:

    1 kg flour
    10 oranges
    10 tablespoons olive oil
    10 tablespoons of sugar
    1 teaspoon cinnamon
    1 teaspoon aniseed
    1 teaspoon baking powder (bicarbonate)
    1 pinch of salt
    Sunflower oil for frying
    Cinnamon sugar for coating the doughnuts

Preparation:

1. Heat the olive oil. When the oil starts to smoke, add the aniseed and remove the pan from the heat.

2. Mix the flour, sugar, salt, cinnamon, the baking powder and the grated rind of one orange in a deep bowl.

3. Gradually stir in the olive oil with aniseed, and the orange juice and mix the dough until it becomes smooth. Leave to stand for 30 minutes.

4. Take small pieces of dough, roll them into little balls, flatten them slightly and make a hole in the middle with your finger.

5. Fry them in plenty of hot sunflower oil over a moderate heat. Dry on absorbent kitchen paper and coat them with the sugar and cinnamon mixture.

ROSCOS DE NARANJA DE PERIANA

Orange Doughnuts of Periana

Here is another recipe for Roscos de Naranja (Orange doughnuts), this time from Periana in Andalucía, using yeast to produce the dough.

Ingredients:

    2 Eggs
    10 tablespoons of oil
    10 tablespoons of orange juice
    10 tablespoons of sugar
    0.5 kg of Flour
    1 sachet of dried yeast
    1 tablespoon of ground cinnamon
    Grated lemon peel
    Olive oil

Preparation:

1. Beat the eggs in a bowl.

2. Add the sugar, oil, orange, cinnamon, grated lemon peel, flour and yeast.

3. Beat the ingredients together into a smooth mix.

4. When the dough thickens, oil your hands and manually knead the dough for about 10 minutes.

5. Make the fritters either round, like a doughnut, or straight, like a stick.

6. In the meantime, on a medium heat, warm up a pan of olive oil for frying.

7. Fry the doughnuts until they are golden brown, making sure not to let the oil get too hot.

8. When they are fried, place on some kitchen roll to drain and sprinkle each doughnut with sugar.

ROSCOS DE VINO DE MÁLAGA
Wine Doughnuts of Málaga

Ingredients:

    1 kg of butter or lard (at room temperature)
    1 cup of olive oil (toasted)
    1 glass of white wine
    400 g caster sugar
    15 g ground cinnamon (according to taste)
    20 ground cloves
    2 glasses of dry brandy
    3 kg flour
    Icing sugar (to coat the doughnuts)

Preparation:

1. Beat the butter. Gradually add the olive oil and the wine, stirring constantly.

2. Add the sugar, cinnamon, cloves, brandy and flour, stirring continuously to form a consistent dough.

3. Take small pieces of the dough and make them into doughnuts. Place them on an oven tray lined with baking paper.

4. Put the tray in the oven and bake at 180ºC for 15 minutes or until golden brown.

4. Remove the doughnuts from the oven and allow them to cool. Once cold, sprinkle them with some water and coat with icing sugar.

5. Finally, let them stand for a few minutes for the sugar to set, and then wrap them in kitchen paper to keep them moist until they are to be served.

ROQUITAS DE ALMENDRAS

Little Almond and Chocolate rocks

This is a little recipe that combines ingredients of the old and the new world. It wasn't so long ago that we could see chocolate coated almonds being made on the streets of Spain's towns and cities. Here is a slightly modernised version.

Ingredients:

    100 g raw or roasted almonds
    25 g candied orange
    150 g chocolate fondant
    0.5 tablespoon grated orange peel
    0.25 teaspoon ginger powder (a pinch)

Preparation:

1. Toast the raw almonds in a frying pan without fat, stirring constantly to prevent burning. Let them cool. Meanwhile, chop the candied orange into small pieces.

2. Chop up the chocolate and melt it in a double boiler (au bain marie), over a low heat, stirring as required. Remove it from the heat and add the orange peel and ginger. Add the almonds and candied orange and mix all ingredients together well.

3. Cover a shallow oven tray with baking paper and, with the help of two spoons, form small blobs of almonds and chocolate and drop them onto the paper.

4. Place the tray into the refrigerator until the chocolate is solid and the "little rocks" are easily peeled off the paper.

SOPA DE ALMENDRAS DE LAS DOS CASTILLAS
Almond Soup of the two Castillas

No, this is not a soup. Despite the name, it is in fact a dessert, and a very old one at that. It is a traditional Christmas Eve dessert from the old kingdom of Castilla (now Madrid, Castilla-La Mancha and Castilla y Léon), made with crushed almonds in cream or milk.

Prior to the 20th century the dish was made only with water and known as "leche de almendras" - almond milk, because during Christmas Eve religious obligations forbade the use of meat and milk. Traditionally, the dish is served in clay bowls and decorated with pine nuts.

Ingredients:

    0.5 litre of milk
    200 g chopped toasted almonds, ground in a mortar
    1 lemon rind
    1 stick of cinnamon
    100 g of pine nuts
    10 slices of baguette previously toasted
    Ground cinnamon
    200 g of sugar

Preparation:

1. Heat the milk in a fire-proof casserole dish with the lemon rind and the cinnamon stick. When it reaches boiling point, stir continuously for about 3 minutes. Remove the lemon and cinnamon stick.

2. In a separate bowl, put the bread, the pine nuts and the ground toasted almonds. Sprinkle with sugar and cinnamon and then add the milk and dissolve. Use a little more milk than is necessary, because when the soup cools, it will thicken.

3. When all is thoroughly mixed, remove from the heat.

4. Present the dish in a clay pot and decorate with chopped toasted almonds and some pine nuts.

SOPA DULCE DEL VALLE DEL JERTE DE EXTREMADURA

Sweet soup of the Jerte Valley of Extremadura

This is a typical Christmas dessert of the Jerte Valley in Cáceres province, in the region of Extremadura.

Ingredients:

    0.5 litre milk
    100 g shelled walnuts (or almonds)
    0.5 kg bread, sliced
    0.5 kg apples, diced
    300 g honey
    100 g peanuts
    Olive oil

Preparation:

1. Fry the bread slices and the chopped apples in some olive oil. Once fried and drained, put alternate layers of bread and apple in an ovenproof earthenware dish.

2. Preheat the oven to 250°C.

3. Mix the honey with the milk and add this to the bread and apple layers in the dish. Place the dish in the oven until the mixture is well cooked.

4. Once cooked, cover the top with the chopped walnuts (or almonds) and peanuts, place the dish back in the oven until the crust is golden brown.

5. Leave the dish to cool and serve.

TARTA DE SIDRA DE ASTURIAS
Cider Tart of Asturias

Ingredients:

    1 Genoese sponge
    2 Apples
    125 ml milk
    250 ml cider
    100 g of sweet apple preserve (see index for recipe)
    4 egg yolks
    250 g sugar
    4 sheets of gelatine
    500 ml whipped cream

Preparation:

1. Slice the apples and boil them in water with sugar (4 tbsp.) until soft. Put aside.

2. Boil the milk, add the cider, and when this mix starts to boil again, add the sweet apple preserve, the egg yolks beaten with the sugar (until it becomes whitish) and finally add the gelatine sheets.

3. Remove from the heat, allow the mixture to cool and then add the whipped cream.

4. Place the apple slices in the bottom of the cake tin in such a way that the first slices are half on the base and half up the side of the mould. Then add the creamy cider mix, being careful not to dislodge the slices of apple. Finally cover the cream with the Genoese sponge cake.

5. Put the tart in the freezer until set. Decorate it with some of the sweet apple preserve that has been blended.

6. Note: The cake tin should be lined with a circle of baking paper on the bottom and a strip of baking paper going around the side.

TARTA DE TURRÓN DE CANTABRIA
Nougat tart of Cantabria

This is a delicious dessert to enjoy at family gatherings during Christmas. It comes from Cantabria and Asturias and is typical of the many different tarts made with soft nougat.

Ingredients:

    300 g of soft nougat
    100 g of icing sugar
    1 litre of cream
    3 egg yolks and 3 egg whites
    Melting chocolate for the sauce

Preparation:

1. Whip the cream and add the egg yolks and the beaten egg whites, the sugar, and the melted nougat, so that the mixture takes on the consistency of a paste.

2. Fill some pudding moulds with this paste and put them in the freezer for 6 hours.

3. When frozen, remove them from the moulds and serve them with a hot chocolate sauce.

TARTA DE SANTIAGO

St. James' Cake of Santiago, Galicia

This delicious almond cake is named in honour of Santiago (St. James), the patron saint of Spain. It is said that his remains are buried in the city of Santiago de Compostela, Galicia. During the Middle-ages, the pilgrimage to Santiago was the most important pilgrimage of the Christian world. Today, many people still make the trip to Santiago; not just for religious reasons, but as a cultural, historical visit.

The cake's origin is not certain, but it may have been brought to Galicia by a pilgrim. Today, this cake is sold all over Santiago de Compostela and is popular with tourists and pilgrims alike. It is also a very popular Christmas sweet throughout Spain.

Ingredients (serves 8 approx):

>2.6 cups ground almonds
>0.75 cup flour
>1.25 cup sugar
>4 eggs
>8 tbsp butter at room temperature
>0.5 tsp baking powder
>0.5 cup water
>Grated zest of 1 lemon
>Icing sugar to decorate

Preparation:

1. Blanch the almonds and then, using a grinder or a food processor, grind them until fine and set aside.

2. Heat the oven to 180°C. Grease a round 20cm baking tin.

3. In a large mixing bowl, beat the eggs and sugar together. Add the butter, flour, baking powder and water and mix well (with an electric hand mixer).

4. Stir the almonds into the dough. Add the grated lemon rind and stir until thoroughly mixed.

5. Pour the cake mix into the cake tin. Bake in the oven on the middle shelf at 180°C for approximately 45-50 minutes. Check after 45 minutes. It is done if a toothpick inserted into the centre of the cake comes out clean.

6. The traditional way to decorate the cake is to sprinkle icing sugar on the top, with a cut-out of the sword of St. James or a cross in the middle. Place the template of the cross in the centre of the cake and dust the top with the sugar. A small flour sifter works well for this.

TRONCO DE NAVIDAD
Christmas Trunk

The Christmas Trunk is not originally Spanish at all, but French, and still known as the "Buche de Noel". It is thought to have originated with an innovative French pastry chef (in the late 1800s) who came up with the idea of replacing the real 'Yule' log (an ancient tradition of celebrating Christmas and the winter solstice by burning a wooden log in the hearth) with a cake that was log shaped. It is basically a large Swiss roll with a rich filling, completely coated in chocolate and made to resemble a log.

There are now many recipes for this throughout Europe, but Spain still manages to produce some of the richest and most sinful versions of this delicious rolled and filled cake. This recipe uses chestnut jam which is a particular favourite in southern Spain, but many other fillings can be substituted.

Ingredients (serves 4):

> 75 g flour
> 75 g sugar
> 3 eggs
> 1 jar of sweet chestnut jam
> 1 tablet of chocolate fondant (250 g)
> 100 ml cream
> 50 g butter
> Icing sugar

Preparation:

1. Whisk the eggs with the sugar until the mix has doubled in volume. Add the flour through a sieve and mix gently.

2. Pour the mixture into a baking tray lined with baking paper, greased and floured. Bake at 180°C for 8-10 minutes.

3. Turn the warm cake onto a clean, smooth, lightly floured, kitchen towel, remove and discard the baking paper and then roll up the cake with the towel. Leave to cool for 30 minutes before filling.

4. Fill the roll with chestnut jam and re-roll it.

5. Coat the "log" with a chocolate fondant, which is melted in a microwave or "au bain marie" together with the cream and butter.

6. Use a fork to create the appearance of a trunk in the melted chocolate, sprinkle icing sugar on it and decorate with a Christmas theme of your choice (holly, stars etc.).

TRUCHAS DE NAVIDAD DE LAS ISLAS CANARIAS
Almond and Sweet potato fritters of the Canary Islands

This is a delicious traditional Christmas recipe influenced by the strong connections between the Canary Islands and Spain's new conquests, using a mixture of ingredients from both "worlds" - almonds from the old world and sweet potato from the new world.

They are called "truchas" because of their shape which resembles a trout.

A variation of this recipe uses raisins (150 g soaked in orange blossom water) blended into the filling mixture. The "truchas" were traditionally deep fried in olive oil until browned, but they can also be baked and this makes them a little lighter.

Ingredients (makes 24 truchas):

Crust:

> 700 g puff pastry (ready made)
>
> Or

500 g white flour
2 heaped tsp sugar
Pinch of salt
Approximately 250 ml cold water
225 g butter

Filling:

> 1 kg white or orange sweet potato
> 2 star anise to boil with the potatoes
> 100 g sugar
> 1 egg yolk
> 100 g whole peeled almonds
> 0.5 tsp cinnamon
> 1 tsp anise liquor (to taste)
> Zest from 1 lemon
> Icing sugar for dusting

Preparation:

1. To make the pastry from scratch, place the flour, sugar and salt in a large mixing bowl. Cut the butter into tablespoon-size pieces and add to

the flour, cutting with a fork to mix. Sprinkle in a few tablespoons of the cold water and continue to mix with a fork. Add some more water and gently knead the mixture just enough so that it becomes a smooth dough, no longer sticking to your hands. If the dough is kneaded too long, it will become tough. Cover the dough in the bowl and place in the refrigerator while the filling is prepared.

2. Clean the sweet potatoes and place them whole and unpeeled in a pot. Cover them with water; add one or two star anis to flavour the potatoes. Bring to the boil and cook for approximately 20-30 minutes until soft. The potatoes are cooked when you can easily insert a fork into the thickest part of the potato. Drain and place them on a plate, allowing them to completely cool.

3. Grate the lemon zest onto a plate. Grind the almonds in a mortar or blender. Separate the yolk of one egg into a small bowl for later.

4. When the potatoes are cool enough to handle, remove the skin. It should rub off easily. Cut the potatoes into large chunks, place them in a mixing bowl and mash with a potato masher. Add the lemon zest, ground almonds, cinnamon and anise liquor. Stir together, add in the sugar and mix thoroughly.

5. Pre-heat the oven to 200°C whilst making the "truchas".

6. Lightly flour a smooth surface. Roll out the dough thinly and cut out circles of approximately 7 - 8 cm in diameter.

7. On each circle of dough, place a portion of sweet potato filling. Then fold the circles in half to form a semi-circle. Press the edges together with a fork to seal. Place each on baking paper in an oven tray.

8. Whisk the egg yolk and brush the top of each "trucha" with beaten egg yolk. Bake for approximately 15 minutes or until the "truchas" turn golden brown. Remove from the oven and let them cool for about 10 minutes.

9. Dust with icing sugar and serve warm. They can also be reheated to eat later.

TURRÓN DE ALICANTE
Hard Nougat of Alicante

The nougat of Alicante is often referred to as "hard nougat". The recipe is very old, and it is still made in pretty much the same way as it always was. The Nougat of Alicante has been in production for centuries and is believed to originate from original Arabic recipes.

There are several theories about the exact origins of nougat, but the one that seems most likely, according to food historians, suggests that nougat was created by the Arabs, who were trying to come up with a portable source of nutrients that would remain in good condition for long periods and was easy to transport by their armies, without the risk of intoxication or degradation.

Whatever the exact origin, the Turrón of Alicante today is considered to be a product of exceptional quality. It enjoys a D.O. (denomination of origin) status.

What follows is a basic recipe. It requires the use of some shallow wooden moulds to form the nougat, but you can improvise with metal cake tins.

Ingredients:

    350 g of honey
    200 g of sugar
    2 egg whites
    650 g of toasted almonds (chopped up)
    3 tablespoons of water
    4 drops of aniseed liquor
    1 pack of wafers

Preparation:

1. Whisk the egg whites until stiff.

2. Mix the water and sugar in a saucepan on low heat until obtaining a consistent syrup.

3. In another saucepan heat the honey. Once it is liquefied, add it to the syrup.

4. Remove from the heat and mix well with a wooden spoon and put the mix on the heat again until it turns into a caramel-like substance.

5. Add the chopped almonds, the anis liquor and the egg whites.

6. Stir with a spatula or wooden spoon until you have a consistent mixture.

7. Line the moulds with parchment paper and wafers. Pour in the mix.

8. Smooth the top of the mix with a spatula.

9. Put a wooden board on top of the mould with a weight. Leave the nougat to set for a few days.

TURRÓN BLANDO O DE JIJONA
Soft Nougat in the style of Turrón de Jijona

Turrón or Nougat is another example of how the production of almonds dominates Spanish and other European confectionary at Christmas time. Turrón has its roots in the Moorish period of Spain. It appears to have originated in the Andalucían Arab kingdoms prior to the Christian conquest of Spain. The Arab culinary tradition of the time included a similar dessert named "turun", so it seems that nougat or turrón production was introduced into the Arab Kingdoms of Al-Andaluz after they started cultivating almonds in the Caliphate of Cordoba some time after the 10th century AD.

There is also evidence of a similar confection, named cupedia or cupeto, produced in Ancient Rome and probably adopted by the Arab world as they colonised the remnants of the Roman Empire in the Levant. At any rate, Turrón or Torró has been known at least since the 15th century in the city of Jijona / Xixona in Alicante.

Spanish turrón may be roughly classified as:

- Hard (the Alicante variety): A compact block of whole almonds in a brittle mass of eggs, honey and sugar; 60% almonds.

- Soft (the Jijona variety): Similar, but the almonds are reduced to a paste. The addition of oil makes the mix more chewy and sticky; 64% almonds.

What follows is a recipe for the soft nougat or Turrón de Jijona, a very popular traditional Christmas sweet. This type of nougat, manufactured in Jijona in the Valencia region, is highly prized and carries a D.O. (designation of origin). It consists of a ground mass of honey, sugar and almonds.

Ingredients:

    300 g Toasted almonds
    200 g Honey
    200 g Sugar
    50 g Toasted Hazelnuts
    50 g Pine kernels
    1 teaspoon cinnamon

Preparation:

1. Peel and very finely chop the almonds, hazelnuts and pine kernels.

2. Put the honey with the sugar in a saucepan. Heat the mixture for a few minutes, stirring all the time.

3. When the sugar has completely dissolved, pour the mix over the nuts and combine well.

4. Pour the mixture into a wooden or aluminium mould. The mould should be low and rectangular.

4. Place a weight on top and let the mould stand for 4-5 days in the fridge, to create the shape and allow the mix to consolidate, after which the turrón is ready to eat.

Tip: The variety of almond most popular for this particular nougat is the Marcona almond which is a small round almond.

TURRÓN DE GOFIO CANARIO

Almond and Honey Turron of the Canaries

This sweet is only produced in Gran Canaria and is made with sugar, "gofio" (a flour made from roasted grains), almonds, honey, anise and lemon. In many ways it resembles nougat.

Ingredients:

    1 kg gofio (preferably mixed wheat & millet)
    1 kg Honey
    410 ml condensed milk
    250 g unsalted butter - softened to room temperature
    Grated zest of 1 lemon (or more, according to taste)
    300 g crushed toasted almonds.

Preparation:

1. Put the gofio in a bowl and add the honey, the condensed milk and the soft butter.

2. Finely grate the lemon rind and add it to the other ingredients in the bowl.

3. Crush the almonds with a mortar and add these to the mixture.

4. Mix until you get consistent, homogenous dough. It can be quite time-consuming and hard work to get a thoroughly consistent mixture!

5. After mixing, shape the mixture into cylindrical "loaves", wrap them separately in foil and store them in the fridge to set. The Turrón will last for up to 6 months in the fridge.

6. When ready to serve, remove a "loaf" from the fridge, slice what you need and return it to the fridge, because when it gets warm, it will soften.

7. Serve this dessert in small quantities - it is very rich.

TURRÓN DE YEMA

Egg Nougat

Egg Nougat is one of the richest and most traditional Christmas sweets in the Catalan cuisine. It was originally created to use the waste egg yolks and pieces of hard and soft nougat left over from other dishes. However, since then, it has developed into a very popular dish in its own right.

Ingredients (2 nougats):

    500 g of ground almonds
    400 g of sugar
    120 g of water
    6 egg yolks
    A pinch of salt
    1 lemon (grated rind)
    2 g cinnamon powder

Preparation:

1. Pour the water in a saucepan, add the sugar and heat slowly until it becomes syrup and takes on a bit of colour. (If you have a thermometer it should be 121°C.)

2. In a separate bowl, mix the ground almonds, the cinnamon, lemon peel, salt and egg yolks. When the syrup is ready, stir it slowly into this almond mixture. Mix well until it becomes a consistent thick paste.

3. Prepare one or more wooden nougat moulds (depending on the size of your moulds) with greaseproof paper for the bases.

4. Pour the egg nougat into the mould(s), cover with greaseproof paper and place a smooth weight on top covering the entire surface of the mould to make sure the top of the nougat becomes smooth and the nougat firm.

5. Let the nougat set for 24 hours and then remove the weight and the mould.

6. Finish off the egg nougat by sprinkling sugar on its surface and subsequently grilling it quickly in the oven.

7. Store the finished egg nougat wrapped in greaseproof paper to prevent it from drying out and hardening too quickly. You can also keep it in an air-tight container until it is ready to serve.

UVAS EN ANIS SECO

Grapes in dry Anis liquor

This is a simple but favourite treat for Christmas, often made in rural Andalucía. During the grape season, place fresh grapes (or raisins if there are no grapes) in a preserving jar and fill it up with dry Anis liquor and put it aside until Christmas. This produces a delicious anis flavoured grape which is a wonderful addition to a Christmas dessert.

Ingredients:

Grapes or raisins
Dry Anis Liquor
Apple
Cinnamon sticks

Preparation:

1. Wash the grapes or raisins. If using raisins, allow them to soak in water for a while until they swell up.

2. Fill a jar with the grapes or raisins. In layers add the slices of apple (not too thin) and some cinnamon stick.

3. Fill the jar with Anis liquor making sure to cover the fruit.

4. Close, and store in a dark place until Christmas.

5. Serve cold.

YEMAS DE SANTA TERESA DE ÁVILA
Yolks of Ávila

Yemas de Santa Teresa (Egg yolks of Saint Theresa of Ávila) originate in the province of Ávila in Castilla y León. These little sweets are well known across Spain and very popular at Christmas time.

They have a long history. Some food historians believe them to have originated in Andalucía in the middle ages and to be of Arab origin. Meanwhile others say that they came from the nuns of a monastery in Ávila, and became popular during the life of Saint Theresa of Ávila.

The truth is probably closer to the latter story, because mediaeval winemakers often used egg whites to help purify wine. They did not have any use for the yolks and so gave their egg yolks to the nuns, who traditionally prepared pastries and sweets to sell. The nuns then used the yolks to create the "yemas". They have been commercialised in Ávila since 1860, but are still made in many domestic kitchens to celebrate the feast day of St. Theresa, but also around other feast days such as Christmas.

Ingredients (6-8 balls):

> 75 ml water
> 100 g sugar
> Peel from 0.5 lemon
> 6 egg yolks
> 1 cup of icing sugar

Preparation:

1. Make a syrup by dissolving the sugar, whilst bringing the water to a boil. Add the lemon peel. Continue to simmer until the mixture is a thick syrup, stirring frequently to prevent burning. Remove from the heat, and remove the lemon peel from the syrup.

2. Lightly beat the egg yolks, using a whisk. Pour them into the sauce pan with the syrup and then put the pan on a very low heat and stir the mixture slowly and continuously for 3-4 minutes with a whisk, until the yolks begin to solidify. The mixture will start to pull away from the sides and bottom of the pan as it cooks. Remove from heat and spoon onto a plate. Allow to cool.

3. When the mixture is cool, sprinkle powdered sugar onto a surface. Form the "yemas" into a ball about the size of a walnut, coating then in sugar.

4. Place the "yemas" on a plate and chill in the refrigerator. Serve on a plate, or in individual paper cake cups.

---oOo---

2.5 Breads and Tortillas

CORONA DE QUESOS Y NUECES
Crown of Cheese and Walnut bread

The origin of this savoury bread isn't quite clear, but variations of this recipe seem to be related to the traditional "Rosco del Reyes", which is eaten on the "Día de los Reyes", the Feast of Epiphany on January 6th, but in this case the Rosco is savoury rather than sweet.

There are many variations on the Rosco theme that are traditional to Christmas, with a wide range of flavours. This one is a particularly rich cheesy bread. You can use some discretion in the type and amount of cheese you use. A strong cheese which bakes well may be the best to choose.

Ingredients:

>100 ml milk
>1 egg
>1 teaspoon sugar
>0.5 teaspoon salt
>300 g bread flour
>40 g butter
>12 g fresh yeast or 1 packet of dried yeast
>200 g cream cheese
>2 tablespoons milk
>50 g ground walnuts
>75 g blue cheese or similar strong cheese
>100 g chopped walnuts

Preparation:

1. Dissolve the yeast in 50 ml of lukewarm milk. Mix in 50 g of flour and let it stand until it starts to ferment.

2. Mix the egg with the milk, salt and sugar. Add the flour and knead into a dough. Add the butter and knead again before adding the yeast mix to the dough. Knead the dough thoroughly, place it in a bowl, and allow it to rise until it has doubled in volume.

3. In the meantime, prepare the cheese mixture. Thoroughly mix the ground walnuts with the cream cheese and the 2 tablespoons milk. Put aside.

4. Crumble the chopped walnuts and the blue cheese together and set aside.

5. When the dough has risen, roll it out on a smooth, floured surface into a rectangle of about 30 x 35cm.

6. Spread the cream cheese almost to the edges of the dough and then scatter the crumbled walnuts and (blue) cheese mix on top of this.

7. Subsequently, roll the cheese into the dough and extend it into a roll that should be about 50 cm long.

8. Now we want to plat the dough into the "crown", so use a knife to make a cut all the way along the length of the dough roll, but leave one end uncut.

9. Turn the parts in which the filling is visible upwards. Plat the two parts of the dough until you reach the end.

10. When it is all platted, join the two ends and form a ring. Leave the dough to rise again.

11. When the dough has risen, place the "crown" into a preheated oven and bake for 25 minutes at 200°C in an oven tray with baking paper.

12. When baked, remove from the oven and allow to cool on a rack. Serve.

FILLOAS DE GALICIA
Galician Crepes

Filloas de Galician is Galicia's own answer to the crêpe. They have an infinite number of fillings sweet or savoury and are always welcome at any table. Traditionally they were baked on very hot smooth granite rocks and are believed to have a Celtic origin. They are normally eaten at Carnival but also at other religious festivals such as Christmas time. They are always popular!

Ingredients (serves 4):

- 6 eggs
- 0.5 kg of flour
- 1 litre of milk
- 1 litre of chicken stock
- 1 piece of lard or salty butter

Preparation

1. Beat the eggs with the milk and stock in a large bowl, adding a pinch of salt and gradually adding the flour until it is well mixed. Allow the mixture to rest.

2. Grease a non-stick frying pan with some lard or butter.

3. Put into the frying pan on the heat and pour in some batter to cover the bottom of the pan.

4. When the filloa has solidified and browned a little, turn it over to brown the other side.

5. Repeat until there is no more mixture.

6. There are many delicious fillings for filloas including the following: Apple compote with cinnamon, honey, chestnut purée, quince jam or chocolate (there are more). In some areas they are also eaten with ham or cheese or as a plain accompaniment to a stew.

TORRIJA DE CANTABRIA
Dipped toast of Cantabria

Torrijas or dipped toast is very similar to so-called "French toast", but has reached a new level of variation in Spain. Traditionally, it was a way of using up old bread and eaten by the workers as a cheap but tasty high-protein and energy food. The torrija appears to have been first mentioned in the fifteenth century by Juan del Encina with his list of ingredients as "honey and many eggs to make French toast ", and it is described as a dish suitable for "recovery in labour". The first recipes date back to the "Book of Cozina" by Domingo Hernandez de Maceras in 1607 and "Art Cozina by Francisco Martinez Motiño in 1611. In the early twentieth century, torrijas were very common in the taverns of Madrid and served with glasses of wine.

Over the centuries, torrijas became synonymous with Easter in most of Spain, when they are eaten as part of the tradition of abstinence from meat during Lent and on other fast days. However, it is so popular, that many bakeries routinely make and sell torrijas all year round and even keep stale bread to sell to customers wanting to make their own. Only in Cantabria have they also become a traditional Christmas sweet. Here we present the Cantabrian torrija, which is really a richer (and sometimes alcoholic) version of the normal torrija. Any kind of stale bread may be use to make torrijas, but in Spain most people use slices of baguette.

Ingredients:

    1 baguette (from yesterday)
    0.5 litre of milk
    250 g Sugar (or honey)
    1 cinnamon stick
    Cinnamon powder and icing sugar mix
    Grated skin from half an orange
    Eggs
    Olive oil and butter for frying

Preparation:

1. Boil the milk with the cinnamon stick, the sugar (or honey) and the orange skin for a few minutes until completely mixed.

2. Slice the baguette, but not too thinly. Beat a couple of eggs in a bowl.

3. Dip the slices of bread in the milk and sugar mixture, drain them and then coat them in the beaten egg.

4. In a frying pan, heat a little butter and the olive oil.

5. Fry the dipped slices of bread in the hot oil until golden brown.

6. Sometimes a little brandy is dribbled onto the torrijas to prepare them for serving. Coat them lightly with a mixture of cinnamon powder and icing sugar.

TORTILLAS IN GENERAL

The world of tortillas is infinite. The culinary history of the Tortilla goes back a very long time. The Romans called them "ovorum cake", in Mexico they have made them for thousands of years as have the Native American tribes in the US.

The simplest tortilla is a fried, whisked egg (omelette), but up from that they can reach a level of extraordinary sophistication. They can be sweet or savoury, and the range of ingredients includes vegetables, fruits, meat, poultry and fish. They can be made with many kinds of flour. They may be thin, soft, brittle, thick, dry or oily.

Types of Tortillas and how to make them: Here are just a few suggestions for types of tortilla: Mushroom, Asparagus, Pepper, Seafood, Spinach, Fresh herbs, Chorizo. Later we will provide recipes for these.

Tortillas are often served for breakfast or as a snack or tapa during the Christmas holidays. They are popular, easy to make and can be really delicious as well as filling and fairly healthy.

TORTILLA DE PAN RALLADO
Breadcrumb Tortilla

Here is one recipe that shows once again the ingenuity and talent of rural cooks of Andalucía who use the simplest ingredients they have on hand, and are able to prepare delicious dishes from almost nothing.

Ingredients:

    8 eggs
    1 clove of garlic
    50 g breadcrumbs
    Parsley
    Salt

Preparation:

1. Beat the egg whites together first and then add the egg yolks. Add garlic, very finely chopped parsley, and salt.

2. Add the breadcrumbs to the mix, stirring well, till the batter has the right consistency.

3. Bake the tortilla over a low heat, to make sure that it is cooked inside. Shape into a circular shaped "cake".

TORTILLA PIMIENTOS
Pepper Tortilla

Ingredients (serves 4):

    1 red pepper
    1 green pepper
    2 beef tomatoes
    3 slices of boiled ham (optional)
    5 spring onions
    5 cloves of garlic
    4 tablespoons olive oil
    Freshly ground black pepper
    Salt
    4 chopped olives
    4 eggs

Preparation:

Wash the peppers, cut them in half and remove the seeds. Put them on a baking tray and bake them in a pre-heated oven at 250ºC. for about 20 minutes. Remove the tray from the oven; cover the peppers with a damp cloth and leave to cool. Peel the peppers and cut them into thin strips.

Skin the tomatoes, de-seed them and chop them into small pieces. Slice up the ham. Wash the spring onions and cut them into small rings. Peel the garlic and crush.

Heat half the olive oil in a frying pan. Lightly fry the ham, onions and garlic. Add peppers and tomatoes. Season with salt, pepper and olives, and simmer until all liquid is absorbed. Put in a bowl and leave aside.

Put the rest of the oil in the same frying pan and heat up. Whisk the eggs, season with salt and pepper, and pour into the pan. Let them solidify on a low heat for 3-4 minutes.

Spread the vegetable mixture over the eggs in the pan, cover and cook for a further 8-10 minutes. Serve.

TORTILLA DE ESPÁRRAGOS TRIGUEROS
Green asparagus tortilla

Ingredients (serves 4):

    4 spears of asparagus
    3 tablespoons olive oil
    3 tablespoons cream
    4 eggs
    Freshly ground white pepper
    Salt

Preparation:

Wash the asparagus and chop them into small pieces. Set aside the asparagus tips, and boil the bottom halves of the stems in salty water for 10 minutes. Chill immediately in iced water.

Heat 2 tablespoons of olive oil in a pan and fry all the asparagus pieces for about 3 minutes. Remove and put aside.

Whisk the eggs with the cream in a bowl.

Heat the remaining oil in the pan and pour in the egg mixture. Let the mix solidify slightly and arrange the asparagus on top.

Shake the pan to ensure that the asparagus are well-covered with the egg mixture.

Season with salt and pepper, serve hot.

---oOo---

2.6 Christmas drinks

2.6.1 Wine

Preamble: Wine plays an enormously important role in the culinary life of Spain. Few main meals would be taken without some wine to accompany them. We don't have the space to describe all the wines of Spain here, but we can give you an idea about how to find a good wine and how to serve it properly. These days, most wines in Spain are of very good quality. Spain has become a serious international player as a producer of the world's finest wines. The days when Spain was known only for Sherry and Muscatel are long gone. In many ways, Spain is eclipsing France as a producer of high quality wines.

Let us take a look at some of the complexities in choosing a Spanish wine.

2.6.1.1 The Wine Regions of Spain - Classifications

We are not going to attempt a complete evaluation of the wines of Spain, but rather just give the reader an appreciation of the types and diversity of Spanish wines and where they come from. The following list shows the regions which have official Denominación de Origen (D.O.). There are 66 wine regions with this status in Spain.

Aside form the D.O. wine regions, there are many hundreds of fine wines which are not within a D.O. or which choose not to register as a wine with a D.O. Small vineyards often choose not to register. Whilst the D.O. system does provide some guarantee of origin and consistent quality, it doesn't say anything about the palatability of a wine, and wines without D.O. can be superior to D.O. wines and vice versa.

A lower level of classification is the VCIG. : "Vino de Calidad con Indicación Geográfica". This is a starter classification for wine regions climbing the quality ladder. There are two wine regions with this status.

The highest level of classification is the VP. Class, meaning "Vino de Pago": these wine producers aspire to the very highest standards with extremely strict geographical criteria, centring on individual single-estates with an international reputation. There are currently twelve estates with this status: eight in Castilla-La Mancha and three in Navarra and one in Valencia. The number is growing rapidly.

2.6.1.2 Wines - Denominations of Origin in Spain:

Here is the full list of the main D.O's in each region and the names of the wines from these D.O's. It includes the V.P. grade estates.

Autonomous Region	Dominiaciónes de Origen (DO)
Andalucía	Condado de Huelva Jerez-Xeres-Sherry Málaga Manzanilla Sanlúcar de Barrameda Montilla-Moriles Sierras de Málaga
Aragón	Calatayud Campo de Borja Cariñena Somontano Cava
Castilla y León	Arlanza Arribes Bierzo Cigales Ribera del Duero Rueda Tierra de León Tierra del Vino de Zamora Toro Cava (1 producer in Aranda de Duero)

Autonomous Region	Dominiaciónes de Origen (DO)
Castilla-La Mancha	Almansa Campo de La Guardia (VP) Dehesa del Carrizal (VP) Dominio de Valdepusa (VP) Finca Élez (VP) Guijoso (VP) Pago Casa Del Blanco (VP) Pago Calzadilla (VP) Jumilla La Mancha Manchuela Méntrida Mondéjar Pago Florentino (VP) Ribera del Júcar Uclés Valdepeñas
Cataluña	Alella Catalunya Conca de Barberà Costers del Segre Empordà Montsant DO Penedès Pla de Bages Priorat (DOCa) Tarragona Terra Alta Cava
Comunidad de Madrid	Vinos de Madrid
Comunidad Valenciana	Alicante Utiel-Requena ((includes a VP) Valencia Cava

Autonomous Region	Dominiaciónes de Origen (DO)
Extremadura	Ribera del Guadiana Cava
Galicia	Monterrei Rías Baixas Ribeira Sacra Ribeiro Valdeorras
Las Islas Baleares	Binissalem-Mallorca Plà i Llevant
Las Islas Canarias	Abona El Hierro Gran Canaria La Gomera La Palma Lanzarote Tacoronte-Acentejo Valle de Güímar Valle de la Orotava Ycoden-Daute-Isora
Comunidad Foral de Navarra	Navarra Señorío de Arínzano (VP) Prado de Irache (VP) Otazu (VP) Rioja Cava
País Vasco	Txacolí de Bizcaia Txacolí de Getaria Txacolí de Álava Rioja (Alavesa) Cava
Murcia	Alicante Bullas Jumilla Yecla

2.6.1.3 Wines serving recommendations for Spanish wines:

Here we suggest the serving temperatures for Spanish wines:

Young white wines and sherries:	7 to 10° C
Sweet white wines:	6 to 8° C
Aged white wines:	10 to 12° C
Sparkling wines:	6 to 8° C
Rosé wines:	10 to 12° C
Young red wines:	12 to 15° C
Aged red wines:	17 to 18° C

2.6.1.4 Wine Ageing: Reservas, Crianzas etc.

The three most common aging designations on Spanish wine labels are Crianza, Reserva and Gran Reserva.

Crianza: red wines are aged for 2 years with at least 6 months in oak. Crianza whites and rosés must be aged for at least 1 year with at least 6 months in oak.

Reserva: red wines are aged for at least 3 years with at least 1 year in oak. Reserva whites and rosés must be aged for at least 2 years with at least 6 months in oak.

Gran Reserva: wines typically appear in above average vintages with the red wines requiring at least 5 years aging, 18 months of which in oak and a minimum of 36 months in the bottle. Gran Reserva whites and rosés must be aged for at least 4 years with at least 6 months in oak.

2.6.2 Other Christmas drinks:

On the following pages we will describe just a few traditional Christmas drinks from around the country. There are many.

LICOR CAFÉ GALLEGO
Liqueur coffee of Galicia

Ingredients (for 1 litre of liqueur):

    2 litres of Galician aguardiente de bagazo
    320 g of coffee beans
    2 sticks of cinnamon
    2 pieces of star anise
    Juice of half of an orange
    1 lemon
    1 kg of white sugar
    6 ounces of black chocolate
    200 ml water

Preparation:

1. Make a syrup by boiling the water and the sugar for about 10 minutes in a saucepan over a medium heat. Keep stirring to prevent sticking. Put aside when finished.

2. Grind the coffee beans.

3. Take a large container (such as a water bottle) and fill it with the aguardiente, the syrup, the coffee, star anise, cinnamon sticks, the juice of half an orange and the rind of 1 lemon. Break the black chocolate into pieces and add these to the mixture.

4. Leave the mixture to stand for 10 days in a cool, dark place. Every day, shake the container so that the ingredients are well mixed.

5. On the tenth day strain the liquor using 2 filters. For the first filtration use a fine wire sieve. For the second filtration use a fabric strainer to prevent fine debris from entering the coffee liqueur.

6. Put the liquor into a bottle and seal tightly.

7. In three months the coffee liquor is ready to drink, but it does improve with time so do not be afraid to leave it for a year or more. It will only get better.

8. Serve the liquor very cold, if possible directly from the freezer.

PONCHE DE NAVIDAD DE CAFÉ
Christmas Coffee Punch

Ingredients (serves 8-10):

    0.5 litre of coffee
    0.5 kg of sugar
    0.5 litre dry anise liquor
    1 litre of mineral water
    Lemon rind
    1 tablespoon aniseed

Preparation:

1. Put the water, lemon rind and aniseed in a saucepan and bring to the boil. Add the sugar, the anise liquor and the coffee.

2. Remove the mixture from the heat and mix well.

3. This punch is served with homemade Christmas fritters like borrachuelos or any of the Christmas doughnuts (roscos) on Christmas morning.

PONCHE DE MANZANA Y GRANADAS
Apple and Pomegranate Punch

Here is a non-alcoholic punch made with pomegranates and orange juice. Pomegranates are very common in Spain in the winter and this is a fresh, colourful, festive punch.

Ingredients (3 small glasses):

    2 Pomegranates
    1 cup of apple juice
    Half a cinnamon stick
    1 teaspoon of ginger
    2 cups of water
    Juice of 1 orange

Preparation:

1. Cut the pomegranate in half and squeeze the juice from it like you do with an orange.

2. Strain the juice and put it in a small saucepan. Bring to the boil on a moderate heat along with the water, the apple juice, the ginger and the cinnamon.

3. Leave to boil for about 5 minutes, reduce the heat and simmer for about 15 minutes more. (Remove any foam that appears on the surface, especially at the beginning.)

4. Finally, remove from the heat, strain the juice and mix in the orange juice.

5. Serve hot.

RESOLÍ DE MÁLAGA
Spicy Spirit drink of Málaga

In Andalucía and in Castilla-La Mancha, this is a traditional Christmas accompaniment to the many sweet biscuits, mantecados, or roscos of the festive kitchen. But at 18% alcohol, this is only for the adults though! It is a drink very typical of the city of Cuenca in La Mancha and in the tiny village of Alfarnate in Málaga province - where it has been made at Christmas time since well before living memory.

Resolí is a liqueur based on coffee and spices, but apparently the drink is of Arabic origin and developed from a Moorish spiced digestive drink. The modern version contains around 15 - 18% alcohol and the ingredients vary, but generally it consists of dry anise liquor or brandy, coffee, cinnamon, orange and lemon peel, sugar and cloves, diluted with water.

Resolí is a drink with a very distinctive flavour and it is usually taken by itself or with ice after meals and often accompanied by sweets like gingerbread or any of the other many Christmas sweets. It is also commonly drunk at Easter time. Here is a recipe from Alfarnate, where every house makes its own.

Ingredients:

    1 litre of dry brandy
    0.25 kg of ground coffee
    4 cinnamon sticks
    12 whole cloves
    1.5 litre of water
    Half a nutmeg
    1.5 kg of sugar

Preparation:

1. Mix all the ingredients in a container.

2. Allow to marinate for a week.

3. Occasionally stir the liquid.

4. After that week, add a litre and a half of water.

5. Mix and then allow it to settle for one day.

6. Strain the mix through a fine sieve and then add a kilo, or a kilo and a half of sugar. Stir to dissolve and bottle.

7. It is ready to drink immediately.

---oOo---

2.7 Seasonal Tapas, Canapés and Ibéricos

2.7.1 Introduction to Tapas: There are a lot of stories about how tapas came into existence and we won't speculate here on which of these myths are actually true. Suffice it to say that tapas have long been an important part in the Spanish culinary day, either as an evening snack with a drink, or a pre-meal aperitif at any time.

There are many hundreds of tapas in existence and every region in Spain has its own. Traditionally, tapas were just given to a customer with a drink. These days bars often charge for them, but offer you a menu of tapas to choose from. However, in many country bars it often happens that a customer will receive a tapa with a drink without asking, thus maintaining this old tradition of generous hospitality.

Here we have assembled some tapas that we know are popular during the Christmas season, but our list is by no means exhaustive. Many recipes for main course and starters are also often served as tapas in smaller portions.

So how is a canapé different from tapas? Well, in fact it isn't actually different, except linguistically and socially. A canapé is a small quantity of food which is served as an aperitif or hors d'œuvre in exactly the same way as a tapa is served with a drink, usually preceding a meal. The only real difference is that a canapé sounds somewhat more refined than tapa. For the rest the differences are an illusion. Tapas can be any kind of small dish served with any kind of drink at almost any time of day. The same is true of a canapé.

2.7.2 The Ibéricos: During important fiestas like Christmas and New Year, and at other special events, the one food which is always in demand are the famous and delicious Ibérico hams and their associated Ibérico products, like chorizos.

So what is Ibérico ham and why is it so sought after and important?

Definition: "Jamón Ibérico" or Iberian ham is also called "pata negra" and "carna negra" - black hoof. It is a type of cured ham produced almost exclusively in Spain According to the E.U. Denominación de Origen (D.O.) rules for Jamón Ibérico, it may be made from black Iberian pigs or cross-bred pigs as long as they are at least 75% Ibérico. Jamón Ibérico is routinely voted the best ham in the world by the industry in international competitions.

The black Iberian pig lives primarily in the south and southwestern parts of Spain, including the provinces of Salamanca, Ciudad Real, Cáceres, Badajoz, Seville, Córdoba (DO Los Pedroches) and Huelva (DO Jabugo - one of the most famous).

Husbandry: Immediately after weaning, the piglets are fattened on barley and maize for several weeks. The pigs are then allowed to roam in the "dehesa" - which is a mixture of pasture and oak woodland, to feed naturally on grass, herbs, acorns, and roots. When the slaughtering time approaches, the diet of the pigs is limited to olives or acorns for the best quality jamón ibérico, or it may be a mix of acorns and commercial feed for lesser qualities.

Processing: The hams produced from the slaughtered pigs are salted and left to begin drying for two weeks, after which they are rinsed and left to dry for another four to six weeks. The curing process then takes at least twelve months, although some producers cure their jamónes ibéricos for up to 48 months.

Origins and Quality: In particular, the ibérico hams from the towns of Guijuelo in the province of Salamanca and Jabugo in the province of Huelva are known for their excellent quality and both have their own Denominación de Origen (D.O.). Almost the entire town of Jabugo is devoted to the production of Jamón Ibérico; the town's main square is called La plaza Del Jamón (Ham Square).

The hams are labelled according to the pigs' diet, with an acorn diet being the most desirable:

> **- Jamón Ibérico de bellotas:** The finest is called jamón ibérico de bellota (acorn). This ham is from free-range pigs that roam oak forests (called dehesas) along the border between Spain and Portugal, and eat only acorns during the last months of their lives. It is also known as jamón ibérico de Montanera. The exercise and diet have a significant impact on the flavour of the meat; the ham is cured for 36 months.

> **- Jamón Ibérico de recebo:** The next grade is called jamón ibérico de recebo. This ham is from pigs that are pastured and fed a combination of acorns and grain.

> **- Jamón ibérico de cebo:** The third type is called jamón ibérico de cebo, or simply, jamón ibérico. This ham is from pigs that are fed only grain. The ham is cured for 24 months.

Additionally, the word puro (pure, referring to the breed) can be added to the previous qualities when both the father and mother of the slaughtered animal are of pure breed and duly registered on the pedigree books held by official breeders.

The term "pata negra" is also used to refer to jamón ibérico in general, and may refer to any one of the above three types. The term refers to the colour of the pigs' nails, which are white in most traditional pork (Sus domesticus) breeds, but black for the Black Iberian breed. While as a general rule, a black nail should indicate an Ibérico ham, there are cases of counterfeits.

Jamónes de bellota are prized both for their smooth texture and rich, savoury taste. A good ibérico ham has regular flecks of intramuscular fat (marbling). Because of the pig's diet of acorns, much of the fat is oleic acid, a monounsaturated fatty acid that has been shown to lower LDL cholesterol and raise HDL cholesterol.

The fat content is relatively high compared to jamón serrano, thus giving it a very rich taste.

Jamón ibérico is eaten in very thin slices.

Jamón ibérico, which only accounts for about 8% of Spain's cured-ham production, is very expensive and not widely available abroad.

Buying Jamón Iberíco: The front legs of an Ibérico pig are sold as "paletilla". These are somewhat cheaper than the rear legs of the animal which are the true hams - "jamón". There is a significant difference in price between the two and a "paletilla" is quite a bit cheaper than a "jamón".

Preparation and storage: In Spain it is common to see a whole ham resting on a stand in the kitchen, ready for anyone to cut a thin slice for a snack. A whole jamón can easily be stored in your kitchen and used daily for tapas, sandwiches, or in recipes.

Storing a Ham: Store the whole jamón in a cool, dry and ventilated place either resting in a holder (jamonero) or hung by a rope. To preserve the freshness, moisture and flavour of your ham as it is consumed, always cover the sliced area with a moistened cloth or with a piece of the removed fat layer after slicing. If the meat is exposed to the air for some time, discard the first slice of the exposed area, as it will be dry and tough.

If you are using boneless jamón, it needs to be stored in the refrigerator. Boneless hams can be divided into pieces. Serve the jamón at room temperature.

Slicing Jamón Ibérico: Remove the layer of fat from the top and the sides until the meat is exposed. Trim the fat as you slice. Cut small, very thin slices, including some of the marbled fat. Slice downwards with your free hand behind the knife. If you plan to consume the entire ham in a day or two, you can remove the skin and fat completely. If not, it is better only to remove the skin and outer fat layer from the area to be sliced that day. To enjoy the flavour and texture of a fine jamón, slice the ham with a long sharp knife in the following order: first the rump half, then the rump end and lastly the shank.

The meat nearest the bone is difficult to slice well, and can be cut into small chunks for use in soups and stews. The ham bone itself is also excellent for flavouring broths, soups and stews, and may be cut and frozen for later use.

How to Serve Jamón Ibérico: Ibérico ham should be consumed at room temperature when it will have a lustrous appearance. When it is too cold, the fat will appear opaque. Any ham that is cut should be consumed immediately, or covered with a clean moistened cloth, to avoid prolonged exposure of the ham to air.

Generally speaking, the ham should be cut by hand, not using an electric knife or slicer. The heat of an electric knife / slicer damages the texture and taste of the meat. If you buy pre-packed sliced ibérico ham, be sure to check if has been manually sliced or not.

In addition, each time you slice the ham, you should protect the cut area with a cloth moistened with olive oil, or with a piece of the trimmed skin and fat layer, so that the cut area remains fresh. To further protect the ham, you may cover it with a clean cloth.

The Appearance of Jamón: You may notice natural molds and bits of salt on the surface of the ham - these occur naturally in the curing and maturation process. In fact, mold is an indication of a properly aged ham. Simply wipe clean with vegetable oil and a cloth.

> Mold: A thin layer of mold may appear on whole hams. This penicillin-like mold is completely harmless. It can be removed with a clean, damp cloth, with a cloth and oil, or a vegetable brush.

Small white spots or chalky granules may form during the curing process. They are amino acids found in aged meat and cheese products and are perfectly safe to eat.

Iridescent sheen: This effect can be seen on the cut surface of the ham and in certain parts of the meat. The colouring sometimes has a metallic appearance. It is insignificant as far as the quality of the ham is concerned.

Salt: Sometimes salt may form on the surface of the ham in dry conditions. This inorganic salt does not affect the flavour of jamón and can be brushed or wiped away.

White film: This may be seen on the cut surface of whole or boneless hams. The film is mostly comprised of amino acids and salt precipitate and is perfectly safe. We recommend that you simply discard the discoloured slice.

Fat: Whole hams tend to be rather fatty, which protects the meat and helps it keep longer.

Other Ibérico products: Apart from the Ibérico hams, there are of course other Ibérico products of similar quality. These include various chorizos and blood sausages. Similar rules for the production of these products are contained in the Denomination of Origin and these are much sought after products.

Recipes for Jamón Ibérico: Normally Jamón Ibérico is served in very thin slices either by itself or on very thin and bland slices of white bread. Serving anything together with a good Ibérico ham would be considered heresy.

2.7.3 The Tapas recipes: Tapas are something of a moveable feast and recipes come and go in and out of fashion. Here we present a small collection of festive tapas recipes:

ALCACHOFAS CON ALMEJAS DE NAVARRA
Artichokes with clams of Navarra

Artichokes are a popular vegetable in Spain, especially fresh. They are often served sautéed with ham or stuffed with a white sauce with ham or another meat. They are sometimes served cold and combine well with anchovies and piquillo peppers, or with salmon and capers, or fish in olive oil. Here is a typical recipe from Navarra for a dish often served as tapas on Nochebuena.

Ingredients (serves 4):

> 20 artichoke hearts (fresh or from a jar)
> 2 tablespoons olive oil
> 24 clams (cleaned)
> 1 cup vegetable or fish stock
> 2 finely chopped cloves of garlic
> 1 tablespoon flour
> 2 tablespoons dry, white wine

Preparation:

1. Drain the artichoke hearts.

2. Brown the garlic cloves in hot oil in a deep frying pan or an earthenware dish.

3. Add the flour then mix in the white wine and the stock.

4. Add the clams and cook until they open.

5. Then add the artichoke hearts and cook for a few minutes before serving.

BERENJENAS CON MIEL DE CAÑA
Aubergine with molasses

The preparation of aubergines cut into thin slices and decorated with some drops of thick, sweet molasses has become a very popular tapas dish in recent years. It is often served as a tapa, but can also be part of a main course or even a sweet. It is especially favoured on Christmas Eve, because it contains no meat and therefore conforms with the traditional "keeping of the vigil" of Nochebuena.

Ingredients (serves 4):

    2 large aubergines
    1 bottle of beer
    Flour
    1 egg white
    Yeast (the tip of a teaspoon)
    Molasses (to taste)
    Olive oil
    Salt (to taste)

Preparation:

1. Make a batter in a bowl by whisking an egg white until stiff and then stir in the flour, salt and yeast. Then gradually pour in the beer, stirring continuously,, until obtaining a quite thick batter mix (it should be like a thick soup and should not have any lumps).

2. Wash the aubergines, cut them into slices of about 1 centimetre thick and then cut these in half, so you have a lot of semi-circles of aubergine.

3. The half slices of aubergine are dipped into the batter and then fried in a pan with plenty of very hot oil (or, to make them even crispier, in a deep fat fryer).

4. Once browned, take them out and let them drain on a paper towel. Serve hot with a little dribble of molasses poured over them.

BOQUERONES EN VINAGRE

Anchovies marinated in Vinegar

A popular tapa before dinner on the evening of Nochebuena:

Ingredients (12 tapa servings):

      0.5 kg of fresh, whole anchovies
      1 to 2 cups of white wine vinegar
      2 tablespoons of salt
      3 tablespoons of olive oil
      3 cloves of garlic, coarsely chopped
      2 tablespoons of chopped parsley
      Shredded lettuce, to garnish
      Half a lemon, to garnish
      Chopped spring onion, to garnish (optional)
      Bread, to serve

Preparation:

1. Clean and fillet the anchovies.

2. Rinse the fillets in water and place them in iced water for 30 minutes to firm them.

3. Place the anchovies, skin-side down, in a single layer in a non-reactive container (glass or ceramic). Pour over the vinegar -enough to cover the fish- and the salt.

4. Cover and refrigerate for at least 6 hours or up to 24 hours. The fillets will turn white and opaque.

5. Before serving, drain off all the vinegar marinade and rinse the anchovies in cold water.

6. Drain well and pat dry. Arrange them skin-side down, like spokes of a wheel, on a serving dish. Sprinkle with oil, garlic and parsley.

7. Garnish the dish with lettuce, place the half lemon in the centre, and a little chopped spring onion. Serve with bread.

BROCHETAS DE GAMBAS Y BACON

Prawn and Bacon Brochettes

This is a very popular and delicious tapa often served on special occasions throughout Spain. It is especially popular in the Basque country. It is perfect for a Christmas reception and very suitable to be served with a chilled white wine.

Ingredients:

    24 medium-large fresh headless prawns, peeled
    150 g thinly sliced bacon (or jamón)
    Ground black pepper
    2 lemons, quartered
    1 tablespoon olive oil

Preparation:

1. Cut the bacon (or jamón) into pieces large enough to wrap easily around the prawns.

2. Place the wrapped prawns on a board and skewer them through the fattest part and the tail, making sure the bacon is firmly fixed. Season generously and drizzle with the olive oil.

3. On a high heat grill or barbecue the prawn and bacon brochettes for 2-3 minutes on each side, so the bacon becomes crisp.

4. An alternative method is to roast these in a hot oven (220°C) on an oiled baking tray for 8-10 minutes. Squeeze with the juice of the lemon and serve immediately.

CHAMPIÑONES AL AJILLO
Garlic Mushrooms

This is a delicious tapa that is found in many parts of Spain and there are many variations, some using wild mushrooms. This simple variant is a favourite as a winter and Christmas tapa in the south of Spain where wild mushrooms are readily found. But it can also be made with button or horse mushrooms from the supermarket.

Ingredients (serves 4):

>2 tablespoons chopped parsley
>0.5 teaspoon dried red chilli chopped
>4 cups mushrooms cut in quarters
>6 cloves garlic, finely chopped
>2 tablespoons lemon juice
>0.5 cup olive oil
>3 tablespoons dry sherry
>0.25 teaspoon paprika powder
>Salt and pepper, to taste

Preparation:

1. Heat the olive oil in a frying pan and sauté the mushrooms over a high heat for about 2 minutes, stirring constantly.

2. Lower the heat and add the garlic, sherry, lemon juice, dried chilli, paprika powder, salt and pepper.

3. Cook for about 5 minutes or until the garlic and mushrooms are softened.

4. Remove from the heat, sprinkle with chopped parsley, and serve on small earthenware platters. This goes very well with a chilled Manzanilla wine.

GAMBAS A LA PLANCHA

Grilled shrimp

Grilled shrimp with a chilled Fino sherry is a popular tapas especially in coastal areas and is a special treat at Christmas time. This simple recipe could be found in almost any coastal town.

Ingredients (serves 6):

    2 teaspoons sea salt
    Juice of 1 lemon
    0.5 cup olive oil
    24 medium-large shrimp (0.5kg) in the shell with heads

Preparation:

1. In a bowl, whisk together the olive oil, lemon juice, and salt until well blended. Dip the shrimp briefly into the mixture to coat lightly.

2. Heat a dry skillet over high heat.

3. When the pan is very hot, working in batches, add the shrimp in a single layer without crowding. Sear for 1 minute.

4. Reduce the heat to medium and continue cooking for 1 minute. Turn the shrimp, increase the heat to high, and sear for 2 more minutes, or until golden.

5. Keep the shrimp warm on an ovenproof platter in a low oven. Cook the rest of the shrimps in the same way.

6. When all the shrimps are cooked, arrange on a platter and serve immediately with lemon.

PAPAS ARRUGADAS CON MOJO PICÓN
Wrinkled potatoes with hot pepper sauce

Potatoes have been cultivated in the Islas Canarias since the 17th century when they were brought back from the Americas. The people of the Canarias call these potatoes "papas", which is the native American name, while in the rest of Spain they are usually called "patatas". These "wrinkled potatoes" are a traditional Christmas dish, served with a "mojo" or sauce. The "mojo" is made with garlic and peppers, is slightly piquant and very tasty. The two are often served together as a starter, side dish or tapa at Christmas time.

Mojo Picón - Garlic and pepper sauce:
Ingredients (serves 8):

> 5 garlic cloves
> 1 teaspoon cumin seed
> 2-3 small dried chilli peppers
> Salt
> 30 g breadcrumbs
> 0.5 teaspoon paprika powder
> 45 ml red wine vinegar
> 75 ml olive oil
> 0.5 cup water as required

Preparation:

1. Using a mortar and pestle, grind the cumin, garlic, and chillies with some salt to taste. The mixture should be mashed well.

2. Add the paprika powder, the vinegar and oil, and continue to blend.

3. Add bread crumbs and mash together

4. Gradually add water until the sauce has the desired consistency.

5. Pour the mojo over the potatoes and serve.

Ingredients (serves 6-8 as a tapa):

> 1.25 kg small potatoes
>
> 2 Tbsp coarse sea salt

Preparation:

1. Clean the potatoes and remove "eyes" - do not peel them. Place the potatoes in a large pot and boil them in water with the salt for 15-20 minutes until cooked.

2. Remove from the heat and pour off the water. Put the pot with the potatoes back on the stove, allowing any remaining water to dry off. You should see a layer of salt form on the dry skins which will then wrinkle.

3. Serve the "papas" with the Mojo Picón.

TAPA COJONUDOS DE BURGOS
Fried Quail Eggs with Chorizo or Morcilla

"Cojonudos" are another simple, but tasty tapa made by topping a slice of baguette with a fried quail egg and a slice of fried chorizo sausage. A similar tapa can be made with a small slice of morcilla (black pudding) instead of chorizo sausage. Quail eggs are about a third of the size of chicken eggs, are mottled grey and white. They are available by the dozen in most supermarkets in Spain and are a very popular ingredient in "tapa" dishes.

Ingredients (serves 4-6):

    1 dozen quail eggs
    12 slices of baguette
    12 Slices of chorizo (0.5cm thick)
    Olive oil for frying

Preparation:

1. Arrange the slices of baguette on a large dinner plate or serving platter.

2. In a frying pan, fry quail eggs 2 at a time in a little olive oil. Be careful not to over-heat the pan because the eggs burn easily. As you remove each egg, place each on top of a slice of baguette. Note: Quail eggs are quite hard. Crack them open by giving them a quick, sharp tap with the blade of a small knife. Remove the knife and separate the halves.

3. Cut chorizo into slices of about 0.5 cm thick. In the same pan lightly fry the chorizo slices. Remove them one at a time and place them on top of the egg on each slice of baguette. If you use morcilla (black sausage) instead, cut it a little thicker than the chorizo and then do exactly the same.

ENSALADA DE PIMIENTOS ASADOS

Grilled Pepper salad

A salad made with grilled peppers makes an excellent and popular festive tapa.

Ingredients:

    2 red peppers
    2 green or yellow peppers for roasting
    1 or 2 ripe tomatoes
    1 large onion
    Vinegar (to taste)
    Olive oil
    Salt (to taste)

Preparation:

1. Roast the peppers together with the tomatoes. When they are roasted, place them in a sealed container to cool and release their juices.

2. Once cooled, peel the peppers, cut them into strips and put them in a bowl. Peel and mince the tomatoes and add them to the peppers. Keep the juices from both.

3. Pour the juices from the peppers and tomatoes into a bowl, sieve them, and add a little seasoning, some vinegar, and a dash of olive oil. Stir the mixture and put the chopped-up onion on top.

4. This salad is good by itself but is also an ideal compliment to eat with freshly fried whitebait.

ENSALADA PIPIRRANA
Mixed "Pipirrana" Salad

Pipirrana is a refreshing and nutritious salad, very tasty, easy and quick to prepare. Many local dishes don't have a strict method of preparation or an exact list of ingredients. They developed over time and many variants evolved throughout the years. As popular dishes, families and villages have made them with whatever ingredients were affordable or seasonal. Pipirrana is a typical example of one of these ad-hoc dishes. Basically, it is a salad prepared with whatever fresh salad vegetables you have. It's a good emergency salad when unexpected guests arrive for Christmas dinner.

Ingredients (serves 4):

> 200 g of cooked cod (optional)
> 1 cucumber
> 2 cloves of garlic
> Half an onion
> Marinated olives
> 2 tomatoes
> 1 medium green pepper
> 3 bread slices
> 2 tablespoons olive oil
> 2 tablespoons of wine vinegar
> Salt
> Black pepper

Preparation:

1. Wash the peppers, remove the seeds, and chop into small cubes.

2. Peel and dice the cucumber and tomatoes. Chop the garlic and onion very finely.

3. Mix all the vegetables, add the cod (cut into little pieces) and dress with the vinegar, oil, pepper and salt, or prepare a vinaigrette with these ingredients, leave to stand for an hour and then dress.

4. Chop olives into very small pieces and sprinkle them on the salad.

5. Refrigerate for half an hour before serving.

6. Serve with bread.

PINTXOS DE AHUMADO CON FRUTAS - PAÍS VASCO
Smoked Fish and fruit Pintxos of the Basque country

The combination of smoked fish with fresh fruit makes a very tasty and popular tapa and is especially appreciated in the Basque country. In this recipe we have suggested to use smoked mackerel but more traditionally you could just use salted cod and any smoked fish that is available together with seasonal fruits and olives. In the Basque country it is often served with one of the local white wines of the region.

Ingredients (12 tapas):

    12 green olives halved
    6 very small tomatoes, halved) e.g. Cherry tomatoes)
    12 mixed green and red grapes, halved (or passion fruit)
    0.5 kg assorted berries as available (strawberries, raspberries)
    200 g smoked salmon
    200 g smoked trout
    200 g smoked mackerel (or salted cod after de-salting)
    1 lemon, quartered
    Freshly ground black pepper

Preparation:

1. Cut the fish into 2-3 cm pieces.

2. Use the skewers and alternate pieces of the three fish, folding where necessary, with the tomato, fruit and olives.

3. Season lightly with pepper and cover with the juice from the lemon.

TAPA JAMÓN, QUESO Y CHORIZO CON PAN
Tapa of Ham, Cheese and Chorizo with Bread

This is a very simple, but delicious tapa that everyone will enjoy. It involves very little cooking and can be put together at the last minute.

Ingredients:

    2 French-style baguettes
    250 g Manchego cheese
    125 g Serrano ham
    500 g Chorizo

Preparation:

1. Slice the baguette, making slices of about 1 cm thick.

2. Slice the Manchego cheese, approximately 0.5 cm thick.

3. If you have a whole piece of jamón, slice it into paper-thin slices to fit on the top of the baguette slices.

4. Slice the chorizo into pieces about 0.5 cm thick, ready for frying (which is optional). Some people prefer to simply slice the chorizo and serve it; others prefer it lightly fried in olive oil.

5. Place a large heavy-bottomed frying pan,on the heat with a little olive oil. Fry the chorizo slices for 5-10 minutes, turning as necessary. Remove as soon as the chorizo is cooked.

6. Place the baguette slices on the platter. Place one piece of cheese and a piece of ham on each one. On others, place a piece of chorizo. Serve.

TORTILLA A LA CAZADORA

Fresh mushroom Tortilla

Ingredients (serves 4):

 4 tablespoons of olive oil
 300 g mixed mushrooms, finely sliced
 50 g Serrano ham, diced
 4 eggs
 Freshly ground black pepper
 Salt
 1 tablespoon of parsley

Preparation:

Heat 3 tablespoons of oil in a frying pan. Fry the mushrooms on high heat until all the juices have evaporated. Add the ham and fry with the mushrooms for a moment. Take the mixture out of the pan and put aside. Heat the rest of the oil in the same pan. Beat the eggs in a bowl and season with pepper, salt and parsley. Add the mushroom mixture to the eggs in the bowl, stir well and slowly fry the tortilla in the oil. It can be served hot or cold.

TORTILLA DE ESPINACAS
Spinach Tortilla

Ingredients (serves 4):

    300 g spinach leaves (frozen)
    1 clove of garlic
    Freshly ground white pepper
    Salt
    Freshly grated nutmeg
    4 tablespoons of olive oil
    4 eggs
    3 tablespoons of cream

Preparation:

Let the spinach slowly thaw and drain well. Crush the garlic and mix it with a little oil. Heat 1 tablespoon of oil in a pan and stir-fry the spinach for 5 minutes. Season the spinach with garlic, pepper, salt and nutmeg. Whisk the eggs together with the cream. Heat the remaining oil in a pan, pour in the egg mix and cover this immediately with the spinach. Let it cook on medium heat for ca. 8 minutes. Serve hot.

TORTILLA DE HIERBAS AROMÁTICAS
Tortilla with fresh herbs

Ingredients (serves 4):

    1 teaspoon of fresh tarragon, finely chopped
    1 teaspoon of fresh oregano leaves
    1 teaspoon of fresh thyme leaves
    1 teaspoon of fresh parsley, chopped
    4 eggs
    3 tablespoons of cream
    Freshly ground white pepper
    Salt
    Nutmeg
    3 tablespoons of olive oil
    2 tablespoons of grated Manchego cheese

Preparation:

Mix the fresh herbs with the eggs and the cream in a bowl. Season this with pepper, salt and freshly grated nutmeg. Heat the oil in a frying pan. Make 2 thin tortillas with the egg mixture. Take them out of the pan and roll them up. Place in an oven-proof dish and sprinkle with the grated cheese. Briefly bake under a grill until the cheese melts and browns slightly. Serve hot.

TORTILLA DE CHORIZO
Chorizo Tortilla

Ingredients (serves 2):

    150 g chorizo, diced
    1 boiled potato, diced
    3 eggs
    1 tablespoon of olive oil
    Freshly ground black pepper
    1 pinch of salt

Preparation:

Fry the chorizo in a frying pan without adding any oil, until the fat starts to run. Add the diced potato and fry both until crisp. Remove from the pan. Whisk the eggs with pepper and a pinch of salt. Add the potato/chorizo mix. Heat the oil in the frying pan, add the egg mix and fry on both sides for about 4 minutes. Serve.

---oOo---

3.0 Dining, Serving and Restaurant etiquette in Spain

General Information: Lunch is the main meal of the day in most of Spain (but particularly in the South of Spain). However, at Christmas time, dinner is the main meal on Christmas Eve and New Year's Eve.

The structure of lunch or dinner is much less fixed than in Northern Europe, but the general structure is:

    Entrantes ("Primer Plato") - Starters

    Plato Principal ("Segundo Plato") - Main Course

    Postres - Sweet

Dinner is more informal than lunch and may start as a series of tapas, gradually developing into dinner. It is normal to eat quite lightly at dinner time and only have a main course. This is not true during the Christmas celebrations, when dinners are long leisurely affairs consisting of many courses.

Timing:

- Lunch starts from about 13:30 and generally continues up to 16:00 (or later).

- Dinner will not start before 20:00 and may continue until midnight (at least).

Etiquette: Normally a meal is set as the course arrives, so don't expect a table set with 5 layers of knives and forks when you arrive.

In most restaurants (even the best) a course will probably be entirely cleared and the table reset for each course. Even in a small restaurant, your table will be redressed as the waiter sees fit. Leave it to the waiter; he sees this as his responsibility, whilst yours is to enjoy the food he brings you.

Waiting: Waiters in Spain tend to be professionals. Most have been formally trained and, generally speaking, the standards of service are very high indeed. However, do not confuse professionalism with "high-speed eating" - in Spain they are opposites. Food is a leisure activity, to be enjoyed without haste; it is NOT a utilitarian bodily function as it has become in Northern Europe or North America.

Generally, when you enter a restaurant you will be noted immediately by the waiters. Usually the pace of eating in Spain is deliberately very leisurely, so the waiter will leave you to settle at your table for a few minutes. It is normal NOT to have a waiter on your elbow within 15 seconds! The idea is that you are not being rushed. But you can be sure that you have been seen.

Don't go to a restaurant to eat in a hurry. That is a contradiction of the entire raison d'être of a restaurant - it is a place to rest, relax, and not be rushed, but to enjoy a good meal in a calm and convivial atmosphere. If you are in a hurry, then go to a fast food place.

It is normal to order a drink first whilst reading the menu.

What to order: Flexibility is the main thing about eating out in a Spanish restaurant. You can basically have what you want in whatever order you want to have it. The main thing is to tell the waiter. Some customers like to have dishes served separately, such as meat and vegetable dishes, some prefer them together. Just tell the waiter how you would like it.

A salad, soup or gazpacho is normally served as a first course in Spain. However, some soups are main course soups and may be ordered as such. Gazpachos are generally served during the hotter months of the summer, but are also served as a special Christmas dish.

Bread is usually included with most menus and generally doesn't need to be ordered separately.

Mixing and sharing dishes - Combining dishes or asking for off-menu dishes: You should never be frightened to ask for something that isn't on the menu or is a variation of a menu dish. If the kitchen can do it, they will be happy to make it for you. In even the most modest, rural restaurants in Spain the chef will do his/her utmost to oblige a customer. It is quite unlike the attitude that prevails in many northern European restaurants, where the menu is strictly "non-negotiable"! Unlike most Northern European countries, the menu in a Spanish restaurant is only a guide. So if you want something special, you should always ask for it. If they have the ingredients, you can be sure that the restaurant will try to oblige you.

It is interesting to explore the habit of sharing dishes, which is so normal in Spain. The Northern European habit of having a dish entirely to oneself, doesn't really work in Spain. A meal in Spain is much more a truly shared experience, and that means that dishes are quite normally tasted and shared by everyone. It is common for a waiter in a restaurant to automatically bring extra spoons or forks for the other diners when one person orders a particular dish. Sadly, in Northern Europe we have forgotten how to share in this way and the habit may come as a surprise for the unsuspecting Northern European visitor.

The "Sobremesa": After a meal it is usual for diners to linger for a very long time, and several hours is not unusual. In Northern Europe, we tend to eat and go, thinking that the restaurant needs the table. In Spain, the opposite is true... when you sit at a table it becomes yours for the day. Have lunch (or dinner) and stay for as long as you want, regardless of whether you order more or not; it doesn't matter.

Tipping in a restaurant: It is normal to tip for good service. 10% is normal and many happy customers give more.

---oOo---

List of recipes - Spanish names

Starters, Salads and Gazpachos	**Page**
Ajoblanco de Almáchar	80
Cardo con béchamel de Aragón	82
Ensalada el Remojón	83
Gazpacho de Almendras y pasas	84
Parpuchas de Málaga	85
Patatas al Romero	86
Patatas a la Sidra de Asturias	87
Tortillitas de Coliflor	88

Soups	
Crema de Andaricas (nécoras) de Asturias	90
Sopa Cachorreña de Málaga	91
Sopa de Ajo - Sopa Castellana	89
Sopa de Cebolla	92
Sopa de Galets o Caldo de Navidad de Cataluña	94

Goat's meat	
Cabrito a la Miel	96
Cabritu a la Sidra de Asturias	98
Choto al Ajillo de Alcaucín	99
Choto a la Nerjeña o Cabrito en Salsa de Almendras	100

Lamb	**Page**
Cordero Asado al horno	102
Cordero al Chilindrón	103
Cordero de Navidad a la Miel	105
Cordero al Romero con puré de Ajos	107
Paletilla de Cordero	108

Rabbit	
Conejo estofado de Navidad	109
Conejo Guisado al Muscatel de El Borge	110
Conejo en Salsa de Nueces	111

Pork	
Filetes de Lomo al Vino (Andalucía)	113
Lombarda Navidena	112
Lomo Relleno al Horno	114

Poultry	
Capón Relleno (Frutos seccs) para Navidad	116
Capón Relleno de Higos y Trufas al Oloroso de Jerez	118
Pato al Horno con Peras Caramelizadas de Cataluña	119
Pavo con Trufas	121
Pechuga de Pavo con Salsa de Almendras	123
Perdices al Vino Muscatel de Sedella, Málaga	124
Pollo Relleno de Navidad	125

Stews and Fricassees	**Page**
Cardo de Navidad de Navarra	127
Cardo de Nochebuena de Aragón	128
Cocido de Tagarninas y Cardos de Málaga	129
Fabada Asturiana	130
Gachas Manchegas	132
Marmitako	133
Pote Asturiano de Berza	135

Casseroles	
Cardo de Navidad de Cataluña	137
Cazuela de Fideos a la Marenga	139

Fish	
Bacalao Ajoarriero de Aragón	141
Bacalao con Coliflor a la Gallega	143
Bacalao a la Vizcaína	144
Langostinos de Sanlúcar	146
Mejillones a la Asturiana	147
Merluza y Almejas en Salsa Verde	148
Salmón al Cava	150

Sweets and Confectionary	
Alfajores Andaluces de Medina-Sidonia	151
Almonds Garrapiñadas	153
Bizcocho de Navidad Con Fruta Escarchada	154
Borrachinos de Asturias	155
Borrachuelos de Navidad de Málaga	156
Budín de Navidad	158
Buñuelos de Manzana a la Canela	159

Sweets and Confectionary (cont.)	Page
Casadielles de Asturias (I)	160
Casadielles de Asturias (Ii)	162
Churros	163
Cordiales de Murcia	164
Crespillos de Barbastro	165
Dulce de Manzana	166
Escaldao de Asturias	167
Galletas de Anís	168
Galletitas de Vainilla	169
Galette de Pérouges de Cataluña	170
Guirlache de Aragón	171
Hojaldrinas	172
Mantecados de Navidad	173
Mantecados de Aceite de Navidad	174
Mantecados de Alfarnate	175
Mantecados Manchegos	176
Marquesas de Navidad	178
Mazapán, Tradicional Dulce de Navidad	179
Marzipan - Figuritas de mazapán	181
Melindres de Galicia	183
Nevaditos de Cantabria	184
Pan de Cádiz	185
Pan de Higo	187
Pastel de Gloria o Tetillas de Monja	188
Pastelito de Gloria	190
Pastelillos de Cabello de Ángel de Murcia	191
Las Peladillas de Casinos	192
Peras al Vino de Málaga	193
Pestiños	194

Sweets and Confectionary (cont.)	Page
Pestiños de Málaga	195
Polvorones de Estepa	196
Polvorones de Chocolate	197
Prestines de Extremadura	198
Puré de Castañas con Queso de Afuega'l Pitu	199
Roscón de Reyes	200
Roscos de Anis	203
Roscos Carreros de Málaga	204
Roscos Duros de Navidad	205
Roscos de Huevo	206
Roscos de Minuto de Alfarnate	207
Roscos de Naranja	208
Roscos de Naranja de Periana	209
Roscos de Vino de Málaga	210
Roquitas de Almendras	211
Sopa de Almendras de Las Dos Castillas	212
Sopa dulce del Valle del Jerte de Extremadura	213
Tarta de Sidra de Asturias	214
Tarta de Turrón de Cantabria	215
Tarta de Santiago	216
Tronco de Navidad	218
Truchas de Navidad de Las Islas Canarias	220
Turrón de Alicante	222
Turrón Blando O de Jijona	224
Turrón de Gofio Canario	226
Turrón de Yema	227
Uvas En Anis Seco	228
Yemas de Santa Teresa de Ávila	229

Breads and Tortillas

Corona de Quesos Y Nueces	231
Filloas de Galicia	233
Torrija de Cantabria	234
Tortilla de Pan rallado	236
Tortilla Pimientos	237
Tortilla de Espárragos trigueros	238

Christmas Drinks

Licor Café Gallego	244
Ponche de Navidad De Café	245
Ponche de Manzana Y Granadas	246
Resolí de Málaga	247

Tapas

Alcachofas con Almejas de Navarra	254
Berenjenas con Miel De Caña	255
Boquerones en Vinagre	256
Brochetas de Gambas y Bacon	257
Champiñones al ajillo	258
Ensalada de Pimientos Asados	263
Ensalada Pipirrana	264
Gambas a la plancha	259
Papas Arrugadas con Mojo Picón	260
Pintxos de Ahumado con Frutas - País Vasco	265
Tapa Cojonudos de Burgos	262
Tapa Jamón, Queso y Chorizo con Pan	266
Tortilla a la Cazadora	267
Tortilla de Chorizo	270

Tortilla de Espinacas   268
Tortilla de Hierbas Aromáticas 269

List of recipes - English names

Starters, Salads and Gazpachos	**Page**
Almond and Raisin gazpacho	84
Aragonese Cardos in Béchamel sauce	82
Cauliflower Fritters	88
Cod Pancakes of Málaga	85
Garlic Soup of Almáchar	80
Potatoes in Cider from Asturias	87
Potatoes with Rosemary	86
Salad "El Remojón"	83

Soups

Cod and Orange Soup of Málaga	91
Crab Cream Soup of Asturias	90
Garlic Soup of Castilla	89
Onion Soup	92
Pasta broth of Cataluña	94

Goat's meat

Kid Goat in Almond Sauce from Andalucía	100
Kid Goat in Cider from Asturias	98
Kid Goat in Garlic from Alcaucin	99
Kid Goat in Honey	96

Lamb	Page
Christmas Lamb with Honey	105
Lamb and Rosemary with garlic purée	1107
Lamb in Red Pepper sauce	103
Roast Marinated Lamb	102
Shoulder of Lamb	

Rabbit	
Rabbit in Walnut Sauce	111
Rabbit Stew	109
Rabbit Stew with Muscatel from El Borge, Málaga	110

Pork	
Baked Stuffed Loin	114
Christmas Red Cabbage with Bacon	112
Loin fillets in a wine sauce (Andalucía)	113

Poultry	
Christmas stuffed Chicken	125
Partridge in Muscatel wine from Sedella, Málaga	124
Roast Turkey with Truffles	121
Roasted Duck with caramelised Pears of Cataluña	119
Stuffed Capon - Figs, Truffles and Oloroso Sherry	118
Stuffed Capon - Fruit and Nuts	116
Turkey Breast with Almond Sauce	123

Stews and Fricassees	Page
Asturian Bean and Chorizo Stew	130
Asturian Leaf Kale Stew	135
Cardos in Almond sauce of Aragón	128
Christmas Cardo Stew of Navarra	127
Fresh Bonito and Potato Stew	133
Savoury Porridge of La Mancha	132
Thistle and Chickpea stew of Málaga	129

Casseroles	
Christmas Cardo casserole of Cataluña	137
Pasta and fish casserole "a la marenga"	139

Fish	
Cod Ajoarriero of Aragón	141
Cod and Cauliflower of Galicia	143
Cod Stew of Biscay	144
Hake Fillets with Clams in Salsa Verde	148
Mussels in the Asturian style	147
Prawns from Sanlúcar in Cadiz	146
Salmon with Cava	150

Sweets and Confectionary	
"Ladyfingers" of Galicia	183
Almond and Honey Turron of the Canaries	226
Almond and olive oil Christmas Biscuits	174
Almond and Sweet potato Fritters of the Canary Islands	220
Almond Christmas Biscuits	173
Almond Soup of the two Castillas	212

Sweets and Confectionary (cont.)	Page
Angel hair Pasties of Murcia	191
Anis and Honey fritters of Extremadura	198
Anis Biscuits	168
Anis Doughnuts	203
Apple and cinnamon doughnuts	159
Borage fritters of Barbastro	165
Bread dumplings in syrup of Asturias	155
Bread Pudding of Asturias	167
Catalan Sugar Cake of Pérouges	170
Chestnut purée with cottage cheese	199
Chocolate Shortbread	197
Christmas biscuits of Alfarnate	175
Christmas cake with candied fruit	154
Christmas Trunk	218
Churros	163
Cider Tart of Asturias	214
Crispy Christmas doughnuts	205
Doughnut "volcanoes" of Málaga	204
Egg Doughnuts	206
Egg Nougat	227
Fig Loaf	187
Marzipan figures	
Filled Almond Sweet of Murcia	164
Fruit Marzipan of Cadiz	185
Gloria Cakes - Almond Meringues	188
Grapes in dry Anis liquor	228
Hard Nougat of Alicante	222
Little Almond and Chocolate rocks	211
Little Glory Cakes	190

Sweets and Confectionary (cont.)	Page
Marquesa Christmas Almond Cakes	178
Marzipan, the traditional Christmas sweet	179
Nougat of Aragón	171
Nougat tart of Cantabria	215
One minute Rosco doughnuts from Alfarnate	207
Orange Doughnuts	208
Orange Doughnuts of Periana	209
Pears in wine from Málaga	193
Pestiños ("Angel Wings") of Málaga	195
Ring of the Three Kings	200
Shortbread biscuits of La Mancha	176
Shortbreads of Estepa (Seville)	196
Snow Cakes of Cantabria	184
Soft Nougat in the style of Turrón de Jijona	224
Spanish Christmas pudding	158
Spicebread of Medina-Sidonia	151
St. James' Cake of Santiago, Galicia	216
Sugared Almonds of Valencia	192
Sugared Roasted Almonds	153
Sweet Apple Preserve	166
Sweet Christmas fritters of Málaga	156
Sweet Fritters	194
Sweet soup of the Jerte Valley of Extremadura	213
Vanilla biscuits	169
Walnut Pasties of Asturias (I)	160
Walnut Pasties of Asturias (II)	162
Wine and Orange Christmas cakes	172
Wine Doughnuts of Málaga	210
Yolks of Ávila	229

Breads and Tortillas	**Page**
Breadcrumb Tortilla	236
Crown of Cheese and Walnut bread	231
Dipped toast of Cantabria	234
Galician Crepes	233
Green asparagus tortilla	238
Pepper Tortilla	237

Christmas Drinks	
Apple and Pomegranate Punch	246
Christmas Coffee Punch	245
Liqueur coffee of Galicia	244
Spicy Spirit drink of Málaga	247

Tapas	
Anchovies marinated in Vinegar	256
Artichokes with clams of Navarra	254
Aubergine with molasses	255
Chorizo Tortilla	270
Fresh mushroom Tortilla	267
Fried Quail Eggs with Chorizo or Morcilla	262
Garlic Mushrooms	258
Grilled Pepper salad	263
Grilled Shrimp	259
Mixed "Pipirrana" Salad	264
Prawn and Bacon Brochettes	257
Smoked Fish and Fruit pintxos of the Basque Country	265
Spinach Tortilla	268
Tapa of Ham, Cheese and Chorizo with Bread	266

Tapas (cont)	Page
Tortilla with fresh herbs	268
Wrinkled potatoes with hot pepper sauce	260

About the author

Malcolm Coxall, the author, is the proprietor of the family's 110 acre farm in the Axarquía of southern Andalucía in Spain. The farm has been certified as organic since 1999 and produces olives, almonds and culinary herbs. It incorporates a small factory for the packing of organic herbs and dried fruits and nuts.

Malcolm also provides business, marketing and IT consultancy to other organic food producers in the region. He has published articles on sustainable agriculture, organic food production, forest biodiversity, environmental protection and environmental economics. He is also author of the book "Traditional Recipes of the Axarquía". He is active in the European food and environmental movement, and has taken several successful legal actions in defence of European environmental standards in the European Court of Justice.

Malcolm is passionate about food sovereignty and the maintenance of local food production. He believes that culinary diversity, agricultural sustainability and traditional gastronomy have much to teach a generation that has basically forgotten how food is grown and prepared.

"Truly good food is local, ethical, diverse, organic and slow. How and what we eat defines who we are as a society. Societies that knowingly eat chemically adulterated junk foods, produced in heartless factory farms, reveal an intrinsic social, political and health malaise. They reveal their lack of sustainability, an inherent insecurity and a disconnection from their natural and social context. Contrast this careless mentality with those societies which treasure their land, their natural environment, their people, their traditional cuisine and the quality and purity of their food. Then explain to me again why we need fast food and how "factory agriculture" fits in with human and environmental well-being and sustainability. To be sustainable, what we really need to do is to start to understand food again, beginning with the basics both on the farm and in the kitchen.

We could do worse than to try to understand and (more importantly) enjoy our own local gastronomic heritage again. Not only is this worthwhile and important, but it is also great fun to discover how to make and enjoy real food again."

September 2013

---oOo---

www.ingramcontent.com/pod-product-compliance
Lightning Source LLC
Chambersburg PA
CBHW070637160426
43194CB00009B/1482